Jossey-Bass Teacher

Jossey-Bass Teacher provides K–12 teachers with essential knowledge and tools to create a positive and lifelong impact on student learning. Trusted and experienced educational mentors offer practical classroom-tested and theory-based teaching resources for improving teaching practice in a broad range of grade levels and subject areas. From one educator to another, we want to be your first source to make every day your best day in teaching. *Jossey-Bass Teacher* resources serve two types of informational needs—essential knowledge and essential tools.

Essential knowledge resources provide the foundation, strategies, and methods from which teachers may design curriculum and instruction to challenge and excite their students. Connecting theory to practice, essential knowledge books rely on a solid research base and time-tested methods, offering the best ideas and guidance from many of the most experienced and well-respected experts in the field.

Essential tools save teachers time and effort by offering proven, ready-to-use materials for in-class use. Our publications include activities, assessments, exercises, instruments, games, ready reference, and more. They enhance an entire course of study, a weekly lesson, or a daily plan. These essential tools provide insightful, practical, and comprehensive materials on topics that matter most to K–12 teachers.

Biology Inquiries

Standards-Based Labs, Assessments, and Discussion Lessons

MARTIN SHIELDS

JOSSEY-BASS
A Wiley Imprint
www.josseybass.com

Published by Jossey-Bass
A Wiley Imprint
989 Market Street, San Francisco, CA 94103-1741   www.josseybass.com

Jossey-Bass books and products are available through most bookstores. To contact Jossey-Bass directly call our Customer Care Department within the U.S. at 800-956-7739, outside the U.S. at 317-572-3986, or fax 317-572-4002.

Jossey-Bass also publishes its books in a variety of electronic formats. Some content that appears in print may not be available in electronic books.

ISBN-13: 978-0-7879-7652-1
ISBN-10: 0-7879-7652-0

Printed in the United States of America
FIRST EDITION
PB Printing   10 9 8

About This Book

Organization

The lesson entries in this book are organized into chapters corresponding to content standards of the *National Science Education Standards*. The first chapter of entries, "Science as Inquiry," correlates with content standard A. The next six chapters of lessons correspond to the six "fundamental concepts and principles" of content standard C, Life Science. The final chapter connects to content standard F, Science in Personal and Social Perspectives.

Some of the book's lessons are short and can be completed in as little as twenty minutes. Others are extended investigations that take days or weeks to complete. Some of the entries are inquiry labs, some are assessments, and others are discussion-centered lessons. Many of the lessons are inquiries, most are constructivist, many are both. All of the offerings strive to stimulate active learning, to be student-centered, to be standards-based.

The approaches of inquiry and constructivism recognize that student understanding takes time to develop. The focus, then, should be on sequences of related learning experiences rather than on single, stand-alone lessons. Some of the entries in this book are presented as pieces of a series. With others it is assumed that they will be connected to other related lessons by the teacher.

Who Is the Book For?

It is hoped that this book will provide useful lesson ideas for teachers of all experience levels. Detailed implementation tips are provided as guidance for those less familiar with student-centered, minds-on teaching.

As a high school biology teacher, I wrote the entries while drawing from my grade 9 to 12 experiences. However, most of the lessons are either useable or easily adaptable for middle school levels. Many might also be useful in a community college classroom. In inquiry lessons there are usually many different levels of content acquisition that can be achieved. This makes such lessons easily adaptable for both varied age and ability levels.

How to Use the Book

Reproducible student handouts are provided for most of the lessons. In a number of cases (especially the nonlabs), these handouts could serve simply as a guide for class-wide discussion topics. Distributed as handouts they offer the option of students collaborating on the questions or of individual student writing and reflection. Some sections of certain handouts would be appropriate for outside of class assignments.

The teacher pages of the lesson entries are divided into the following sections:

- *Topic connections.* A short list of biology content topics that are addressed by the lesson.

- *Introduction.* This section provides an overview of the lesson. Common student misconceptions addressed by the lesson are discussed here.

- *Materials, time approximation, preparation, safety precautions.* These sections provide information to help the teacher plan to use the lesson.

- *Implementation strategy.* This section of the teacher pages gives tips for successfully using the lesson. Strategies for constructivist and inquiry-based approaches are included here.

- *Possible responses for selected student handout questions.* Included as part of the Implementation Strategy section, this provides responses that could be reasonably expected for certain questions. Some questions are not covered because possible responses will be so varied depending on the group and situation.

- *Lesson outline.* This section gives a suggested sequence to the events of the lesson.

- *Reference.* This section gives the original source (for the author) of the core lesson idea or any works that supplied data or content information.

Many of the book's entries include a "content acquisition" or "background information" portion in the middle of the lesson outline. These segments recommend that content learning occur via Web research, readings, or other lessons. Such segments may appear as gaps in the middle of the lesson. However, they are left open because there are so many different ways that the goal can be achieved. How it is accomplished depends on available resources as well as the needs, style, and interests of both students and teacher.

Sources for Lessons

Some of the lesson ideas are original. Some are adapted from referenced sources. Others are inquiry and/or constructivist modifications of traditional cookbook labs or lessons.

Acknowledgments

I WOULD LIKE TO THANK a number of people who helped to improve this book. Mary Scorese of Pascack Hills High School field-tested some of the lessons and offered valuable feedback from the trenches. Jane Kinkle of Grover Cleveland Middle School reviewed the manuscript and offered many useful suggestions.

Thanks to Fran Zak and Borislaw Bilash of Pascack Valley High School for the mushroom omelets. I owe a special debt to Borislaw for inviting me into the *A Demo a Day* series for my first book-writing experience.

Kate Gagnon of Jossey-Bass graciously helped me prepare the manuscript for publication. My editor, Dr. Steve Thompson, has been tremendously supportive of this project from the very beginning.

Thank you to the National Association of Biology Teachers, National Academies Press, and McGraw-Hill for allowing me to reprint material from their publications. And thank you to many of my students at Pascack Hills for allowing me to photograph them and/or their work for inclusion in this book.

Most of all I would like to thank my wife, Phyllis. For three years she has heard more about this book than anyone should have to. She has improved the manuscript immensely for clarity and style. And she has supported the project (and me) in so many ways. And apologies to Noah and Phoebe. I know I spent far too much time this summer in front of the computer working on this project and not enough outside playing baseball! I dedicate this book to Phyl, Noah, and Phoebes.

Contents

Preface

INQUIRY, guided inquiry, constructivism, the learning cycle, the 5 E's, PBL, "minds-on," active learning . . . help. We're agog in buzzwords. But wait, there's hope. The more you learn of these reform approaches to science teaching, the more you realize their commonalities. In essence they are linked by what they are not. They are *not* knowledge transmission models. They address the flaws of the traditional lecture and cookbook lab formats. They reject the classroom in which passive students simply receive information from teachers. They reject lab exercises in which students follow step-by-step instructions to merely verify what they've previously learned. In short, these reform approaches require significant cognitive sweat from the learner.

For a while now education resources have promoted "hands-on" activities as a panacea to improve learning. Hands-on means that students are busy doing something, that they are kinesthetically involved. This does not, however, guarantee that students are busy learning. Many hands-on lessons are effective. But the ones that succeed do so because they go beyond engaging the body of the learner—they also engage the mind. They challenge the student by requiring thought processes such as questioning, analyzing, designing, debating, reflecting, and communicating.

This book presents lessons based on the approaches of inquiry and constructivism. Many of the lessons are hands-on. But all of them are minds-on. That is, they aim to significantly *engage the mind of the learner.* The broad goals of inquiry and constructivism are to develop deep understanding of scientific ideas rather than shallow memorization of facts and vocabulary. These approaches are promoted by every major science and science education organization. They are central to the *National Science Education Standards.* And classrooms steeped in the challenges of inquiry are vibrant places to be for both student and teacher.

This reform approach to teaching science requires a trade-off. Inquiry and constructivist lessons take more time to implement than teacher-centered strategies. This comes as no surprise. Teaching for true understanding *should* take longer than asking only for superficial memorization. But which is more valuable to a learner? Which is more useful? Which is more lasting? Referred to as "less is more," such an approach covers fewer topics but results in more understanding, more real learning.

Biology teachers are hearing the drumbeat of the call for reform. Department supervisors, revised curricula, journal articles, and many state standards implore science teachers to make their lessons more constructivist, more inquiry-based and more standards-based. This book aims to help biology teachers respond to this call to action.

A number of books provide excellent theoretical explanations of inquiry and constructivism. Some, including the *Standards,* include broad case study descriptions of inquiry lessons that help the reader to visualize how they unfold. As a complement to those works, this book offers a variety of accessible, detailed lesson ideas to help you start. It fills an available niche. Many busy educators would like to transform their teaching approaches, but they lack the time and/or tools to do so. The lessons in this book can be used tomorrow. And the entries explain the nuances of constructivist, inquiry-based implementation that can make the experiences rich ones for students.

About the Author

MARTIN SHIELDS teaches biology and AP biology at Pascack Hills High School in Montvale, New Jersey. He received a B.A. in biology from Hobart College in 1985. In 1991 he earned a master's of science for teachers of biological sciences degree from the University of Montana. His master's research focused on the behavioral ecology of bighorn sheep (*O. canadensis*) and the implications of bighorn social structure on the conservation of genetic diversity.

Shields has served on advisory committees for the Biological Sciences Curriculum Study (BSCS). He has been published in *The Science Teacher* and *The American Biology Teacher*. He co-authored *A Demo a Day: A Year of Biological Demonstrations,* published by Flinn Scientific, Inc. He has presented frequently at state and national conferences. Shields was an Access Excellence Fellow and, in 2000, was chosen for the Presidential Award for Excellence in Math and Science Teaching.

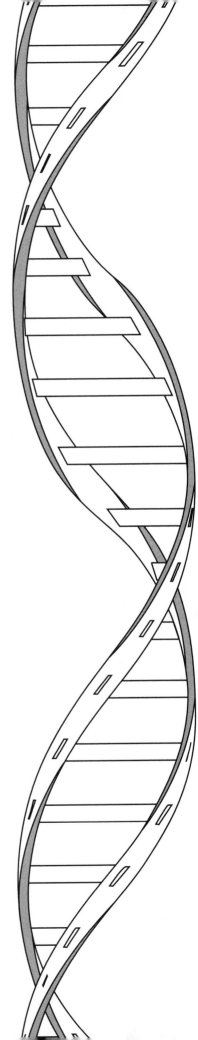

Chapter 1

Introduction

What exactly does inquiry mean? What is standards-based science teaching? What is the constructivist approach? And, why should we include these ideas in our lesson designs? This first chapter addresses these basic questions with an overview of the theory on which the book's lessons are based. The term *inquiry* has assumed many faces in education. The chapter describes the different forms of inquiry distinguished in the *National Science Education Standards*. Constructivism is introduced and a list of more detailed resources for these topics is provided.

What Is Standards-Based Teaching?

THE *NATIONAL SCIENCE EDUCATION STANDARDS* (the *Standards*) was published by the National Research Council (NRC). The *Standards* was developed over four years with input from tens of thousands of scientists and educators. The work is not a curriculum. That is, it does not provide lists of content topics that should be mastered in the way that many state standards do. The life science content standards, for example, focus on general themes that should be emphasized by teachers, such as the molecular basis of heredity. The national standards are a broad guide, a vision, for effective science education. They offer research-supported prescriptions for how best to develop scientifically literate students.

Standards-based teaching mobilizes the vision of the *Standards*. It employs strategies derived from learning theory research such as constructivism. It is steeped in inquiry. It strives for deep understanding of science content over superficial memorization of facts.

The *National Science Education Standards* are available for purchase in print or for free online from National Academy Press. Leonard, Penick, and Douglas (2002) offer a useful twenty-point checklist and rubric for teachers to self evaluate the extent to which they are standards-based.

Inquiry

The chorus from the acronymed science and science education organizations (AAAS, NRC, NSTA, NABT, BSCS) coalesces around the primacy of inquiry. The *Standards* advise that science teachers should employ varied strategies, but inquiry is clearly positioned as the central approach in the document. In fact, the NRC even published a separate volume focusing solely on inquiry in the science classroom (NRC, 2000). The *Standards* define inquiry as:

> *A multifaceted activity that involves making observations; posing questions; examining books and other sources of information to see what is already known; planning investigations; reviewing what is already known in light of experimental evidence; using tools to gather, analyze, and interpret data; proposing answers, explanations, and predictions; and communicating the results. Inquiry requires identification of assumptions, use of critical and logical thinking, and consideration of alternative explanations. (p. 23)*

The National Science Teachers Association position statement on scientific inquiry (2004) proclaims that "understanding science content is significantly enhanced when ideas are anchored to inquiry experiences." They recommend that all K-12 teachers make inquiry the centerpiece of the science classroom.

Scientific Inquiry Versus Inquiry Learning

An important distinction is carved in the *Standards* between the type of inquiry practiced by scientists and inquiry as an approach to teaching science content in the classroom. However, both are essential components of a science curriculum. Scientific inquiry refers to designing and conducting scientific investigations. According to the *Standards*, students should learn how to do scientific inquiry (abilities) and to comprehend how science is done (understandings). In essence, scientific inquiry should be taught as both process and content in a biology class. But "abilities necessary to do scientific inquiry" means more than just the science process skills that are traditionally taught such as observing, measuring, and experimenting. The *Standards* promote a more complete integration of science process skills with the evaluation, interpretation and explanation of data (NRC, 2000).

On the other hand, inquiry in the *Standards* also refers to a classroom strategy for teaching any other science content such as photosynthesis or molecular biology. Such an inquiry approach involves the learning of concepts through inquiry investigations. For example, students might discover for themselves in an inquiry that plants respire by collecting and evaluating data showing a net oxygen consumption in the absence of light.

It is clear that the *Standards* aim to move teachers away from the traditional stand-alone "scientific method" or "science process" unit that often initiates a course. Instead, science inquiry abilities should be developed continually throughout a course and in the context of new biology content learning.

Inquiry Learning Defined

The NRC (2000) provides and explains a working definition of an inquiry approach to teaching science. Their definition centers on "Five Essential Features of Classroom Inquiry." (Bybee, 2002) summarizes the five essential features as:

1. Learners engage in scientifically oriented questions.
2. Learners give priority to evidence in responding to questions.
3. Learners formulate explanations from evidence.
4. Learners connect explanations to scientific knowledge.
5. Learners communicate and justify explanations.

As much as possible each of these features is pursued by students with significant input and sometimes self-initiation. Traditional cookbook labs and activities do not achieve these features. Typically such labs provide the student with a scientific question, an introduction that answers the question, a step-by-step procedure and directions on how to analyze the data and explain the results. Inquiries, on the other hand, begin with questions that may be developed or refined by students. Then they often require students to devise ways to answer the questions. Learners collect and interpret data, using it as evidence to support new understandings. Content learning then occurs as students evaluate their data in the context of scientific knowledge gleaned from book, teacher, or Web resources. Finally, scientific explanations are proposed, debated, and defended by learners. Volkmann and Abell (2003) offer an "inquiry analysis tool" to assess whether a lab activity includes the essential features of inquiry.

In general, inquiries involve less pre-lab than found in cookbook activities. First, students are not presented with the ideas to be learned in the beginning of the lesson. Instead they develop understanding of the concepts throughout the experience—and especially toward the end. New terminology is introduced after exploration. Second, there usually is not a long explanation of a procedure before an inquiry lab because students are more involved in developing the investigative approach themselves during the activity. Inquiry labs often begin with just a brief introduction to some possible materials, important safety notes, and sometimes a brief demonstration of relevant equipment or a data-collecting approach.

Partial Versus Full Inquiries

Inquiry learning activities that consist of all five of the "essential features" are considered *full inquiries. Partial inquiries* include only some of the five features. A partial inquiry might, for instance, provide experimental data for learners to manipulate, analyze, and explain. Both types of activities have value for the biology classroom. Partial inquiries can address a specific science process ability. They can form part of a sequence of experiences that together include all five features of inquiry. But many full inquiries should be used throughout a biology course.

Open Versus Guided Inquiry

Inquiries vary in the balance between student self-direction and teacher guidance. The NRC (2000) recommends that inquiries of different degrees of "openness" be employed by teachers. Specific biology content concepts are probably best taught through more structured, guided inquiries that focus learners on the intended outcomes. After all, students can't be expected to rediscover hundreds of years of biological knowledge through self-initiated questions. And some starting information or guidance is often necessary to raise the inquiry to higher levels. More open inquiries better develop scientific investigation abilities. These focus more on learning to do biological research than learning a specific biology concept. Clark, Clough, and Berg (2000) address this issue well:

> *In rethinking laboratory activities, too often a false dichotomy is presented to teachers that students must either passively follow a cookbook laboratory procedure or, at the other extreme, investigate a question of their own choosing. These extremes miss the large and fertile middle ground that is typically more pedagogically sound than either end of the continuum. (p. 40)*

In Investigating Osmosis in Plant Cells the prime objective is developing understanding of osmosis in plants. So the learners are given a teacher-initiated question to investigate. They experience the five essential features of inquiry, and they delve deeply into osmosis. On the other hand, Investigating Plant Growth is a more open inquiry in which learners choose their own questions to investigate. With groups investigating different variables, the biology concept learning varies across the class. But all students experience scientific inquiry from beginning to end and at a depth that isn't possible in the osmosis example. Termite Trails Mystery exemplifies an inquiry in which students initially explore their own questions, but then discussion guides the group toward investigating one central topic.

Initiating Inquiry: Discrepant Events

Inquiry begins with questions. Sometimes questions are offered by the teacher and students are challenged to develop a means of finding answers and explanations. Or questions can be generated by students out of previous learning, readings, discussions, or explorations. One way to jump-start the inquiry process involves discrepant events. An occurrence that is discrepant to students is one that is contrary or inconsistent with what they were expecting. In Termite Trails Mystery, for example, a termite dropped onto paper begins to follow a red ink trail. This is strange and unexpected to the students. Discrepant events pique student curiosity. They capture attention and, most importantly, they motivate students to learn more about the observed occurrence. With a mystery to be solved, learners are primed for inquiry. They have a reason to design, conduct, and interpret experiments. They have a purpose for using books and Web resources to acquire scientific knowledge. Other lessons involving discrepant events include Red Dot Special, What Is Life? Glue Goblins, Mendel's Data, Cold-Blooded Thermometers, and Water Discrepancies.

Converting Cookbook Labs to Inquiry

Developing an inquiry-based classroom does not have to require reinventing the wheel. Many traditional labs and activities can fairly easily be modified into inquiry experiences. Generally, this involves simply reversing the organization of the lesson. Instead of concepts first followed by an "experiment" to verify the concepts, reposition the investigative part to the beginning. Begin with questions. Then students collect and interpret data. Eventually students are exposed to the concepts via teacher, book, or Web resources. They then further develop understanding by evaluating their lab experiences and data in light of accepted scientific knowledge.

The content information is back-loaded in an inquiry. It follows a period of seeking explanations for mysteries, solutions to challenges, and approaches to explorations. This is similar to watching a baseball game in that students are much more excited when the outcome is unknown than they would be in watching a replay (Alberts, 2000).

In a modified cookbook lab, the procedure is either deleted or greatly reduced. Instead of a step-by-step recipe, students may be presented with some general guidelines or suggested approaches. The use of a new data-collecting tool might be explained. Some possible materials to use may (or may not) be listed. Students create their own experimental designs. Each lab group in a class may develop a different approach to exploring the topic of the lab.

Investigating Osmosis in Plant Cells and The Osmosis Inquiry Egg are examples of classic labs that were modified into inquiries. Llewellyn (2002) and Clark (2000) offer many useful strategies for converting labs into inquiries.

Questioning in an Inquiry Classroom

Questioning comprises the core of inquiry. Often, students generate questions to investigate. They question their own ideas and those of their classmates. And teachers continually question students to find out what they know and to challenge them to think. In an inquiry-oriented classroom, teacher questions go well beyond asking for recall of facts. Instead, questions intend to draw students out, to prompt learners to develop an understanding of concepts. For real learning to occur, students have to be held accountable for being engaged. Inquiry questions don't let the recipient off the hook—they require the student to explain, to analyze, to justify.

The following list contains examples of responses and questions frequently heard in inquiry-oriented classrooms:

- Good question. What do *you* think? (as a typical response to students' questions)
- Interesting. Why do you think that?
- Interesting idea. How could you test that?
- Interesting idea. What evidence do you have for it?
- Is there another possible explanation for that?
- What kinds of data could help answer that question?
- What can you conclude from that?
- How do you explain these observations/data/results?
- What are some hypotheses for that?
- What information would you need to research before investigating that topic?
- How confident are you of these results? Why?
- What else could have led to these experimental results?
- What are the variables in this experiment?
- What are the constants in this experiment?
- What further questions are raised by these results/conclusions?
- Good start. How could we improve on that idea?
- What can you now conclude about your hypothesis?
- How do you justify your conclusion/explanation?

- How could that experiment be made even better?
- What will that experiment tell you? How will it do that?
- What kind of data will you collect? Why?
- Can you think of any other data that would provide even more information?
- What mathematical analysis can you do to your data to get more information out of it?
- Does everyone agree with that statement/conclusion/reasoning?
- Who has some constructive feedback for this group?

"The Lab Didn't Work"

An attraction of cookbook labs for teachers is their predictable, consistent results. Students as well as teachers become molded to the lab experience where everyone knows the expected lab result and most groups either get that result or fudge their data to look like they did! If students don't achieve the expected, they conclude that either "the lab didn't work" or they "messed up." But with inquiries there is not usually one right answer or outcome. Instead, the emphasis is on "What results did you get and how do you explain them (whether expected or not)?"

True, the inquiry-oriented lab atmosphere can seem messy at times for student and teacher. But if it all leads to serious thinking about the biology concepts and scientific process, then the experience is successful no matter how messy. Let's look at an example. In The Osmosis Inquiry Egg students investigating salt as a variable often very reasonably predict that an egg in salt water will lose mass. But even in very salty (20 percent) solutions, the eggs do not lose mass. I have had students observe such results and proclaim, "It didn't work" or "We messed up" or, the best of all, "The egg is messed up." I lead them away from this sort of thinking with a short discussion. I ask if those are the only possible explanations they can think of. I emphasize that data is data. Their task is to explain the data they got. It is critical to emphasize to the students that they will not be penalized for getting "strange data" or for missing "the right" explanation. They need to focus on developing logical explanations. A sincere and complete effort at this is what matters.

In the case of the egg in salt water, maybe the egg is hypertonic to the solution. Or maybe the salt didn't completely go into solution. Or maybe the membrane is permeable to salt. I don't know the exact answer, *but that doesn't matter.* What matters is students doing what scientists do—using their minds to develop possible explanations, alternative explanations, and justifications with a combination of logic and biological knowledge. Students may actually learn more about a topic like osmosis when they have to explain surprising results.

Assessing Inquiry Investigations

Assessment takes many forms and serves many purposes in the science classroom. Two books that explore the subject in detail are *Classroom Management and the National Science Education Standards* by the NRC (2001) and *Science Educator's Guide to Laboratory*

Assessment by Doran, Chan, Tamir, and Lenhart (2002). The following provides just a few suggestions for assessments to follow an inquiry lab after a brief overview of the topic.

Three types of assessment occur in the inquiry-based, constructivist classroom. They provide feedback to students that helps them to further develop understanding.

1. Diagnostic Assessment

These inform the teacher (and students) of learners' prior knowledge. What do they know? What preconceptions and misconceptions do they have? These assessments are never graded. Their purpose is to determine where the students are so the teacher can decide on areas that need to be addressed. They also help students to clearly identify their own preconceptions so that they can specifically compare them to new experiences and explanations. Many of the entries in this book begin with questions and discussions to assess prior knowledge. Also, strategies such as concept maps, drawings, Venn diagrams, and others can be used. Prior knowledge assessment is critical for a constructivist approach to teaching.

2. Formative Assessment

Formative assessments occur frequently. They are informal and usually not graded. Formative assessment provides feedback to students. It helps them further their understanding of skills or concepts. It takes the form of questioning, discussing, critiquing, peer critiquing, self-critiquing, and other techniques.

Formative assessment is assessment in that it gauges student abilities and understandings but it is teaching in that it also helps the student to improve those abilities and understandings. All of the lessons in this book include questions, discussions, feedback sessions, and reflections that serve as formative assessment.

3. Summative Assessment

Summative assessments occur at the end of an activity, unit of study, or course. Tests, lab reports, and other graded assessments fall in this category. A summative assessment attempts to quantify the level of student achievement. What did they learn? What do they now know or know how to do? How well can they explain certain concepts? There is, of course, overlap among the types of assessment. For instance, many summative tasks can also involve a formative component or be used in a formative way.

Scientific Reporting

Central to scientific inquiry is the communication of goals, procedures, experimental approaches, results, and explanations. There are a number of ways that students can report on their investigations. These develop scientific reporting abilities and inform the teacher of student achievement.

Lab reports are an important format for communicating scientific information that students should experience. However, scientists communicate their results in many other ways as well. And student interest is heightened if a variety of strategies for assessing labs are used.

Mini posters (Williamson, 2002) are used by students to create a scaled-down version of a scientific poster like the ones used by researchers at conferences. By taping or gluing two file folders together, they make a three-paneled, self-standing mini poster on which they present information on their investigation (see Figure 1.1). On the due date students set up their mini posters, and they circulate among those of others, reviewing and critiquing them. The posters fold into an 8–1/2 x 11-inch size for storage. If a section (or more) of the mini poster is deemed to need revision, it is easy for a student to rework that section only and then tape it on top of the original version of the section. An advantage to the small poster size is that it forces students to be concise. See the outline in Worksheet 1.1 for the sections that could be included in a mini poster or scientific lab report paper. Worksheet 1.1 could also be used as a handout for reference.

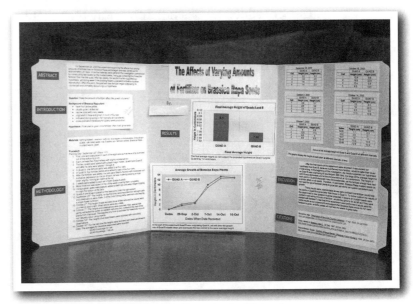

Figure 1.1. Example of a Miniposter

Oral presentations can take many forms. Students can use posters, overhead transparences, PowerPoint® slides, and so on. Often inquiry investigations lead different student groups in different experimental directions, so presentations promote concept learning among the audience as they learn about an investigation that is different from their own. Presentations also allow for modeling of skills, abilities, and approaches. Students observing exceptional presentations learn what "could have been done" and the achievement bar is raised for all.

More importantly, oral presentations facilitate formative feedback discussions that advance understanding for everyone in the class. During or after presentations the teacher questions presenters and/or audience members about statements made, experimental design flaws, faulty logic, content misconceptions, and so forth. The teacher should also encourage peer critiquing. Productive questions include, "Does anybody see a flaw in the experimental design?" or "Does everyone agree with that statement/claim/conclusion?" or "What else could have been done?"

Reflections encourage students throughout an investigation to think about what they are doing. In class or at home journal writing encourages student thinking on questions, experimental designs, conclusions, and biology concept explanations and applications. These are ongoing formative assessments. They aid the learners in constructing new understanding for themselves.

Narrative lab reports (Licata, 1999) are a periodic alternative to formal lab reports that focus students more on the concepts than on the structure of the reporting. In a continuous essay, students "tell the story" of the inquiry. They can be focused on addressing central questions such as:

- What was I looking for?
- How did I look for it?
- What did I find?
- What does this mean?

Data tables, graphs, sketches, and *calculations* can be embedded in the body of the essay or added to the end. Either way they should be discussed in the narrative.

Sections for a Scientific Paper or Poster

I. The Title
The title should be descriptive. It should be brief *but* it should also indicate the variable(s) that were tested. A poor title: *Plant Experiment.* A better one: *Investigation of the Effects of Mozart's Music on* Brassica rapa *growth.*

II. The Abstract
A one- or two-paragraph summary. The abstract condenses the entire report into a brief, clear, quickly readable overview.

III. Introduction
Background information: What is the experimental topic? What is known about the topic? What is unknown? How does this study fit into that context? Define and explain the major scientific concepts.
Questions and hypothesis: Explicitly state the experimental question being investigated. State any hypotheses being investigated and if/then predictions.

IV. Methods and Materials
Procedure: Listed numbered steps. What exactly was done (written in past tense) in enough detail so others could replicate your experiment. But keep it concise.
Materials: What materials were used?
Statistical/mathematical analysis: What calculations (for example, mean of height increase in plants exposed to. . .) were made?

V. Results
1. Data tables and graphs go here.

2. Describe the results but do not interpret them here. Interpretation of results goes in "Discussion."

VI. Discussion
Address the original question and hypothesis. Did the experiment answer the question? Did the results support the hypothesis? *Refer to the data* to back up conclusions.

Explain the data. If the results were unexpected, why were they? Even if results were expected, what other possible explanations are there?

Biological meaning, implications, context, and "big picture." Any generalizations and new predictions can be described here.

Areas of future research should be described.

VII. Literature Cited
Bibliography of all sources used for background information.
Adapted from: Ambrose, H., Ambrose, K., Emlen, D., & Bright, K. (2002). *A handbook of biological investigations* (6th ed.). Winston-Salem, NC: Hunter Textbooks.

Constructivism

A growing body of evidence supports the infusion of constructivist learning theory into science lessons. Central to constructivism is the notion that humans actively construct knowledge based on interactions with the physical world and social interactions with others. Learning does not happen by receiving information. Rather it occurs as people actively build new understandings for themselves. Also, people enter learning opportunities with pre-existing understandings that were constructed through previous experiences.

Implications for Biology Teachers

Two primary insights from constructivism need attention from biology teachers:

1. Knowledge is actively constructed by learners. Our students are ultimately responsible for developing their own new comprehension. Lasting learning will not occur via an active teacher transmitting information to passive recipients. Teachers instead need to guide students through the process of constructing new knowledge for themselves.

2. Students come to class with previously constructed knowledge based on their past experiences. These preconceptions, many of which are misconceptions, are hard to displace! Research shows that unless students acknowledge and address their preconceptions on concepts studied in class they do not abandon them (NSTA, 2003).

Constructivist Lessons

Some of the essential aspects of a constructivist lesson include:

1. *Determine student prior knowledge.* Assess students for their preconceptions on the topic(s) to be learned. This can be done via concept maps, free-association brainstorming, drawings, discussions, and so on. Many of the lessons in this book begin with discussions to elicit prior knowledge. It is critical that students not be criticized for their ideas that are misconceptions. Instead, strategies should be employed to help students recognize and decide themselves that certain prior knowledge needs to be modified or replaced.

2. *Students construct new and better understandings.* This should begin at the level of what students know and believe (preconceptions). Students engage in inquiry activities, discussions, research, and so on to build new knowledge. The process should be active, requiring much interaction, analysis, evaluation, explanation, justification, and communication.

3. *Students reflect on their learning.* If preconceptions are going to be altered or replaced, then students need to think about how new information integrates

with previously held beliefs. Via journal writing, focused questions, and discussions, learners compare where they are now to where they were before. In short, they directly address the extent to which their thinking on a subject has changed.

Trumbull (1999) points out that constructivist learning should involve dialogue, argument, and reference to evidence. Such actions help students to construct new understanding. It is also important for students to use biology content in varied situations. Such knowledge transfer facilitates deep and lasting learning.

Many of the lessons in this book follow a constructivist approach in one way or another. For instance, Are Humans Still Evolving? begins by eliciting misconceptions and finishes with students reflecting on how their thinking has changed. Bacon Diffusion exemplifies how a traditional demonstration can be modified into a constructivist introduction to a concept. A number of sources listed in the references such as Yager (1991), Llewellyn (2002), and Zelia and Geraldo (1999) go into more depth on constructivism in science education.

Questioning in Constructivist Lessons

The following are examples of teacher questions that would be supported by constructivist learning theory. Of course, all of the inquiry-oriented questions listed earlier would also fit here.

Prior Knowledge Assessment
- What do you know about . . . ?
- What comes to mind when you think of . . . ?
- What causes . . . ?
- How do you explain . . . ?

Reflection Questions
- Think back to our first discussion on this topic. Many people believed . . . . What do you now think of that idea?
- Why do you now think differently about that?
- How has your thinking on . . . . changed after this lab/activity/unit?
- How effective was your experimental plan?
- Why did we do this activity/lab/lesson? Did it help you learn? Explain.

Develop Your Own Inquiries

The *Standards,* an inquiry approach, and constructivism all point toward extended in-depth student-generated investigations. Many of the best biology learning experiences will germinate out of student interests and locally relevant issues.

Resources for Educators

In addition to the *Standards,* the National Research Council has published expanded books on inquiry (NRC, 2000) and assessment (NRC, 2001). These works are highly recommended. The National Science Teacher's Association's (2003) publication, *Pathways to the Science Standards,* helps to explain the *Standards* and provides excellent examples of each standard being implemented in the classroom.

The Biological Sciences Curriculum Study (BSCS) has promoted the inquiry approach since the 1950s. BSCS has developed a "5 E" model for implementing constructivist inquiry lessons. It provides a template for including the essential components of effective science learning. The five phases of the model are Engage, Explore, Explain, Elaborate, and Evaluate. See the BSCS Web site for much information as well as access to resources. Their Web address is www.bscs.org.

The Access Excellence Web site, www.accessexcellence.org, contains many standards-based lesson ideas, science education reform articles, discussions, and more.

Membership in NSTA provides their journal, *The Science Teacher,* which is ripe with ideas on inquiry, constructivism, and national standards. Their Web site offers many more resources at www.nsta.org. The National Association of Biology Teachers' journal, *The American Biology Teacher,* often includes inquiry-oriented ideas and discussions. Their Web site is www.nabt.org.

The Exploratorium, www.exploratorium.com, has an institute dedicated to promoting inquiry-based science learning.

References

Alberts, B. (2000). Some thoughts of a scientist on inquiry. In J. Minstrell, and E. van Zee (Eds.), *Inquiring into inquiry learning and teaching in science* (pp. 3–13). Washington, DC: American Association for the Advancement of Science.

Bybee, R. (2002). Scientific inquiry, student learning and the science curriculum. In R. Bybee (Ed.), *Learning science and the science of learning* (pp. 25–35). Arlington, VA: NSTA Press.

Clark, R., Clough, M., & Berg, C. (2000). Modifying cookbook labs. *The Science Teacher, 67*(7), 40–43.

Doran, R., Chan, F., Tamir, P., & Lenhart, C. (2002). *Science educator's guide to laboratory assessment.* Arlington, VA: NSTA Press.

Leonard, W., Penick, J., & Douglas, R. (2002). What does it mean to be standards-based? *The Science Teacher, 69*(4), 36–39.

Licata, K. (1999). Narrative lab reports. *The Science Teacher, 66*(3), 20–22.

Llewellyn, D. (2002) *Inquire within: Implementing inquiry-based science standards.* Thousand Oaks, CA: Corwin.

National Research Council. (1996). *National science education standards.* Washington, DC: National Academy Press.

National Research Council. (2000). *Inquiry and the national science education standards: A guide for teaching and learning.* Washington, DC: National Academy Press.

National Research Council. (2001). *Classroom assessment and the national science education standards.* Washington, DC: National Academy Press.

National Science Teachers Association. (2004). Position statement on scientific inquiry. Accessed at www.nsta.org.

Texley, J., & Wild, A. (Eds.). (2003). *Pathways to the science standards* (2nd ed.). Arlington, VA: NSTA Press.

Trumbull, D. (1999). *The new science teacher: Cultivating good practice.* New York: Teacher's College Press.

Yager, R. (2000). The constructivist learning model. *The Science Teacher, 67*(1), 44–45.

Volkmann, M., & Abell, S. (2003). Rethinking laboratories: tools for converting cookbook labs into inquiry. *The Science Teacher, 70*(6), 38–41.

Williamson, B. (2002). *A segment of a presentation included an explanation of the idea of using mini-posters to assess investigations.* NSTA national convention, San Diego, California.

Zelia, J., & Geraldo, A. (1999). A course for critical constructivism through action research: A case study from biology. *Research in Science and Technological Education, 17*(1), 5–17.

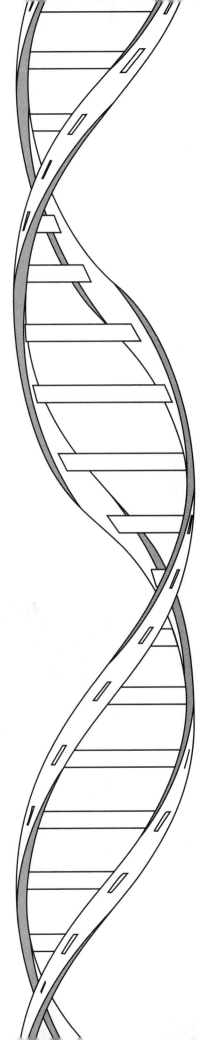

Chapter 2

Science as Inquiry

Developing Inquiry Abilities and Understanding

The lessons in this chapter aim to develop both an understanding of the nature of science and the ability to think and act like a scientist. Many of the lessons in the other chapters of the book focus on these outcomes as well, but the lessons here are more generically focused on scientific inquiry. Most would work well early in a course, but they also could be integrated into any content unit in a biology curriculum.

The Inquiry Cubes

In this minds-on inquiry, students use observations and deductive reasoning to make predictions about unknown sides of three patterned cubes.

Topic Connections

Scientific Inquiry, Nature of Science, Role of Technology

Introduction

This inquiry begins with students sitting in a circle around a large numbered cube. At first students make and record observations based solely on what they can see from their seats. Eventually they solicit information about the cube from others in the room and, using all available evidence, they try to predict the numbers on the bottom side of the cube. This first cube is a die numbered 1 through 6.

The next two cubes are progressively more complex. The second one is numbered in sequence from 2 through 12. With 12 as the hidden number, the students at first will predict either 0 or 12 for the bottom because they could both continue the visible sequence of 2 through 10. However, observing that opposite sides sum to 14 allows them to *more confidently* predict 12 to be on the bottom because 2 is on top.

Patterned with two numbers and a name per side, the third cube increases the challenge considerably. Here, students experience the importance of clearly recording every observation if they are to successfully discern a pattern from the evidence. Multiple hypotheses are offered, debated, and tested. The usefulness of technology is introduced as students use a small mirror to view one corner of the hidden cube side.

The Inquiry Cubes introduce many of the central skills of scientific investigation and the nature of science. After experiencing the cubes students are surveyed for prior knowledge on scientific inquiry. Subsequently, new concepts are acquired and then applied by students to their experiences with the cubes.

Figure 2.1. Two Inquiry Cubes

Materials

- Cardboard or construction paper, enough to make three cubes approximately 12 inches by 12 inches by 12 inches
- Clear tape
- Markers: black, red
- Mirror, pocket-sized

Time Approximation

Cubes #1 and #2 require about 15 minutes. Cube #3 requires about 25 minutes.

The cubes can be done in succession over one long period or they can be broken up (one per day or one per week).

Preparation

Cut large (12 inches by 12 inches by 12 inches) squares out of cardboard or construction paper. The sturdier the cubes are made, the better they will last from year to year. After writing the numbers, names, and any other information on the squares, tape them into cubes (Fig 2.1).

The sides for the cubes should be as follows:

Cube #1

- Number each side from 1 to 6 with the black marker
- Draw diagonal lines in pencil across each *even* numbered side
- Make the cube so that opposite sides add up to 7 (1 and 6 are opposite each other, 2 and 5, 3 and 4). When making the cube, be sure that the numbers on the four sides (1, 3, 4, 6) will be right-side-up when the cube is sitting with 2 on the bottom.

Cube #2

- Number each side 2, 4, 6, 8, 10, and 12 with the black marker
- Make the cube so that opposite sides add up to 14
- When making the cube, orient the four sides (4, 6, 8, 10) so that the numbers will be right-side-up when the cube is sitting with 12 on the bottom

Cube #3

- Use Figure 2.2 as a model for making the cube
- All numbers should be black
- Names should be colored as follows:

  Frank and Francene—red

  Rob and Roberta—blue

  Alma and Alfred—black
- Names and numbers should be right-side-up when Francene is on the bottom

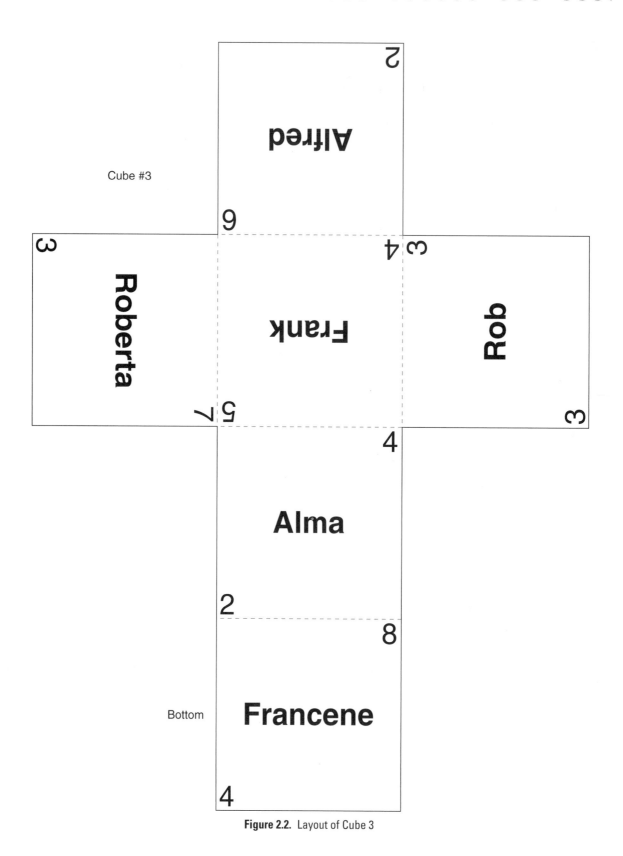

Cube #3

Bottom

Figure 2.2. Layout of Cube 3

Lesson Outline

1. Arrange the class in a circle. Place Cube #1 in the middle of the circle of students so that the number "2" is on the bottom. Be careful not to reveal the bottom of the cube.

2. Have the students make and record as many observations about the cube as they can. Do not let them get up to look at other parts of the cube.

3. Ask the students what questions they have about the cube. These might include:

   • What is on the other side?

   • What is inside?

   • What is on the bottom?

4. One at a time allow student volunteers to ask any other student any question about the cube. In this way students will acquire more data about the cube.

5. Now point out that the question, "What is on the bottom of the cube?" cannot be resolved as easily as some of the others. Focus their thinking on this question.

6. Solicit student hypotheses for what exactly is on the bottom of the cube. For each prediction ask the students what observations serve as evidence to support that idea. See "Implementation Strategies" for examples. Challenge them to explain their reasoning. Facilitate debate or discussion between students with conflicting ideas (this is more of an issue with Cube #2 and especially with #3)

7. Remove Cube #1 without students seeing the bottom.

8. Repeat the above procedure with Cube #2. This time position the cube with the number "12" on the bottom.

9. Repeat the procedure with Cube #3 with some modifications (position the cube with "Francene" on the bottom). After they have made observations and solicited information about the cube from each other, ask them whether they have all of the information sorted out. The cube is complex enough that there likely will be some confusion at this point. Students will be asking others to repeat their descriptions of the cube's sides. Lead the students to realize, if they haven't already, that they should have been writing down information when classmates were sharing it. Allow for another round of observation sharing, if necessary, so that everyone can record all available information for the five exposed sides.

   Next, have the students work in small groups to exchange ideas and develop hypotheses for the hidden side of the cube. Then have the groups share their predictions with the class.

   The class will likely generate three or four reasonable hypotheses for this cube. After facilitating debate on these, allow the students to use some technology to help them collect more information about the unseen side. Tell them that they can use a small pocket mirror to view one corner of the bottom side. Inform them that because of government cutbacks to their research budget they can only afford to use this expensive technology to view one corner. Have the class debate and then decide which corner to view. Then let a student lift one corner only slightly (*no more than 1 inch!*) and view it with the mirror. Any new data is shared with the class, and, if possible, hypotheses are refined.

10. Distribute the student worksheet. Use its first section to assess prior knowledge on the nature of science.

11. Introduce the students to explanations or discussions of scientific inquiry. This can be done in many ways, including teacher-facilitated discussions, readings, and Web/library research. The book *Teaching About Evolution and the Nature of Science* (National Academy of Sciences, 1998) is an excellent content source for this topic.

12. Have the students complete the "Connecting to the Cubes" section of the worksheet. Then lead a discussion on the elements of scientific inquiry experienced in The Inquiry Cubes activity.

Implementation Strategy

- Press students to continually search for additional observations, patterns, and evidence. Especially with the first cube, they may want to hastily make a conclusion. Stress the value of being increasingly confident of proposed explanations.

- Students will fall into the trap of equating their assumptions with facts. Often, with Cube #1 for example, a student will say something like "There is a 2 on the bottom because it is a die." Respond to such claims with questions like "So you say there *must* be a 2 on the bottom . . . there's no other possibility?" or "So you're *absolutely certain* that there's a 2 on the bottom?"

- Focus on the language of scientific conclusions. Students will want to conclude for the first two cubes with certainty. Guide them to phrase their thinking more cautiously in ways such as: "The evidence suggests that . . ." or "We can predict with some confidence that . . ." or "The prediction that is most strongly supported by evidence is. . . ."

- Do not reveal the bottom of the cubes at the end! This reinforces an important aspect of the nature of science. Rarely does a researcher know with absolute certainty that he or she is right. Paleontologists dating the age of a hominid fossil can't eventually "peek" to see if they are correct.

  Also if you are teaching multiple sections of a class, the "answers" would no doubt be shared to members of later periods.

- When making the cubes, you could leave the bottom side blank to prevent the students from accidentally seeing the number. With Cube #3 you could leave the name off of the bottom side (Francene), but you would still have to include the numbers for the "using technology" part of the activity.

- Begin the class period with the first cube in the center of the room. Enhance the drama of the mysterious cube by telling the students nothing about it or what they will be doing with it.

- Important observations and deductions that students could make about the cubes:

Cube #1

- Viewable numbers are 1, 3, 4, 5, 6
- Even-numbered sides have diagonal lines
- Opposite sides add up to 7
- There seems to be a sequence missing one number

Cube #2

- Viewable numbers are 2, 4, 6, 8, 10
- Opposite numbers add up to 14
- There seems to be a sequence by two's

Cube #3

- The sides include names and numbers
- Numbers in the lower left are the same on opposite sides
- Opposite side names are the same color
- Each opposite side is a similar name for the opposite gender
- Numbers in the upper right correspond with the number of letters in the name on that side
- Numbers in the lower-left corner correspond with the number of letters shared between names on opposite sides
- Numbers in the upper right form the sequence: 3, 4, 5, 6, 7
- Upper-right numbers on opposite sides sum to 10

Possible Responses for Student Worksheet Questions

1. Possibilities include questioning, hypothesizing/predicting, observing, recording data, collaborating, using deductive reasoning, concluding, using technology.

2. Measurement, mathematical analysis, repetition, large sample sizes, online or journal research, experimentation.

Reference

National Academy of Sciences. (1998). *Teaching about evolution and the nature of science.* Washington, DC: National Academy Press.

*Adapted from an activity developed by Biological Sciences Curriculum Study, Colorado Springs, Colorado. The idea for cube #2 came from a posting by Susan Plati, Brookline High School, Brookline, Massachusetts, on an Access Excellence list serv.

WORKSHEET 2.1
The Inquiry Cubes

Introductory Brainstorm

What are scientists and what do they do? How is science done? Brainstorm on these questions. Put your ideas in the space below in the form of a concept map or a list of ideas/concepts/terms that come to mind.

Connecting to the Cubes

1. List and briefly explain all of the ways that you were acting/thinking like a scientist during the Inquiry Cube experiences:

   _____

   _____

   _____

   _____

   _____

   _____

   _____

2. What are some important aspects of science that you *did not* encounter during the experiences?

   _____

   _____

   _____

   _____

   _____

   _____

   _____

She Turned Me into a Newt
(I Got Better)

In this introduction to scientific thinking, students create, justify, critique, and debate proposals for testing various common superstitions.

Topic Connections

Scientific Inquiry, Skepticism

Introduction

Does coffee stunt a child's growth? Should you feed a cold and starve a fever? Does an apple a day really keep the doctor away? Many superstitions and sayings are accepted by people simply because they have heard them repeatedly. In this lesson students design and critique experimental proposals to test the validity of various superstitions. Familiarity with the popular statements engages learners from the beginning.

Initially all of the student groups develop a plan for testing the statement "An apple a day keeps the doctor away." As groups present their plans to the class, other students and you critique the underlying logic of the experimental designs. In this way skeptical scientific thinking is developed. Simultaneously there can be an introduction (or review) of the central language of scientific inquiry, including words like hypothesis, independent/dependent variable, controls/constants, and so on. Eventually learners build on their newly reformed understanding of science inquiry by applying it to another superstition of their choice.

In the discussions students explain and justify their ideas. They also critique and debate each other's proposals. Such critical thinking is central to both developing understanding and to the process of scientific inquiry.

The film *Monty Python and the Holy Grail* includes two segments that parody scientific thinking. In one, King Arthur's claim that swallows carried his squire's two coconuts to England is hilariously scrutinized by two guards. In the other, peasants are asked to provide evidence that a woman is indeed a witch. One character proclaims that she turned him into a newt (he got better). Both scenes involve if/then statements, alternative hypotheses, skeptical thinking, and even controls. The short segments are a fun supplement to this lesson. Viewing can be followed by a discussion of the sometimes valid, but mostly very faulty, application of scientific thinking.

Materials

- Overhead transparencies, mini whiteboards, or poster paper
- Video or DVD of *Monty Python and the Holy Grail* (optional)

  The two segments are "Coconuts" Chapter 2, 4 minutes to 7 minutes into the film and "Witch Village" Chapter 6, 17 minutes to 21 minutes into the film

Time Approximation

Part I—"An apple a day. . ." experimental design, presentations, and discussion: 45 minutes

Part II—Second superstition: 35 minutes (or could be shortened if the second experimental designs were done as homework)

Optional video segments: 15 minutes with discussion

Lesson Outline

The First Experimental Design

1. Distribute the student worksheet or write "An apple a day keeps the doctor away" on the board. Ask students whether they have heard the statement before and if they think it is true. Ask them how we know when a claim is true.

2. Break the learners into groups of three or four. Each group will design an experiment to test the "An apple a day . . ." claim. In bullet or outline form the groups put their experimental design on an overhead transparency, a mini whiteboard, or poster paper.

3. Have about four groups share their plans with the class. After a group presents, encourage class members to politely critique the plan. Point out problems, logical inconsistencies, and so forth. Guide them to realize areas for improvement (such as increasing sample size or repeating the experiment).

4. Lead a class-wide discussion in which students summarize the essential features of science inquiry. Also have them explain common problem areas that can invalidate or weaken an experiment.

The Second Experimental Design

1. Student groups (or individuals) choose a superstition from the listing on the student worksheet.

2. They design an experiment to test the claim. This time their designs are written on notebook paper. This step could be completed in class or at home.

3. Students exchange their experimental plans with other groups or individual students. After reading each other's plans, they make notes critiquing the experimental design. Groups/students who exchanged plans then get together to discuss their ideas for improving each other's experiments.

Monty Python

1. Show the two segments of *Monty Python and the Holy Grail.*

2. Lead a discussion. Ask in what ways did the characters think scientifically? In what ways was their thinking sound? In what ways was it flawed?

Implementation Strategy

- The lesson works well with all ability levels. The level of sophistication of ideas will vary with different groups, but all will advance their understanding of scientific inquiry.

- Use this lesson early in a course. Even more advanced groups can use a review of the essentials of science process. Also, the lesson reveals to you how well the students understand scientific inquiry. This information can help guide the choice of lessons to follow.

- It is important for the presenting of the first experimental designs to be oral and to the whole class. This is the core portion of the lesson. The public critiquing and debating helps all of the students to advance their understanding. And under your guidance, misconceptions can be directly addressed.

- Be aware of the experimental plans as they are being developed. That way, if you don't have time for every group to present, you can pick the ones that are the most unique or that raise the most interesting points for discussion.

- As much as possible, encourage students to politely critique the experimental designs of groups that present them. But also critique them yourself by asking pointed questions and facilitating discussion.

- The second experimental design is in essence an assessment. Here students take what they have learned and apply it to a new situation. These experimental plans should show significant improvement over the first ("An apple a day . . .") ones.

- Possible considerations/issues/variables to raise in discussion:
  - *Sample size*—How many people should be studied? For how long? How many times (repetition)?
  - *Variables*—Characteristics of people such as age, weight, gender, genetic differences, and so on
  - *Data*—How collected? How measured? Quantifiable?

Reference

Hoefnagels, M., & Rippel, S. (2003). Using superstitions and sayings to teach experimental design in beginning and advanced biology classes. *The American Biology Teacher, 65*(4), 263–268.

Name _____   Date _____

"An Apple a Day Keeps the Doctor Away"

We have all heard this and many other similar claims throughout our lives. But how do we know if they are true?

Your Task

Part I

1. In small groups, discuss and develop a plan for how you could test the "An apple a day ..." statement to see if it is valid.

2. In bullet or outline form, put your experimental plan onto a transparency or poster paper. Be prepared to explain your design to the class.

3. When other groups present their ideas, take note of aspects of their plans that could be improved. By politely sharing your critique of another group's experiment you will be helping everyone to learn more about scientific inquiry.

Part II

1. Choose a statement from the list below.

2. Design an experiment to test the validity of that claim. Explain your experimental plan in writing.

3. You will be exchanging this plan with another group/student for constructive criticism.

Statements for Experimental Designing

- Eating chocolate causes zits.

- Shaving makes hair grow back more densely.

- Drinking coffee will stunt a child's growth.

- If you swim immediately after eating, you will get cramps.

- If you go outside when your head is wet, you'll catch a cold.

- Feed a cold, starve a fever.

- Break a mirror and you will have seven years of bad luck.

- If you blow out all the candles on your birthday cake with the first puff, you will get your wish.

- The full moon makes people restless.

- Eating carrots improves eyesight.

- If you cross your eyes too often, they will stay that way.

- Reading in dim light damages a person's eyes.

Storytelling Graphing

Students decide how to graph a data set. Graphs are then compared and evaluated for effectiveness.

Topic Connections
Inquiry Abilities, Data Analysis, Communicating Results

Introduction
A good graph tells a story. It arranges and displays data in a way that communicates a trend, a distinction or a notable pattern. Graphs clarify. And they communicate efficiently. An effective graph can quickly reveal the bottom line of an experiment in a way words could not. But not all graphs are created equal. Because of their design, some graphs communicate more information (or more interesting information) than others.

In this lesson, students are challenged to make two to three different graphs of the same data set. They will ask for, but will not receive, guidance as to the types of graphs to make, the grouping of the data, the variables for each axis, and other issues. Instead, they will grapple with the task of making different graphs that communicate something about the data, graphs that "tell a story." Eventually a variety of the student graphs will be displayed, critiqued, and discussed. In the end, students will learn from each other about different approaches to effective graphing.

The lesson calls for using student heights for the data set. However, any set of measurements will do. Since the *National Science Education Standards* call for teaching process skills in the context of content learning, you could infuse this lesson into any early year lab or project.

Materials
- Meter sticks
- Graph paper

Time Approximation
20 minutes to measure and exchange data (Graphs can be completed as a home assignment.) and 20 to 30 minutes to observe, critique, and discuss the graphs

Lesson Outline

Day One
1. In pairs students measure each other and record their heights and names on a blackboard or overhead transparency.
2. Students copy the class data into a table in their notebooks.

3. At home, students make two or three different graphs of the data. They are told only that their graphs should "tell a story" about the data.

Day Two

1. Have a number of students draw one of their graphs on the board in the classroom. Choose the students so that a variety of graph types are represented. Be sure that some of the least effective and some of the most effective graphs are put on the board.

2. Ask the students to consider which graphs convey the most information. Which ones the least? Lead a discussion comparing the possible graphs for the data.

Implementation Strategy

- Any set of quantitative measurements can be used. An advantage to using student heights is the added number of variables to be considered such as gender, names, ninth versus tenth grade, and so on. And interest is always heightened when the study topics are the students themselves.

- Students will want more specific instructions for making the graphs, but don't provide it. Leave them to ponder the possibilities of line versus bar versus pie, what to put on each axis, and so on.

- Although computer-assisted graphing is an important skill to learn, it is recommended that this lesson require pen and graph paper to completely focus the student on designing the graphs themselves.

Possible Student Graph Designs and a Critique

No Grouping

- Height on the Y axis, student names on X axis (line or bar graph)
- Same as above but students arranged in ascending order

These two approaches provide little new information beyond the original data table. The only story they tell is "the class contains many students of varying heights."

Averaging

- Bar graphs of male versus female average heights or other averages

These provide more useful and interesting information than nongrouped graphs

Grouping

- Bar or pie graph of groupings on X axis and "number of students" on Y axis. Groupings could be something like 141 to 145 cm, 146 to 150 cm, and so on.

These graphs relate substantial information. They convey "the story" of where most people in the class fall, how wide the range of the class is, and other information. Even more information is revealed if two or more of this sort are combined on one page comparing genders, for example.

- Discussion of the graphs opens an opportunity to raise the concept of normal distributions and bell curves.

WORKSHEET 2.3
Storytelling Graphing

Graphs communicate information about data. In short, they tell a story. With an effective graph a researcher can quickly show a reader or an audience the outcome of an experiment or an interesting trend. In this activity you will be challenged to make two or three graphs that communicate something about a group of numbers.

The Initial Task

1. Determine your height in centimeters. You might want to work with a partner for this.

2. Record your name and height on the blackboard or other area recommended by the teacher.

3. Make a data table to record the height of every student in the class.

The Challenge

1. Make two or three graphs that visually "tell a story" about the data. The graphs can be of any type that you choose. They can be organized in any way that you choose. There is not one "right" way to do this. There are many possible ways to graph the same data.

Analysis

Look carefully at the different types of graphs made by your classmates.

1. For each graph think about this: "What additional information does the graph give me beyond what is in the data table?"

   _____

   _____

   _____

2. Which two graphs communicate the most interesting "story"? In what way?

   _____

   _____

   _____

3. What other factors contribute to the effectiveness of a graph?

   _____

   _____

   _____

Crossed Knives: A Pattern Game

Students struggle to detect a simple pattern that is revealed through careful and creative observation.

Topic Connections

Scientific Inquiry

Introduction

This brief partial inquiry challenges students to expand their focus of observation. Sitting in a circle, the class begins slowly passing around a pair of butter knives. As they are received by a student, proclaim either "They are crossed" or "They are uncrossed." Students assume the statement is referring to the knives, but you are actually commenting on the legs of the person holding the knives.

When students believe they have detected the pattern, encourage them to test their hypothesis by substituting for you in making the statement. Gradually more and more students join in. Sometimes student hypotheses work only once or twice before it becomes apparent that the pattern has not been solved and a point is thus made about the value of experimental replication. Early in the lesson pause the game and have students discuss their observations. Upon being encouraged to expand their focus and to record and evaluate their observations, a number of students more easily detect the pattern.

Materials

Knives, two plastic or butter knives that are not sharp

Time Approximation

20 minutes

Lesson Outline

1. Arrange the class in a circle that includes yourself.
2. Give an explanation of the game. Tell the class that the two knives will be passed around the circle from one person to the next. Inform them that you will make a statement every time the knives are received by a person. The students' challenge is to carefully observe and to determine the pattern that is occurring. Be very clear to the students that if they think they have the pattern, they should not say it out loud to anyone. Instead, students should volunteer to test their hypotheses by making the statement in place of you.

3. Have the students begin slowly passing the knives around the circle. When a student receives the knives, say either "They are crossed" or "They are uncrossed" as determined by the status of the receiving student's legs at the time.

4. Continue for a couple of turns around the circle. Let students try their own hypotheses by making the statement for you. Correct them if they are wrong or ask other students who seem to have "gotten it" to make the correction.

5. After a couple of times around, pause the game. Ask the students what they need in order to solve the mystery. Encourage them to make a list of their observations to that point. After a few minutes of listing, have students share their observations, but do not have them discuss possible patterns—just observations.

6. Tell the students that the game will resume, but that this time they should more carefully look for and record as wide an array of observations as they can.

7. Resume the game. Continue until a majority of students have detected the pattern.

8. Use the student worksheet questions as a guide for discussion.

Implementation Strategy

- This lesson can be used during any unit of a biology course. Consider using it after a full inquiry in which student-made observations were more narrow than they could have been.

- For the game to work, the class needs to be seated in a circle with student legs observable to everyone in the group. If all student legs are not easily visible, then you might have to move yourself to see, and that could give away the pattern.

- Implore students not to blurt out the pattern when they discover it. Also ask them not to share it with nearby students during the game.

- When you pause the game to discuss observations, ask that students who have detected the pattern not share the one key observation (leg crossing).

- You may have to slow students down if they pass the knives too quickly to allow for sufficient observation time.

Possible Responses to Student Worksheet Questions

1. Value of careful, detailed observation; focusing on every detail—you never know which ones will end up being trivial and which significant—value of recording observations to document, remember, evaluate.

2. Hypothesizing, observing, recording observations, testing hypotheses, evaluating data.

3. This shows the importance of replicating experiments. Scientists should test hypotheses multiple times to verify support.

Reflection and Assessment

Have the students respond to the questions on the student worksheet in written form and/or via a classwide discussion. For an assessment, have students design a new pattern game challenge that requires careful, broad observation to solve.

Source

Dan Griesback, New Teacher's Institute, Rutgers University, 1993.

WORKSHEET 2.4
Crossed Knives

1. Why did we do this pattern game activity in biology class? What was the point? What lessons were learned from it?

   _____

   _____

   _____

   _____

   _____

   _____

2. In what ways did you think or act like a scientist in this game?

   _____

   _____

   _____

   _____

   _____

   _____

3. Student hypotheses in the game sometimes were supported at first but then were not. What should scientists do to be sure that a hypothesis is a good one?

   _____

   _____

   _____

   _____

   _____

   _____

4. Design a new pattern game that challenges people to be carefully and broadly observant. Explain how it would work:

   _____

   _____

   _____

   _____

   _____

   _____

The Distraction Stick: Another Pattern Game

Students struggle to detect a simple pattern that is hidden by distracting irrelevant actions.

Topic Connections

Atmosphere of Inquiry, Hypothesizing, Observing, Skepticism

Introduction

Science extracts meaning from a seeming chaos of actions and processes. Scientists look for patterns. Events that occur repeatedly may be meaningful.

This brief partial inquiry challenges students to find a subtle but predictable pattern. They question, hypothesize, collect evidence, and debate the meaning of the evidence. The lesson is an engaging way to use a short time period on one of those days when the classroom mood could use some lightening! It also helps to perpetuate an atmosphere of inquiry, of questioning, probing, and looking beyond the obvious with a critical eye.

In the game you bait students into searching for a visual pattern (that doesn't exist) by making random motions with a meter stick. Meanwhile, the true pattern is that for every round of the game the first person making a sound is the one who is "it." After a few rounds of the game, students discuss their evidence and attempt to develop hypotheses. More trials ensue. Along the way students are encouraged to test their hypotheses by leading a few rounds of the game.

Materials

Meter stick

Time Approximation

20 minutes

Lesson Outline

1. Students arrange themselves in a circle.

2. Stand inside the circle with a meter stick or broom handle.

3. Explain that in "the stick game" there will be a pattern, detectable over multiple rounds of the game, and their challenge is to find it.

4. Tell the class that if someone thinks he or she has found the pattern, to not call out what it is. Instead the student should test the hypothesis. He or she could volunteer to lead a few rounds of the game or could simply observe further rounds to see if his or her hypothesis is supported.

Teacher Pages

5. Begin each round of the game by announcing, "Let the stick game begin." As you finish the phrase, bang the meter stick on the ground.

6. Make a mental note of the first student who makes a sound after you have banged the meter stick to start the game. This student is the one who is "it."

7. Wave the stick around in dramatic but random motions. Periodically point the stick at certain students, invent sequences of motions, make dramatic eye contact with some. In short, trick the students into thinking that there is something in your motions that determines or signifies who is "it."

8. Suddenly stop the motions and announce who the "it" student is.

9. After four or five rounds of the game, pause and have students discuss with others nearby. They should discuss their observations and any evidence they have for their hypotheses.

10. Resume more trials of the game.

11. If a student proclaims to "get it" then have him or her test the hypothesis by leading two or three rounds of the game.

12. Have students complete the worksheet questions or lead a discussion on the topics.

Implementation Strategy

- The lesson can be useful during any unit of a biology course. Consider connecting it to a full inquiry in which students had trouble noticing important but subtle patterns.

- Implore students not to blurt out the pattern when they discover it and ask them not to share it with nearby students. Instead, students "in the know" should lead some rounds of the game.

- It is possible that no students will discover the pattern. You might leave it undiscovered—scientists can't just give up and ask for "the answer." You could briefly do further trials at future times to prolong the atmosphere of inquiry.

Source

Patrick E. Fitzpatrick, 1994 Access Excellence Fellow, Westminster Schools, Atlanta, Georgia.

Name _____   Date _____

The Distraction Stick

1. Why did we do the stick game in biology class? What was the point? What lessons were learned from it?

   _____

   _____

   _____

   _____

   _____

   _____

   _____

2. In what ways did you act and/or think like a scientist during the experience?

   _____

   _____

   _____

   _____

   _____

   _____

   _____

   _____

3. Discuss some examples of patterns in biology that would be important for a researcher to discover.

   _____

   _____

   _____

   _____

   _____

   _____

   _____

   _____

Case Study Study

Students analyze and discuss case studies of biological research to advance their understanding of scientific inquiry.

Topic Connections

Scientific Inquiry, Nature of Science

Introduction

This reading and discussion lesson addresses the "understandings of scientific inquiry" outlined in the *National Science Education Standards*. Learners read descriptions of biological research programs in articles from popular journals such as *Scientific American* and *Discover*. Students analyze the case studies for features that are central to successful scientific inquiry. Then in small and large group sessions students discuss, debate, and critique the investigations.

Introductory biology textbooks sometimes promote the misconception that science always involves controlled experimentation as part of rigid scientific method. While controlled experiments are extremely important to many studies, they are irrelevant to many others. In addition to the logic of controlling variables, learners should develop an understanding of the features that are common to the majority of scientific inquiries. These features include attention to historical and current scientific knowledge, varied sources of scientific questions, use of technology, use of math, evidence-based logical explanations, the defending and communicating of results and—throughout it all—skeptical thinking.

Materials

Science magazine or journal articles, one per student, hard copy or online link (see "Implementation Strategy").

Time Approximation

- Reading the article will vary; can be completed outside of class
- Small group discussion: 20 to 30 minutes
- Classwide discussion: 30 minutes

Lesson Outline

1. Distribute the student worksheet. Students read the article assigned or they choose from a list of possibilities (see "Implementation Strategy"). They take notes on the discussion questions. (This can also be assigned as homework.)

2. In groups of four, students discuss their ideas for the discussion questions. The group should prepare to share their ideas with the class in the next phase.

3. Divide the discussion questions among the groups in the class. Have each group present their ideas for two or three of the questions. After each presentation, facilitate whole-class discussion/debate on the ideas presented by a group.

4. As homework, have the students write on the reflection topics on the student worksheets.

Implementation Strategy

- There are many possible variants on the Lesson Outline. As written, the lesson allows for in-depth teacher-facilitated analysis of one article. This allows for more detailed and focused attention to some of the nuances of scientific inquiry. This approach could be used periodically throughout a course. Articles could be chosen for various content units, and they could be analyzed for scientific inquiry features as well as for new biology concept knowledge.

  Alternatively, students could choose an article to analyze from a list you provide. Groups of four or five could study the same article and eventually present it to other groups who read a different article. In this approach, the class is exposed to a variety of types of biological research.

- *Scientific American* and *Discover* articles are generally comprehensible to secondary students. Not all articles are appropriate. Choose ones that describe an investigation/inquiry/research program. These types of articles will discuss the researchers and their questions, motivations, and approaches. The References list below includes some articles that would work.

  Date of publication is not a critical issue, since the lesson focuses on timeless features of scientific inquiry. Even very old articles on classic studies could be used.

  Scientific American and *Discover* have archived past issues online. Access is available to subscribers. Libraries may have institutional site licenses.

- Advanced high school students may benefit from reading and analyzing primary sources. This lesson plan could be used with articles from biology research journals. Some of these are making past issues available online for free. The Public Library of Science has a free online biology research journal. See their Web site at www.plosbiology.org.

- The lesson also would work well with book accounts of biological research. Books such as *The Double Helix* by James Watson or *The Beak of the Finch* by Jonathan Weiner could be used.

Some Research Case Study Articles

Blaustein, A., & Wake, D. (1995, April). The puzzle of declining amphibian populations. *Scientific American,* pp. 52–57.

Blaustein, A., & Johnson, P. (2003, February). Explaining frog deformities. *Scientific American, 288,* 60–65.

Cattaneo, E. (2002, December). The enigma of Huntington's Disease. *Scientific American, 287,* 93–97.

Grossman, D. (2004, January). Spring forward. *Scientific American, 290,* 85–91.

Jablonski, N., & Chaplin, G. (2002, October). Skin deep. *Scientific American, 287,* 75–81.

Lenley, B. (2004, February). What does science say you should eat? *Discover, 25,* 43–49.

McClintock, J. (2004, November). This is your ancestor. *Discover, 25,* 64–69.

Pauly, D., & Watson, R. (2003, July). The last fish. *Scientific American, 289,* 43–47.

Willet, W., & Stampfer, M. (2003, January). Rebuilding the food pyramid. *Scientific American, 288,* 64–71.

Yeoman, B. (2003, July). Can we trust research done with lab mice? *Discover, 24,* 65–72.

References

Bybee, R. (2000). Teaching science as inquiry. In J. Minstrell & E. van Zee (Eds.), *Inquiring into inquiry learning and teaching in science* (pp. 20–46). Washington, DC: American Association for the Advancement of Science.

Watson, J. (1968). *The double helix.* New York: Atheneum.

Weiner, J. (1994). *The beak of the finch.* New York: Knopf.

Name _____ Date _____

Case Study Study

You will be reading an article about a scientific investigation. The article may be written by a scientific researcher, a team of researchers, or a journalist. The investigation may involve a series of experiments or extensive observations. Or the inquiry may be an analysis of data from other studies conducted by different researchers or organizations. There are many different ways to answer scientific questions. However, some features are central to scientific inquiry. The questions below focus on some of the fundamental aspects of science.

Your Task
Take notes on the discussion questions below as you read the article you have been given. Be prepared to discuss the topics as they relate to the article and science in general.

Discussion Questions
1. What primary question(s) do the researcher or researchers focus on?

   _____

   _____

2. What led the scientist(s) to conduct the investigation? What about the topic interested or motivated them?

   _____

   _____

3. How did historical and/or current scientific knowledge influence the scientists in:

   (a) Their research design or approach?

   (b) Their interpretations and analysis?

   _____

   _____

4. How did technology improve the researchers' ability to collect, organize, and manipulate data?

   _____

   _____

5. Does the article reveal any ways that mathematics helped the scientists in their investigation? If not, what kind of math do you think was used in designing, analyzing, and communicating about the investigation?

   _____

   _____

Case Study Study, *Cont'd.*

6. Are the researchers' conclusions based on evidence? Are their explanations logical? Explain.

_____

_____

_____

7. Do the researchers suggest areas for further study? If not, can you think of any?

_____

_____

_____

8. Skepticism is a hallmark of scientific thinking. In what ways do the researchers express skepticism of:

   (a) Other research studies or conclusions?

   (b) Their own data?

_____

_____

In what ways are you skeptical of:

   (a) The research design or approach?

   (b) The researchers' conclusions?

_____

_____

Reflection

1. How has your thinking changed on how science is carried out?

_____

_____

_____

2. What are some central features of scientific inquiry? What distinguishes scientific thinking from other ways of thinking about the world?

_____

_____

_____

Investigating Plant Growth

Students develop their own questions and experiments for a long-term study of variables affecting plant growth and development.

Topic Connections

Scientific Inquiry, Plant Growth and Development, Angiosperm Life Cycle, Environmental Stresses

Introduction

Being fairly easy to cultivate in the classroom, plants offer excellent opportunities for developing scientific inquiry abilities in students. Over the course of weeks or months, students can collect and analyze significant quantities of data. The long-term nature of such investigations can provide a better quality science experience than single lab period lessons.

This inquiry begins with students briefly learning the normally recommended method of growing a plant from seed. Then groups raise questions about variables that could affect the growth of the species. Groups then develop an experimental plan to test their hypotheses for one or more of the questions. Over the next weeks students collect data of their own choosing. As much as possible, decisions are left to the students; they decide on questions, hypotheses, experimental designs, the type of data to collect, and how to organize and eventually present their data effectively. Along the way, periodic student-student and teacher-student discussions include constructive criticisms and pointed questions that help students improve their understanding of how to do a scientific investigation. Of course, the inquiry also provides opportunities for learning about germination, growth, development, flowering, and seed development.

Wisconsin Fast Plants® or Wards Rapid Radishes® work very well for this inquiry. Their lighting and watering systems ensure reliable growth, and their rapid development allows students to see the entire life cycle in five to six weeks. Of course, any easy-to-grow plant, such as radishes or beans, could be used. This lesson is written for the Wisconsin Fast Plant® system, but it is easily adaptable for any plant in any growing system.

Materials

- Seeds: Twenty-four per lab group minimum if using one of the rapid growth plant systems (twelve seeds per quad)
- Light bank
- Potting soil
- Quads: Two per experiment
- Fertilizer pellets
- Watering system

Time Approximation

- Four to eight weeks overall
- Day 1: 45 to 60 minutes for introduction and experimental design and critiquing session
- Day 2: 30 minutes to set up the experiments
- Thereafter: Periodically allow 5 minutes at the beginning or end of class for data collection

Preparation

If using Wisconsin Fast Plants® or Ward's Rapid Radishes®, consult their instructions for growing the plants. Fast Plants are available from Carolina Biological Supply Company. Rapid Radishes are sold by Ward's Natural Science.

If using other plants, germinate the seeds before having the students plant them. For beans, soak them in water for six hours or so. Then spread them out on moistened paper towels, roll the paper towels up, and put them in sealable sandwich bags. Also spray water into the bags before sealing them. The idea is that germinating seeds need constant exposure to moisture. After twenty-four hours, spray more water into the bags. After forty-eight hours the seeds should be sprouting and ready for planting. For more detailed planting and growing instructions for a plant species, check with a local garden store, contact a biological supply company, or do a Web search for that species.

Lesson Outline

Day One

1. Inform the students that they are going to grow some plants. Via overhead transparency, handout, or presentation, explain how to set the plants up for optimal growth. Point out how much soil, fertilizer, water, light, and such are recommended.

2. Students brainstorm on variables. Ask students to get into lab groups and come up with a list of factors that might effect the growth of the plants.

3. Next have them pick one or two questions that they would like to investigate with these plants. If they need some guidance here, tell them they could alter some aspect of the way the plants are normally grown—or they could introduce some new factor if they are curious about its effect on plant growth. They should also develop hypotheses for their questions.

4. For the experimental design, have the groups develop an experimental plan to test one or two of their hypotheses. Set parameters for materials before they begin. For example, you might need to limit the number of quads/pots or the number of seeds that a group can use for an experiment based on

availability. With Fast Plants® you should allow at least two quads per experiment so they can be exposed to different treatments/conditions.

5. For a session on experimental designs, lead a discussion where each group shares their experimental plan. Encourage students to offer constructive criticism of other groups' plans. Ask pointed questions to guide students into noticing/understanding major flaws in their experimental approaches. Try to strike a balance between helping students to improve their experiments and leaving issues to be discovered by them on their own.

Day Two

1. Students set up their experiments.

2. They may need some pointed questions from you to help them realize the importance of carefully labeling the different growth conditions in their experiments.

Data Collection

1. At some point before the seedlings emerge, ask students how they will know whether their experimental variables influenced their plants. Have them brainstorm and discuss forms of evidence that they could look for. Ultimately they must decide what kind of data they will collect. And will they collect quantitative data or qualitative or both?

2. A few days after seed planting, there may be seedlings on which data can be collected. Give students 10 minutes to collect and record data. Reinforce the importance of all group members recording data in a lab book, notebook, or journal in an organized manner.

3. Students then collect data every one to three days for a period of four weeks or so. The most growth change happens early on, so have them collect data more frequently in the first two weeks. Growth slows or even stops once flowering occurs.

Data Analysis

1. When data collection is complete, have students analyze their results. Encourage the use of mathematical analysis such as computation of means, ranges, and standard deviations (in advanced classes).

2. Have them graph the data, which could reveal interesting information. Challenge students to choose and design graphs that will reveal important aspects of their results.

Assessment

An extended full inquiry such as this should conclude with students communicating and justifying their experiments, data, and conclusions/explanations. This could take the form of a scientific mini poster (see "Assessing Inquiry Investigations" in the Introduction), a written report, or an oral presentation.

Additional questions that students should address in their report include:

- How confident are you that your results answer your question?
- How could you improve your experiment?
- What further questions are raised by your results?
- Are your results supported or contradicted by background information (via book or Web research) found on plants?

Implementation Strategy

- The amount of guidance you give will vary depending on the age/experience/ ability levels of the learners. As much as possible try to have groups decide for themselves how to design the experiments, collect data, present data in tables/graphs, and so forth. But guiding, pointed questions and constructive criticisms in whole-class discussions will help students deepen their understanding of scientific inquiry.
- The Wisconsin Fast Plant® kits come with cookbook-style student instructions for experiments. Instead of using those procedures, have the students design their own experiments (as discussed in this lesson).
- Steer groups away from experimental plans that will fail so badly that they will probably not be able to collect data (unless you have enough materials to have them start again with a new plan).
- Some groups may decide on an experiment that is excessively simple so that the project will be easy for them. If you suspect this to be the case, challenge them. Ask, "Is that the most interesting question you could ask about that?" and "Will this experiment tell you anything you don't already know?" For example, a group might propose comparing no fertilizer to normal fertilizer amounts or no fertilizer to many fertilizer pellets. A better choice would be to test the effects of a range of fertilizer quantities.
- Fertilizer for Wisconsin Fast Plants® comes in either a water-soluble powder or small pellets. The pellets make for an easier-to-manipulate variable, although both will work.
- Students will often get results that are unexpected or ambiguous. Some factors, such as genetic variability, are difficult to control. And sample sizes will be so small that the impact of random chance on the results will be significant.
- Press students to explain their results fully, whether they were anticipated or surprising. They should discuss and justify their explanations. They should also show that they have considered and weighed alternative explanations.

- Some possible experiments could include testing the effects of the following on plant growth:

  Amount of fertilizer

  Intensity or duration of light

  Wavelengths of light (Students might build small canopies of colored plastic supported by toothpicks to filter the light by color.)

  Quantity/quality of soil

  Density of seeds/plants

  Salt, sugar, caffeine, motor oil, and so on.

  pH

- If using a Fast Plant® watering system, some experimental quads may need to be isolated if they would expose other group's plants to an unintended variable (such as salt leeching into the watering mat).

- Data to collect might include height, number of leaves, length of stems, color of leaves, number of flowers.

Scientific Inquiry Assessment

In this assessment students explain everything that they would do to use science to answer a question of their own choosing.

Topic Connections

Scientific Inquiry, any content area

Introduction

This assessment tests student understanding of scientific inquiry. The plan is flexible. The test could be given early in the year or at any later time to assess how well students are comprehending both the subtleties and the broad approaches of science. The test should not replace frequent hands-on assessments of science inquiry abilities, but it serves as a useful supplement. The *Standards* recommend against teaching science process outside of the context of biological content. Development of science inquiry skills and understandings should occur in every topic unit throughout the year. Thus, this test could be used at the conclusion of any content unit or series of units.

Biology textbooks have traditionally emphasized "The Scientific Method" or "The Process of Science." Such descriptions usually focus on controlled experimentation, and the process is related as a series of steps. Without question, an understanding of controlling and manipulating variables in experimentation is essential for students. However, it is inaccurate to teach that all—or even most—science occurs via the same rigid sequence involving a controlled experiment. Many scientists complete long and fruitful research careers without ever having relied on a controlled experiment! Charles Darwin made some pretty significant discoveries without applying the "scientific method" script.

Of course, science does include approaches and ways of thinking that distinguish it (including controlled experimentation), and understanding of these approaches can be tested. The *Standards* identify "abilities necessary to do scientific inquiry" on pages 175 and 176 of the document. Also, the NAS book, *Teaching About Evolution and the Nature of Science,* provides a rich explanation of the many facets of scientific investigation. Both resources are available online as well as in print.

Grading the test can be based on rubrics constructed with student input. Research questions should be individually chosen by the students. This heightens interest and meaning for them.

Materials

- Writing paper
- Graph paper

Time Approximation

- Outside of class: Give students at least one week to develop ideas
- Rubric development: One class period (optional)
- Test: One class period

Lesson Outline

1. Distribute and discuss the student worksheet at least one week before test day.

2. Provide repeated explanation of expectations one or two more times before the test.

3. Rubric development: Have students brainstorm on general elements that should be included in successful test papers or develop a rubric yourself based on what you expect your students to know.

4. Test day: Provide writing paper. Make graph paper available. Without using any notes, students write their tests.

Implementation Strategy

- Strongly recommend that students share their experimental questions with you for feedback well before the test. A poor question makes it difficult to do well on the rest of the test.

- Topic areas for questions can be limited to biological content already studied or can be open. If left open, many will choose humans or pets as research subjects. Such topics give the exercise more meaning for the learners.

- Do not tell the students exactly what must be included, since that is part of what you are testing! The students need to think of and explain how they would go about using science to answer their question.

- Student test papers should explain (in outline or essay form) everything that they would do to answer their question. Also, they will present fictional data and then analysis and conclusions based on that data.

- Some of the concepts that could be expected for inclusion and explanation in the papers include:

   The experimental question (or group of related questions)

   Testable hypothesis/hypotheses, "if/then" prediction(s)

   Observations and/or observational sampling

   Historical/background information search

   Experiment(s)

   Constants

   Appropriate technology used

Large sample sizes

Repetition/verification

Data table(s)

Graph(s)

Statistical analysis

Conclusions, with an explanation of data connected to historical data/
theories; generalizations from results; and error analysis

Areas for continued research

Reference

National Academy of Sciences. (1998). *Teaching about evolution and the nature
of science.* Washington, D.C.: National Academy Press.

WORKSHEET 2.7
Scientific Inquiry Test

This is an opportunity for you to show the extent to which you understand how scientific inquiry is used to answer questions.

The Task

1. You are to think of a question that can be answered using scientific inquiry.

2. You should be prepared to describe (in detail) everything that you would do if you were to use scientific inquiry to answer your question.

   Remember—this is an opportunity for you to demonstrate that you understand *all* of the aspects of doing high-quality science that you have learned about.

Preparation

It is strongly recommended that you prepare your ideas before coming to class on the test day. You will have to write your test in class from memory. It will be important for you to do the creating, planning, and organizing before the day of the test.

Fictional Data

1. You will make up reasonable data (results) for your investigations.

2. You will use the fictional data so that you can describe a full cycle of scientific inquiry.

Evaluation FAQs

1. What should be included?

   Include *all* of the relevant elements of doing science that you have learned about. A rubric may be developed to establish general criteria.

2. Is a graph required? A data table?

   Include *all* of the relevant elements of doing science that you have learned about.

   Do the very best that you are capable of. Strive for excellence. Be as detailed, thorough, and imaginative as you can be. BUT, also be concise enough so that you don't run out of time at the end of the class.

Suggestion

Share your research question with the teacher ahead of time for feedback. Not all questions can be answered by scientific inquiry.

Biology Portfolio

Students make a portfolio to reflect on their biology learning over a semester or year—a constructivist assessment.

Topic Connections

All Biology Concepts, Scientific Inquiry

Introduction

Reflection is a central component of constructing understanding. At the end of a learning period, students benefit from tasks specifically focused on processing their new way of thinking about a topic. Such reflecting promotes a more complete, more lasting replacement of previous misconceptions with new explanations. Reflections may be useful at the end of a lesson, a lab, or a unit of study. A semester or year-end portfolio project offers unique opportunities for broad reflection and assessment on large portions of a biology curriculum.

In this project students choose labs, activities, lessons, or biology topics to represent categories such as "best example of you designing an experiment to test a hypothesis." They then write a reflection explaining why they chose the item/topic and how it represents the category. There are also more open questions at the end that can be answered in journal or short-essay format. All of the items and reflections should be bound and submitted as a portfolio of the student's learning experiences in the course.

For students the portfolio provides closure. They consider how their thinking has changed on various topics, and this helps them to further process and develop new understandings. Thinking broadly about biology also facilitates drawing connections between topics.

For teachers the portfolio is a valuable assessment tool. Reflections reveal how well learners have developed lasting understanding of topics. Conversely, teachers also learn which topics were not taught well enough to result in deep understanding. The portfolio may inform a teacher to devise a new strategy for teaching a topic in the future.

Materials

Manila file jacket folders—legal size (optional)

Time Approximation

Give one to two weeks to complete outside of class

Lesson Outline

1. At the beginning of the year distribute the student worksheet and explain the portfolio.

2. Provide the students with manila file jackets. Have them label them and store them in a box, cabinet, or shelf in the classroom. Otherwise, warn students to save assignments, labs, projects, and other items over the course of the year for possible portfolio use.

3. About two weeks before the portfolio due date, give the portfolio assignment.

Implementation Strategy

- Consider providing each student with a legal-size manila file jacket at the beginning of the school year. This can be a repository for returned work over the course of the year. At the end of the year students have all of their labs, projects, and other assignments in the folder to help them make their portfolios. Provide a box or shelf in the classroom for year-long storage of these folders. Periodically during the year remind students to place their returned work in the folders.

- Using this as a year-end portfolio is recommended. As written, this portfolio could be used more frequently—concluding semesters or quarters—but it requires a substantial amount of student time. Abbreviated versions might be more appropriate for more frequent use.

- Students will want to know how long their reflections should be. If you specify a length, you risk limiting students who otherwise might have written more. The best reflections generally are at least two paragraphs long. The "extended reflections" should be at least one page each.

- It is recommended that you encourage students to organize/design the portfolios however they choose. After all, it is a representation of students' work, so they will appreciate the chance to be expressive in their methods of binding and decorating.

- Objectively grading the portfolios is a challenge. Obviously, if portions are missing, then points should be deducted. Otherwise, differences between portfolios will be in apparent effort and thoughtfulness—difficult criteria to quantify! In a reasonably motivated class, most students submit portfolios that are complete and reflect significant thought. You can discriminate somewhat if some write three sentences per reflection and others write three thoughtful paragraphs. But in general, this is a project where many students earn (well-deserved) high grades.

WORKSHEET 2.8
Biology Portfolio

A portfolio is a collection of work that reflects a person's experiences or accomplishments. Portfolios often include written reflections on the included work. They are usually presented in binders or folders in a way that is well-organized and visually appealing.

You will create a portfolio of your biology learning experiences. For each of the categories listed below you will do two things:

1. *Choose an item to represent the category.*

   The item might be a lab report, project, quiz, homework assignment, or anything else that was returned to you by the teacher. Alternatively, you could include an assignment sheet, a photo of a project, or a piece of a project if it is too large to include.

   If your item is something that you do not have a physical copy of (for example, a biology topic or a class discussion), then think of a way to physically represent it. You might include an image printed from a Web site or textbook, for example, to represent a topic like DNA replication.

2. *Write a reflection for the category.* The reflection should explain how/why your item selection represents the category. The reflections should be clearly titled and arranged in close proximity to the item that they discuss.

Portfolio Categories

For each of the following categories, your portfolio should have a physical representation (item) *and* a written reflection:

1. Best example of you using experimental evidence to arrive at a new understanding of something.

2. Best example of you designing an experiment to test a hypothesis.

3. A lab investigation that did not work well. Include thoughts on how it could have been improved.

4. A sudden insight. A time during the year when "a light bulb went on" and you suddenly understood something that you previously did not.

5. Two things that you studied but still do not understand (two reflections).

6. Choose two labs/activities/lessons/topics from different parts of the year (not the same unit). How were the biology topics in these two things connected/related?

7. A lesson/assignment/topic/class discussion that reveals the impact of biology on society.

8. A lab/activity/topic/discussion that reveals the relevance of biology to your life.

9. A topic you most enjoyed learning about.

Biology Portfolio, *Cont'd.*

Extended Reflections

For these categories you do not include a physical representation. These are written reflections on how you have changed over time as a result of your learning in this course. These reflections should be lengthier, more substantial than the above.

1. How has your thinking on evolution changed as a result of your learning in biology?

2. How has your thinking on interrelatedness and interactions between organisms changed because of your learning in this course?

3. Because of your learning in this course, how do you now think differently about your own body? About its ability to maintain stability (homeostasis)? About your health?

4. How do you now think differently about natural ecosystems and human impacts on the environment?

Portfolio due date: _____

Chapter 3

The Cell

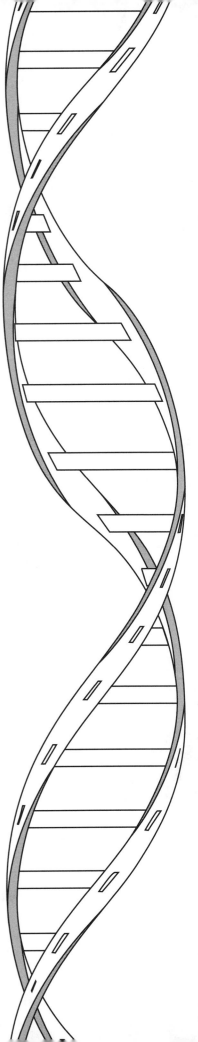

The content standards of the *National Science Education Standards* are not intended as a curriculum list of topics to be memorized. Rather, they are a guide to the central concepts and principles of biology that a student should understand. The lessons in this chapter explore some of the concepts included in the 7–12 Life Science standards that help a learner to understand cells. These concepts include regulation, structure and function, reproduction, cellular chemical reactions, and the cell as the foundation of life.

What Is Life? Part 1: Glue Goblins

Initiate inquiry on the characteristics of organisms using Duco® cement to simulate a life form. This lesson also surveys student preconceptions on the features of living things.

Topic Connections

Characteristics of Organisms, Cells

Introduction

Students harbor many misconceptions about organisms. Some of these stem from a disproportionate familiarity with vertebrate animals. When asked to list features common to all living things, many teenagers will include movement and breathing. Of course, most organisms do not breathe and many do not move. This constructivist introductory lesson draws out student prior knowledge of general life characteristics, and it begins the process of replacing them with scientific understanding.

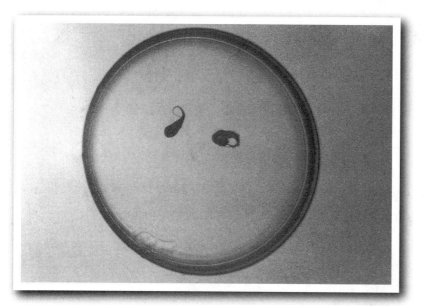

Figure 3.1. Glue Goblin

Life is difficult to define, and sometimes even to recognize. For instance, some scientists consider viruses to be organisms, while others do not. What distinguishes organisms from abiotic (nonliving) things? Consensus is lacking on this, but most biologists agree that there are certain characteristics shared by all organisms, such as metabolism, reproduction, growth, cellular organization, and so on.

In this lesson, students will be challenged to decide whether a mystery object (a drop of Duco® cement in water) is an organism or not.

They then attempt to justify their decision based on observations and their prior conception of life features. An ensuing discussion leads them to question their preconceptions and sets the stage for new concept learning.

Materials

- Petri dishes, two or three
- Duco® brand cement, "Pegamento" type

- Water
- Dropper bottle
- Overhead projector

Time Approximation

20 to 30 minutes; additional time for new concept learning will vary

Preparation

Before class put two or three petri dishes half-full with water near the overhead projector. Also place a dropper bottle filled with water near the projector. *Note:* You will want to practice adding the Duco® cement drop to water before doing it for students.

Lesson Outline

1. Half-fill a petri dish with water and place it on an overhead projector. Following the tips given in "Implementation Strategy," add a drop of Duco® cement to the water in the middle of the dish. If the drop is a good one (moving, not stuck to the side), then turn the overhead projector on. If not, put another petri dish on and try again.

2. Call the students' attention to the overhead screen.

3. Say nothing for a few minutes. Students will call out observations and questions while the cement drop moves erratically around the dish.

4. Ask the students if they think the "thing" is alive and, if it is living, whether it is an organism. Solicit multiple opinions. Be neutral in response to them. Usually most students will think it is alive.

5. Distribute the student worksheet.

6. Have students complete questions 1 through 3 on the worksheet. Have them exchange ideas in small groups after working independently. During this time you might add another drop to the petri dish or add another dish with a new drop in it.

7. Lead a classwide discussion on student responses to the first three questions on the worksheet. Address misconceptions by asking questions. For example, if a student claims that movement shows that the "thing" is living, ask if trees are living and if they move on their own. Or say "OK, trees don't move, so therefore they aren't living. . . ." Challenge the misconceptions, and get the students to think about why they don't make sense.

8. *New concept introduction.* Students learn the generally accepted features common to all organisms. These ideas could be introduced by you, Web research, or reading assignments.

Teacher Pages

Implementation Strategy

- Use this lesson *before* any learning on the characteristics of living things.

- Do not reveal whether the "thing" is an organism or not—even after the lesson is done. For one reason, future use of the lesson could be compromised if students share the information. Also, it is productive to maintain an atmosphere of uncertainty in the classroom. It is inaccurate to project to students that biology consists of easy-to-access, set answers. A more genuine biology inquiry atmosphere is one where people are continually challenged to explain (and re-explain) unknowns based on evidence and reasoning.

- Some tips to prevent students from seeing you add the cement drop to the water:

    Think of an excuse to move any students sitting too close to the overhead projector.

    Add the drop with your back to the class to obscure their view.

    Engage them in a short task at the beginning of class so that they won't be focused on you when adding the drop.

    Dim the classroom lights.

    Wrap the cement tube in paper to cover its bright label.

    Add a drop of water from a dropper bottle so students think the "thing" is coming from that source.

    Do not let students come up to look directly at the petri dish.

    After adding the drop discreetly, hide the cement tube.

    It is best not to move the petri dish after adding the drop of cement—otherwise the drop may stick to the side of the dish. If this happens, use a paper clip or pencil tip to dislodge it.

- Practice adding the Duco® cement before using the lesson. A small, quickly added drop works best. Twist the tube while releasing the glue drop to get a clean break.

- After five or ten minutes the drop slows down (students think it's dying). You might add another at this point. When two drops are put in a dish students may think they are mating or fighting.

- Consider following this lesson with the next two in the book. A series of experiences provides time for the construction of understanding and lasting learning.

Reference

Gentry, C. (1991). Characteristics of life. In D. Sheldon (Ed.), *Favorite labs from outstanding biology teachers* (pp. 64). Reston, VA: NABT.

Name _____ Date _____

What Is Life?

1. While observing the mystery "thing" on the overhead screen, fill in the following:

**Observations Leading You to
Think It Is a Living Thing**

**Observations Leading You to Think
It Is NOT a Living Thing**

What Is Life? *Cont'd.*

2. What is a living thing (organism)? Try to write a definition that defines life (*Note:* This is not asking about living versus dead [once living]. That is an interesting but separate issue.):

_____

_____

_____

_____

_____

_____

_____

3. Make a brainstorm list of features/characteristics that are common to *all* living things:

_____

_____

_____

_____

_____

_____

_____

4. After discussing everyone's responses to the three questions above, what are the best features of living things that were proposed?

_____

_____

_____

_____

_____

_____

_____

What Is Life? Part 2: Investigations

Students design and conduct experiments to decide whether unknown items are living or not.

Topic Connections

Characteristics of Organisms, Cells, Scientific Inquiry

Introduction

In this inquiry, students progress to a deeper understanding of organism characteristics by using the concepts in the design and analysis of experiments. In the process, inquiry abilities are further developed as learners create multiple experiments that often lead to new questions and continued investigation. Conclusions in this lab are rarely simple and straightforward. Rather, students weigh varied and sometimes conflicting evidence in the way that practicing biologists do.

Each group receives a sample of an unknown item or substance. Some will be organisms and some abiotic. The groups have two to four class periods to collect as much evidence as possible to support a conclusion on its status. The point of course is not "getting it right." Instead, students are evaluated on how well they demonstrate an understanding of the characteristics of life and scientific inquiry.

Bromthymol blue is introduced to students as a possible tool to reveal evidence of metabolism. BTB is an indirect CO_2 indicator. It changes from blue to green to yellow as CO_2 lowers the pH of the solution. A change to yellow indicates a larger quantity of CO_2 than a change to green.

Materials

- Containers—glass or plastic specimen dishes or cups/beakers
- Bromthymol blue in any concentration (Dilute to make it last.)
- Drinking straw
- "Unknowns" to be tested—possibilities include:

  yeast

  wheat seeds

  brine shrimp eggs

  brownulated sugar

  algae (filamentous)

  duckweed

  organic sponge

sand

oak galls

whelk egg cases

Time Approximation

- Two complete 45-minute periods over two days for brainstorming, initial design, observations, and experimentation
- Parts of one to three more periods for quick data collection on overnight or ongoing experiments
- One period for group presentations (optional)

Preparation

For each lab group prepare a sample of their "unknown." Put a small quantity of the substance into a container. Glass specimen dishes are ideal. Beakers or cups will also work fine.

Give each group enough of the "unknown" to do multiple experiments, but do not give them all that you have. Keep enough so that you can parcel out more to them over the next few days.

Give a different unknown to each group. Choose from the list under "materials" or use any small, relatively unfamiliar item that you have in multiple quantities.

Dilute bromthymol blue with tap water to stretch out the amount you have. Add water until the BTB is light blue. If using 0.1 percent stock bromthymol blue, then add approximately 400 ml water to 100 ml BTB.

Safety Precaution

Safety goggles should be worn by all students at all times during the lab.

Lesson Outline

1. *Bromthymol blue demonstration.* In front of the class use a drinking straw to gently but steadily blow into a beaker of diluted BTB until it changes to green and then to yellow. Inform the students that BTB can be used as an indicator for the production of carbon dioxide, and this is an indication of metabolism.
2. *Distribution.* Distribute the unknowns to the groups. Distribute the student worksheet and have the students read it.
3. *Brainstorming.* Groups think of lists of questions to ask about their unknown. Then they design plans for answering their questions (see "Implementation Strategy" for examples of possible questions and data-collection approaches).

    Circulate among groups to monitor their ideas. Offer constructive feedback. Make suggestions for possible tools/materials if such guidance seems warranted.

4. *Investigations.* Groups make observations, collect data, run simple experiments, and set up overnight or long-term experiments.

   On the second day, data is collected from overnight experiments and further investigations are planned and conducted. Some groups may need prodding at this point to go further then they have. Remind them that more data, more evidence is always more convincing than less.

5. *Analyzing and Reporting.* Groups discuss their data. They weigh their evidence to frame conclusions on the question of whether or not their unknown is an organism.

   Groups prepare reports on their research. These can be oral or written. For oral presentations, students could make overhead transparencies or use presentation programs such as PowerPoint®.

Implementation Strategy

- Repeatedly stress to the students that the point of the lab is *not* to identify their unknown. Their task is to collect as much convincing evidence as possible to conclude whether or not the unknown is an organism.

- Some possible student approaches are shown in the following lists.

Question	Evidence Collection
Does it produce CO_2?	Expose it/immerse it in Bromthymol blue,
Does it produce waste?	look for color change after various periods
Does it exhibit metabolism?	of time
	Other chemical indicators could be used
Is it comprised of cells?	Microscope observations
Is it highly organized?	Observations—micro or macro
Is there evidence of specialized structures?	
Does it respond to stimuli?	Expose it to variables such as light, temperature changes, sound, touch and so on.
Does it grow?	Observe—compare various size measurements over time
Does it reproduce?	Observe—would need to be quantified
Does it use energy?	Expose it to food/light and look for evidence of consumption or conversion.

Source

Kathryn M. Hopkins, retired educator, Newark, Delaware.

What Is Life? Investigations

You have been presented with a type of thing that may be unfamiliar to you. Your challenge is to investigate this "unknown" to determine whether or not it is an organism.

But first, some questions to consider:

How do you know whether something is an organism or not? What do living things do? What are the characteristics that are common to different life forms? How do you know whether an organism possesses these characteristics? And what if something seems to possess some features of life but not others?

The Task
Your group will investigate your unknown to collect evidence as to whether or not it is a living thing. You should collect as much evidence as possible via observation and experimentation over the next few days.

Important Notes
1. The point of this lab is *not* for you to identify the "unknown." Accurately identifying it will not improve your performance on the lab.

2. You will not be evaluated on whether or not you are "correct" in your final conclusion. Instead, success on this lab depends on:

   • Demonstrated knowledge of the characteristics of organisms

   • Effective use of scientific inquiry, including questioning, observing, experimenting, collecting data, interpreting/analyzing/concluding and reporting

Materials to Use
Anything that you think would be useful as long as it is safe. Check with the teacher.

I. Brainstorming
Upon receiving your "unknown," spend some time brainstorming with your group on a list of questions that you will try to answer. The questions should focus on the features and needs of organisms.

Next, brainstorm on possible ways to collect data that would answer your questions.

Then discuss your ideas with the teacher for feedback and materials availability. Do this before starting to collect data.

II. Investigate
Make observations, conduct experiments. Record all data in a notebook.

What Is Life? Investigations *Cont'd.*

III. Analyze and Report

Consider all evidence and discuss your conclusions with your group. Reports will be either written or oral and should include:

- Questions asked

- Method of answering each question

- Data

- Analysis/Conclusions

What Is Life? *The Andromeda Strain*

In this lesson students interpret a short passage from a science fiction novel that explores the difficulty with defining life.

Topic Connections

Characteristics of Organisms, Cells, Nature of Science

Introduction

Michael Crighton's *The Andromeda Strain* centers on an investigation of a pathogen newly imported from outer space. The researchers struggle to understand the probable organism because it is so unfamiliar to them. In one interesting passage the character Leavitt proposes to his colleagues that black cloth, a watch, and granite are living things. Cloth and the watch, he argues, are living because they exhibit some of the characteristics of organisms. The evidence of granite living, he continues, is simply undetectable to us because we perceive the world in such a shorter time frame than granite lives in.

The Leavitt character does not believe that cloth, watches, and granite are really organisms, but he makes a point that is important for biology students to consider: life is difficult to define. Our definition of life is limited by our experiences that create a frame of reference. We define life based on the life that we have observed, but . . . what if we discover new possible life forms that do not fit currently accepted descriptions of organisms? Would that mean that they are not living or that our definition of life is too narrow?

Viruses do not fit most definitions of organisms. They do not exhibit all of the features of life generally regarded as required, such as cellular structure. But some scientists would argue that our definition of life should be expanded.

The issues raised in this discussion go even broader. It is important for biology students to understand that science does not have all of the answers. Rather, it is a human endeavor to explain our world using the best available evidence at the time. And even in light of the same evidence, respected scientists often disagree completely on the interpretation of that evidence. The classification of organisms, for example, has changed considerably since Aristotle recognized two categories of life forms, animals and plants. Currently, there is substantial debate on the number of kingdoms of life that should be used. Such debate will continue and classification systems will change again. This seeming instability is not a weakness of science but a strength. Ideas are continually held up to the scrutiny of new evidence, new thinking.

Materials

Two-page excerpt from *The Andromeda Strain*
In the original 1969 hardcover edition (available in many libraries) the passage is found on pages 200 to 202. Regardless of the edition, the segment is in Chapter 20, "Routine." It begins:

"Without chemical reactions, there could be no life. Or could there?"

It continues for about thirteen paragraphs, concluding with:

> *His point was clear enough, and they revised their thinking in one important respect. They concluded that it was possible that they might not be able to analyze certain life forms. It was possible that they might not be able to make the slightest headway, the least beginning, in such an analysis.*

Time Approximation

- 20 minutes—to read the passage and write the reflection (can be assigned outside of class)
- 20 minutes—for discussion

Lesson Outline

1. Assign the two-page reading excerpt. Provide the student worksheet for students to complete after reading. If your students use journals, they could write their reflections in them.

2. Ask a number of student volunteers to either read or summarize their reflections.

3. Lead a discussion relating the reading passage to the issues discussed in the introduction.

Implementation Strategy

Teachers usually know the students in a class who are especially insightful. During the discussion of student interpretations, try not to call on these students first. Other students may be reluctant to share their thoughts after exceptional ideas have been offered, and you want to involve as many students in the discussion as possible.

Reference

Crighton, M. (1969). *The Andromeda strain* (pp. 200-202). New York: Knopf.

WORKSHEET 3.3

What Is Life? The Andromeda Strain

Read the assigned passage from Michael Crighton's science fiction novel, *The Andromeda Strain.* Then write one or two paragraphs interpreting the meaning of the passage. Begin your writing with the following prompt.

I think the point Leavitt is making is . . .

_____

_____

_____

_____

_____

_____

_____

_____

_____

_____

_____

_____

_____

_____

_____

_____

_____

_____

_____

_____

_____

_____

_____

Potato Bubbles: An Introduction to Enzymes

Students are challenged to explain the bubbling that occurs when raw potato is mixed with hydrogen peroxide in this brief inquiry.

Topic Connections

Enzymes, Organic Molecules

Introduction

This lesson is an inquiry modification of a classic catalase activity/demonstration. Before learning about enzymes, students observe the foaming reaction that occurs when potato is mixed with hydrogen peroxide. Their curiosity piqued by this unexpected occurrence, learners then attempt to reason through possible explanations. They collect evidence that helps them to rule out certain explanations. Of course, students do not experimentally discover that potatoes contain catalase or all of the details of the chemical reaction. But by struggling to explain an observed mystery, learners are primed to acquire new conceptual information. Knowledge then gleaned from readings or from your sources is integrated with the learners' physical experiences in the construction of new understanding.

Catalase is an enzyme that breaks down hydrogen peroxide, a potentially harmful product of certain cellular reactions. It is found in the cells of aerobic organisms. Hydrogen peroxide spontaneously decomposes into water and oxygen gas:

$$2H_2O_2 \rightarrow 2H_2O + O_2$$

However, the reaction occurs very slowly and does not produce visible bubbles under normal room conditions. Catalase dramatically hastens the reaction, and a foaming of oxygen bubbles is readily apparent. Boiled catalase becomes denatured and will no longer catalyze the reactions.

Materials

- Potato—raw, $1cm^3$ per lab group, per trial
- Hydrogen peroxide—3 percent, 10 ml per lab group per trial
- Beakers—50 ml or 6 oz. plastic cups
- Razors or knives—to cut and crush the potato
- Possibly needed: test tubes, wooden splints and matches, boiling water bath, beef liver, starch powder

Time Approximation

20 to 40 minutes

Preparation

Obtain 3 percent hydrogen peroxide from grocery store or pharmacy. Old hydrogen peroxide found on a prep room shelf may have converted mostly to water. The fresher, the better. Any kind of potato will work. If using beef liver, purchase a small amount from a grocery store.

Consider having a beaker of boiling water ready in the classroom for students to use for boiling potato and/or peroxide. Use a 500 ml beaker about two-thirds filled with water on a hot plate.

Safety Precautions

Caution students to use extreme care when cutting the potato cubes and when subsequently mashing them. Students should wear safety goggles during the inquiry.

Lesson Outline

Observations

1. In small groups have students cut 1 cm^3 cubes of potato.

2. Students carefully mash the potato as much as they can in a few minutes. The mashing could occur in the 50 ml beaker (carefully!) using a glass stirring rod. Or they could use a knife to mince the cube on a hard surface.

3. Students add 10 ml of 3 percent H_2O_2 to the mashed potato in the beaker and observe.

Questions, Hypotheses

1. Circulate among the lab groups and ask them whether their observations raise any questions. Challenge them to come up with possible explanations for their observations and hypotheses for their questions.

Explorations

1. While circulating among the lab groups, challenge them to test some of their hypotheses. Ask: "How could you test that idea?" Let them struggle a bit for a method. Offer them access to any materials that would be safe and time- and cost-effective for them to use. Some groups may need guidance in the form of pointed questions or hints. See "Implementation Strategy" for some possible student explorations.

   At some point focus the class on the bubbles. What are they? Put the formula for hydrogen peroxide (H_2O_2) on the board as a guiding prompt.

Conclusions

1. Lead a classwide discussion in which groups share what they have learned from their explorations. Make a list of hypotheses and supporting or contradicting evidence on the board.

2. Focus the group on the strongest pieces of evidence that at least rule out certain possible explanations.

3. Ask the class what they need (want?) to further explain the foaming potato/H_2O_2 mystery. Their answer, most likely, will be information on potatoes, hydrogen peroxide, or chemical reactions.

Concept Explanation

Students use textbooks, Web sites and/or teacher-led lessons to learn about catalase and the chemical reaction, $2H_2O_2 \rightarrow 2H_2O + O_2$

Student Explanations and Reflection

Students use their new knowledge of enzymes, catalase, and hydrogen peroxide reactions to explain their observations during the inquiry. Students consider how their thinking has changed.

Implementation Strategy

- Use this lesson *before* any learning on enzymes—and catalase in particular—has occurred.

- The lesson calls for minimal introduction. Simply explain to the students what they will be mixing and how to safely cut the potato squares. Be vague in response to queries about why they are doing it.

- Possible students' hypotheses and explorations:

Hypothesis	Exploration	Outcome
Starch is being broken down	Mix starch powder and H_2O_2	No bubbles
Bubbles are H_2	Not testable?	
Bubbles are O_2	Flame test with wooden splint with gas captured in an inverted test tube or beaker	Slight enhancement of burning if the reaction is fresh and the O_2 is captured
The cause/source of the reaction is something in the potato	Mix water or other substances with H_2O_2	No reaction
The cause/source of the reaction is something in the potato	Boil potato for 5 minutes	No reaction!
The cause is the H_2O_2	Mix H_2O_2 and water	No reaction
The cause is the H_2O_2	Boil H_2O_2 for 5 minutes	Reaction with potato still occurs!
It is caused by something found in living things	Mix beef liver with H_2O_2	Reaction occurs

- Give the students the formula for peroxide (H_2O_2) at some point to help them guess that the bubbles could be H_2 or O_2. They might also guess that it could be CO_2 since the potato starch is carbon-based. Ask them how to test the bubbles for type of gas. If you have them, CO_2 or O_2 sensors could be used. They may be familiar with the flame test for O_2 from the past. Otherwise you could introduce it to them.

- By the culmination of the explorations portion of the lesson students may be frustrated at the lack of concrete progress in explaining the bubble reaction. That's OK! Having struggled through this physical and cognitive process they will be especially ready to construct a sound understanding when they acquire the conceptual information to do so.

Name _____   Date _____

WORKSHEET 3.4
Potato Bubbles

Observations (list below):

_____

_____

_____

_____

_____

_____

Questions	Hypotheses

Explorations
List any information acquired from exploring/experimenting with the potato and hydrogen peroxide. List information acquired by other groups as well.

_____

_____

_____

_____

_____

_____

_____

_____

_____

Potato Bubbles *Cont'd.*

Conclusions

What conclusions can be made based on all of the observations and explanations made by the whole class?

_____

_____

_____

_____

_____

_____

Concept Explanation

You will acquire more information about potatoes, hydrogen peroxide and the reaction that was observed.

Student Explanation and Reflection

1. Now explain your initial observations on what happens when potato and hydrogen peroxide are mixed. What causes the reaction to occur so quickly and dramatically? What is the source of the cause? What are the bubbles?

   _____

   _____

   _____

   _____

   _____

2. Explain the results of the explorations carried out by different groups in the class. Do any of them contradict what you now know about the reaction? How do you explain these contradictions?

   _____

   _____

   _____

   _____

   _____

Floating Filter Paper Chips: An Exploration of Enzyme Activity

Students use enzyme-soaked filter paper disks to investigate factors influencing enzyme function.

Topic Connections

Enzymes, Organic Molecules, Metabolic Reactions, Microorganisms

Introduction

In this inquiry students learn a simple tool for measuring enzyme activity. Then they choose a variable that may effect enzyme function and design and conduct experiments on catalyzed reaction rates.

Catalase is the enzyme studied in this lesson. Found in the cells of many organisms, catalase facilitates the conversion of hydrogen peroxide into water and oxygen gas.

$$\text{catalase}$$
$$2H_2O_2 \quad \rightarrow \quad 2H_2O + O_2$$

This decomposition of hydrogen peroxide happens in the absence of the enzyme, but much more slowly. Hydrogen peroxide accumulates in cells as a metabolic byproduct. It can be harmful to cells and catalase functions to eliminate, or at least regulate it. The source of catalase in this inquiry is baker's yeast (*Saccharomyces cerevisiae*).

First, students use a hole punch to make filter paper chips. These discs are filled with catalase by soaking in a solution of baker's yeast. When dropped in a very dilute hydrogen peroxide solution, the catalase-soaked disks sink to the bottom. As the catalase facilitates the H_2O_2 breakdown, bubbles of O_2 accumulate in the filter paper until the disk suddenly floats to the top. The time it takes until the filter paper disk rises to the top is the relative measure of enzyme activity.

After trying and observing the enzyme filter paper disk model, student groups consider variables that might influence the rate of the catalyzed reaction. Enzyme activity is influenced by factors such as temperature, pH, salinity, enzyme concentration, and solute concentration. Students use the filter paper disk model to investigate one of these variables.

Materials

- Hydrogen peroxide, 3 percent
- Baker's yeast, 1 packet
- Filter paper
- Hole punch(es)
- 1-liter beaker or flask for making dilute H_2O_2

- 500-ml beaker or flask for activating yeast
- Smaller beakers (150 to 250 ml) or plastic cups (6 to 9 oz), 5 to 10 per lab group
- Tweezers, 1 per lab group
- Stopwatch or digital watch, 1 per lab group
- Possibly needed (depending on student experiment choices):

  Hydrochloric acid

  Sodium hydroxide

  pH paper or meters

  Graduated cylinders

  Salt

  Hot plates

  Ice

  Thermometers

Time Approximation

90 minutes

Preparation

Activate the yeast by dumping the contents of a packet in about 500 ml of warm water. The yeast will be ready to use in about 30 minutes. For younger students you might label the yeast container "catalase" or "enzyme" to avoid confusion.

Make the H_2O_2 solution by diluting store-bought 3 percent hydrogen peroxide with tap water. Prepare a 1:1000 dilution of 3 percent peroxide to tap water. You may want to adjust the dilution depending on the freshness of the hydrogen peroxide. Test it first. Soak a filter paper disc in the yeast solution. Then add it to about 50 ml of the dilute H_2O_2. It should take from 30 to 60 seconds before the disk rises from the bottom of the beaker and floats. If it takes longer, then add some peroxide to your stock solution. If it takes less, then dilute it further with water. You want to allow for a measurably slower and faster range of rates in the student investigations.

If investigating pH, have the students add the acid or base to make the experimental solutions. But with younger students you might want to prepare a variety of pH solutions yourself that they can use. Simply add HCl or NaOH to the dilute hydrogen peroxide. Keep track of the volumes of acid/base added and add the same volumes of water to other containers to maintain the same concentration in all solutions.

Filter paper is used because normal paper discs will not reliably sink to the bottom of a peroxide solution.

Safety Precautions

Students should wear safety goggles at all times during this inquiry. If some groups choose pH as a variable to explore, you will want to caution them in the use and handling of acids and bases.

Lesson Outline

I. Demonstrating the Tool

1. Distribute the student worksheet.

2. Have students read the introduction and follow the procedure for timing the chemical reaction.

3. Have students repeat the procedure one or two more times. Although there are no experimental variables yet, the times may vary a bit. Lead a discussion on what could cause this. Some possibilities include paper disk lack of uniformity, quantity of catalase absorbed, and so on. Lead students to conclude that they should take the average of repeated trials to reduce the effects of this variability.

II. The Investigation

1. Student groups brainstorm on factors that could influence enzyme activity.

2. Lead a discussion in which groups share their ideas. Help them to isolate factors that would be measurable/testable.

3. Student groups choose a variable and design an experiment to investigate it. You might want to offer other possibilities to the list that was generated by students so that it will include pH, temperature, salinity, substrate concentration, and enzyme concentration. You might point out available materials such as hot plates, ice, acids/bases, graduated cylinders, and salt to help them focus on achievable experiments.

4. *Feedback session.* Groups briefly explain their experimental plans to the class. Other groups and you offer constructive criticisms and probing questions to help students improve their experimental designs.

5. Groups conduct their experiments.

III. Data Analysis and Conclusions

1. Students analyze their data. They compute averages of trials, compare rates, discuss and explain results.

2. Students graph their data.

3. Book or Web research on enzyme structure and factors effecting enzyme activity. This could be done outside of class.

IV. Assessment

See the "Assessing Inquiries" section of the introduction. Student reports could be oral, written, or mini posters.

Implementation Strategy

- The inquiry is best used after learners have at least an introductory understanding of enzymes. But use the lesson *before* any readings or discussions on factors affecting the rates of enzymatic reactions.

- If too many groups choose the same variables, try to steer some away so that a variety of variables are explored by the class as a whole.

- If a group devises an experimental plan that is more simple than they are capable of, then challenge them to improve it. For example, if a group proposes comparing the effects of very hot to very cold, then ask them if they can think of a way to make the experiment more interesting and potentially more revealing.

- Possible experiments:

    pH—Using HCl and NaOH, students make their peroxide solutions acidic and basic. Using pH paper or meters they could make solutions of five to ten different pH levels. Help them realize that adding HCl or NaOH slightly dilutes the concentration of H_2O_2, thus introducing a new variable that must be controlled by adding water of equal volume to other containers.

    Temperature—Using hot plates, ice, and thermometers, students could alter the temperature of various beakers of H_2O_2. The beakers could be heated directly. To cool them beakers could be placed into water baths consisting of dishes or larger beakers with cooler water or ice.

    Salinity—Students dissolve various amounts of salt in different containers of the dilute H_2O_2.

    Substrate or enzyme concentrations—Using graduated cylinders students dilute the yeast suspension or the H_2O_2 solution by various factors.

Reference

Clariana, R. (1994). pH and enzymatic reactions. In R. Moore (Ed.), *Biology labs that work: The best of how-to-do-its* (pp. 22–24). Reston, VA: NABT.

WORKSHEET 3.5
An Exploration of Enzyme Activity?

Introduction

The chemical hydrogen peroxide (H_2O_2) spontaneously decomposes into water and oxygen gas:

$$2H_2O_2 \rightarrow 2H_2O + O_2$$

The reaction happens very slowly, but over a number of years a bottle of peroxide will convert almost entirely into water.

The enzyme catalase dramatically speeds the breakdown of hydrogen peroxide. Catalase exists in the cells of many organisms, including humans, to reduce levels of H_2O_2 that accumulates as a metabolic byproduct. The rate of the catalyzed breakdown of hydrogen peroxide can be measured by the rate of O_2 production. In this investigation the speed with which O_2 bubbles cause a paper disk to rise indicates the relative speed of the reaction. Your source of the enzyme will be baker's yeast (*Saccharomyces cerevisiae*) cells.

I. The Tool for Measuring Reaction Rate

Before conducting an investigation you will learn how to measure the rate of the enzyme catalyzed reaction. Try the following:

1. Use a hole punch to make a disk of filter paper.

2. Drop the filter paper disc into a small beaker with some of the yeast/enzyme solution. Let the disk soak for a few minutes.

3. Fill a small beaker or plastic cup about two-thirds with the hydrogen peroxide solution.

4. Using tweezers, move the filter paper disk from the yeast/enzyme solution into the hydrogen peroxide. The disk will sink to the bottom. Begin timing at the moment the disk touches the bottom.

5. The disk will eventually float to the surface as it fills with O_2 bubbles produced by the breakdown of H_2O_2.

6. Stop timing when the disk reaches the surface.

7. Repeat the above steps one or two more times. Was the reaction time the same for each trial? If not, why not?

II. The Investigation

1. What are some factors that could influence the rate of the enzyme catalyzed breakdown of hydrogen peroxide? In other words, what might influence the effectiveness of catalase at making the reaction occur? Brainstorm with your group and list your ideas in a notebook. Be prepared to discuss your group's ideas with the class.

An Exploration of Enzyme Activity? *Cont'd.*

2. Your group will choose one variable to investigate. You will design an experiment to test if and how your variable influences the activity of the enzyme. Your teacher may point out some possible materials that you could use. Again, be prepared to offer your experimental design to the class for constructive suggestions for improvement.

3. After receiving feedback from other groups and the teacher, go ahead and begin your experiment(s).

III. Data Analysis and Conclusions

1. Make any relevant mathematical calculations of your data in a separate notebook.

2. Graph your data on graph paper or with a spreadsheet program.

3. Discuss and explain the meaning of your data with your group members.

4. Research by using the Web or book resources to find information on enzyme structure and variables that affect enzyme activity.

IV. Report

Your teacher will assign a format for reporting on your investigation. Be sure to include the following in your explanation/discussion of your results:

- How do your experimental findings compare with accepted scientific knowledge of factors affecting enzyme activity? Explain.

- What improvements would you make to your experimental design if you had more time and materials?

Breakfast Is Ready: Bacon Diffusion

A constructivist introductory lesson on diffusion in which students attempt to explain why the odor of cooking bacon spreads through a room.

Topic Connections

Diffusion, Brownian Movement, Concentration Gradients

Introduction

What do your students know about diffusion? What do they think they know? Do they have an intuitive beginning of an understanding of the concept? Or do they harbor misdirected preconceptions that will inhibit new learning unless addressed?

This lesson assesses initial student ideas on diffusion while providing a sensory experience that challenges the learner for an explanation. Student explanations for the "bacon diffusion" reveal to you where instruction should start. Learners begin to build an understanding of diffusion through discussion, debate, and concept application to a shared experience. Many teachers include olfactory experiences (peppermint, vanilla) in units on diffusion, but they are usually reinforcement demonstrations. This lesson moves the experience to the beginning of the unit and challenges students to explain it without new vocabulary words.

When bacon is cooked the added energy sends droplets of fat into the air. Because of Brownian motion and kinetic energy, the fat droplets collide and disperse. The collisions result in diffusion, the net movement of substances from areas of high concentration to lower concentration. The bacon odor diffuses from the area above the fry pan until the molecules are evenly distributed throughout the room and equilibrium has been reached. Be sure to leave the classroom door open so the odor will diffuse into the hallways as well!

Materials

- Bacon
- Fry pan, fork, plate
- Hot plate

Time Approximation

20 to 30 minutes

Lesson Outline

1. Begin cooking bacon just before class starts.

2. While the bacon is cooking periodically ask if anyone smells anything. Ask early enough in the process so that students near the front will smell it while others do not. Continue until everyone in the room smells it.

3. Student explanations: Ask the students to write a one- or two-paragraph explanation of the experience. They should focus on why there was a

transition from no odor to one that was noticeable near the bacon to one that was noticeable throughout the room.

4. Small group idea exchange: In groups of four have students exchange explanations and attempt to come up with one refined explanation that suits them all.

5. Class-wide discussion: Have various students share their group's explanation for the spread of the bacon odor. Do not directly correct them at this point, but remember the misconceptions so that you can directly address them over the next lessons.

6. Provide your version of an explanation. Use handheld models of molecules, drawings, or even your fists to show molecules vibrating, colliding, and dispersing.

7. Move the students closer to a scientific explanation of diffusion. Via lessons, labs, and readings, students learn more about Brownian motion, concentration gradients, and diffusion.

8. Address the misconceptions. At some point either during or after Step 7 remind the students of some of the initial explanations the class had for the bacon experience. Have them consider whether these were valid ideas. Ask them to explain why the ideas were flawed.

Follow-Up

End of unit assessment/reflection: Ask students to relate what they now know about how substances move into, out of, and through cells to what they learned from the bacon diffusion experience. This is an important step! It will help students to more completely replace/modify their preconceptions, and it will help you to assess the success of the teaching unit on diffusion.

Implementation Strategy

- Use this lesson *before* any other lesson or readings on diffusion have been given.
- Turn the hot plate on high and begin cooking the bacon a couple of minutes before students enter the room.
- Students will want to know why you are cooking bacon. Do not tell them the real reason of course. You might tell them that you missed breakfast and are hungry.
- While the bacon is cooking there is time to check homework or perform other such tasks.
- Many alternatives to bacon would work. For instance, you could cook popcorn on a hot plate or light a scented candle.

Reference

Bilash, B., & Shields, M. (2001). *A demo a day: A year of biological demonstrations.* Batavia, IL: Flinn Scientific.

WORKSHEET 3.6
Breakfast Is Ready

Your teacher has been cooking bacon. At first there was not a noticeable odor. Over time people in the front of the room could smell the bacon. Gradually, more and more people noticed the odor. Now everyone in the class should be able to smell it. Eventually, even people outside the classroom will smell the bacon as well.

Your task is to explain what you have just experienced. Why did the bacon aroma first appear? And why did the odor spread throughout the room? Why did some people smell it at first before others could?

Write as much as you can to explain this experience. Don't worry about possibly being "incorrect." The point of this exercise is to attempt to explain the bacon experience *before* you have learned the relevant concepts and terms.

_____

_____

_____

_____

_____

_____

_____

_____

_____

_____

_____

_____

_____

_____

_____

_____

_____

_____

_____

_____

_____

_____

_____

Investigating Osmosis in Plant Cells

Students experimentally approximate the solute concentration of plant cells by exposing them to salt solutions of their own choosing. This is an inquiry revision of a classic lab.

Topic Connections

Osmosis, Plasmolysis, Turgor Pressure, Plant Cells

Introduction

An *Elodea* or onion cell plasmolysis lab has long been a staple of high school biology programs. The traditional procedure is one that walks the student step-by-step through what is essentially a hands-on demonstration. In this inquiry modification of that lab, the student observes plasmolysis and then attempts to explain it. Then students use their new understanding of osmosis in plant cells to design and carry out investigations to determine an approximation of the solute concentration inside *Elodea* cells. Over the course of the inquiry, the depth of student comprehension is tested and further developed.

All cells contain dissolved molecules (solutes) that make them hypertonic to most fresh water sources. Despite the proclivity for water to diffuse into plant cells, they are protected from swelling and bursting by a rigid cell wall. On the other hand, when exposed to exterior hypertonic solutions, plant cells undergo a loss of water known as plasmolysis. After a few minutes in a 10 percent salt solution, for example, an *Elodea* cell looks drastically different. Because of cytoplasmic water/volume loss, the plasma membrane will contract itself away from the cell wall. Under a microscope these plasmolyzed cells will show a circle of green chloroplasts bunched in the cell center by the shrunken cell membrane. The cell wall remains at its original size and shape.

In the investigative part of this lab, students will expose *Elodea* cells to various salt solutions until they get close to one that represents osmotic equilibrium for the cells. A salt concentration that results in only slightly discernible plasmolysis (Figure 3.3) is one that is close to the equilibrium point. Student claims at having discovered the "answer" should be challenged by you and by other lab groups. The most persuasive results will involve many data points and repeated, verified observations.

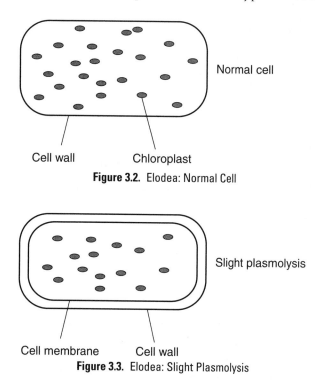

Cell wall   Chloroplast

Figure 3.2. Elodea: Normal Cell

Cell membrane   Cell wall

Figure 3.3. Elodea: Slight Plasmolysis

Normal cell

Slight plasmolysis

In this inquiry you pose the question/problem because the primary objective is expanding understanding of osmosis. Developing scientific inquiry abilities is an important but secondary objective of the lesson. The inquiry approach to the lab facilitates deeper learning of osmosis in plant cells.

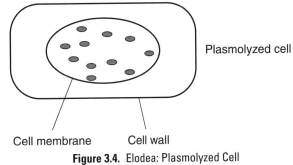

Figure 3.4. Elodea: Plasmolyzed Cell

Materials

- *Elodea* leaves or purple onions
- Salt
- Water, distilled if possible, although tap will work
- Microscopes, slides, cover slips
- Balances
- Graduated cylinders
- Droppers

Time Approximation

70 to 90 minutes

Preparation

Obtain the needed materials. Solution preparation should be done by the students.

Lesson Outline

1. Distribute the student worksheet.
2. Review with students the technique of making a wet mount.
3. Students make and observe *Elodea* wet mounts.
4. Students make 10 percent salt solutions and observe *Elodea* in them.
5. Be sure that all students have seen plasmolyzed cells before they begin the investigation.
6. Why did this happen? Challenge student groups to develop an explanation for why the *Elodea* cells changed in appearance when exposed to salt water. Have them use text/Web resources if needed. Finish this segment with a class-wide discussion. Allow each group to offer their explanation and then encourage students to critique and refine the ideas until there is a sound explanation of the observed plasmolysis.
7. The investigation: Present the experimental challenge to the students. Set them loose to investigate.

    Students should expose *Elodea* cells to various salt concentrations. Those that are hypertonic will yield plasmolyzed cells. Those that are hypotonic to the cells will result in normal-looking cells. An *Elodea* cell in a hypotonic solution will look the same as one in an isotonic solution because the cell wall prevents much cell expansion. So students need to approach the equilibrium point from the hypertonic side. For example, a slide showing slight plasmolysis at 1 percent and another showing no plasmolysis at 0.5 percent could yield a conclusion that the *Elodea* internal solute concentration is between 0.5 percent and 1.0 percent

Assessment

- The student worksheet includes instructions for a lab write-up.
- The investigation also would make a good performance assessment.

Implementation Strategy

- Have lots of salt available!
- The student worksheet tells how to make a 10 percent salt solution. For other concentrations, press your students to figure out for themselves how much salt and water to use. Depending on the math ability level of your group, you may need to help them here. Otherwise, periodically spot-check the groups to see whether they are accurately making the concentrations they intend to.
- For *Elodea* cells the salt concentration that approaches equilibrium is approximately .75 percent. Generally, at 1 percent there is still slight plasmolysis observable. At .5 percent there generally is not. Of course, these numbers could vary with *Elodea* stocks, water sources, and so on.
- Some student groups may start experimenting with higher than 10 percent concentrations at first. Let them learn from their mistake. Usually they will suddenly realize that the equilibrium number must be between 0 and 10 percent
- Often the plasmolysis effect only shows up on *some* cells on a wet mount. Other cells might not be in direct contact with the salt water. Be sure that the students survey the whole slide. If plasmolysis is present in at least some cells, then the solution is probably hypertonic to the *Elodea*.
- More evidence is always better than less. Press the students to try multiple concentrations before making conclusions. Also remind them of the value of verification by repetition.
- Failure to rinse droppers between trials is a common source of error. Probe your students to realize this.
- Students should use a new *Elodea* leaf each time they try a new salt concentration. Slides and cover slips can be reused if rinsed well.

Investigating Osmosis in Plant Cells

Initial Observations

1. Make and observe a wet mount of *Elodea* cells in water. Either here or in a lab note-book, make a sketch of one of the cells. Also record some written observations.

2. Make and observe a wet mount of *Elodea* in a 10 percent salt solution. Make the 10 percent solution by mixing 1 gram of salt with 9 ml of warm water. Make a sketch of a cell that has undergone a change because of the salt water.

3. Why did the cells change? Discuss with your lab partner(s) why the *Elodea* cells were changed by the salt water. Write your explanation below.

_____

_____

_____

The Investigation

Experimental challenge: What is the salt (solute) concentration of an *Elodea* cell? Can you experimentally determine an approximation of this?

Formulate a plan with your partner(s) for how best to collect data to solve the problem. Collect as much evidence as possible to support your conclusion.

Write-Up

Your lab write-up should include the following:

1. Introduction: Explain, define, discuss the relevant concepts.

2. Data: Create a data table(s) and sketches.

Investigating Osmosis in Plant Cells *Cont'd.*

3. Conclusion: Include the following:

   - Explain your observations

   - What is your answer to the problem?

   - Explain how your evidence supports your conclusions

   - Alternative explanations? Possible error sources?

   - Comparison with other groups' findings

4. Follow-up questions: Include responses with your lab write-up:

   - Explain turgor pressure. How is it important to plants?

   - What does winter salting of roads do to roadside plants in the spring when snow melts?

The Osmosis Inquiry Egg

Students investigate osmosis by designing experiments involving animal cells (chicken eggs). The lab is an inquiry modification of a traditional cookbook lab.

Topic Connections

Osmosis, Diffusion, Inquiry Abilities

Introduction

This entry modifies the traditional "Egg Lab" into an inquiry-based investigation. Students use the chicken egg as an experimental animal cell model. With this model they ask questions, design experiments, collect data, and use scientifically accepted ideas to explain their results. Some initial direction may be given, but most decisions should be student-generated, including types/methods of data collection, materials to use, presentation of data, and so on. The multi-day nature of the inquiry encourages extended development of understanding of osmosis and some of the nuances of scientific investigation.

An unfertilized chicken egg, like those sold in grocery stores, is effectively a large single cell surrounded by a calcareous shell. The ovum is the portion known as the yolk. Surrounding the yolk is the potential embryo's water and food source, known as the albumen. Thus, the albumen is an accessory storage portion of the cell—sort of like a plant cell vacuole. The yolk and albumen are contained by two membranes that lie just inside the shell. The acetic acid of vinegar dissolves the calcium carbonate of an egg shell. What remains is a large cell contained by inner and outer membranes. The membranes are selectively permeable and allow for osmosis studies.

A de-shelled raw egg can be handled by students for experimentation. In this inquiry students put eggs into various solutions of their choosing and they collect data over three or four days. An egg in a hypertonic solution will lose water and thus mass, circumference, and so on. An egg in a hypotonic solution will gain water.

Materials

- Raw chicken eggs—at least four per lab group
- Vinegar—enough for all eggs to be submersed
- Styrofoam cups, 16 oz.
- Pancake syrup or corn syrup
- Salt
- Sugar
- Various sodas students may bring
- Other solutions students bring
- Measuring tools—balance, rulers, string

Time Approximation

- 45 to 60 minutes for experimental design, discussion, and set-up
- 10 minutes of each period over three days for data collection

Safety Precautions

Students should wash their hands thoroughly after handling raw eggs. If latex gloves are available, have students wear them when touching the eggs.

Lesson Outline

Day One

1. To begin the shell removal process put eggs in vinegar. Leave them for 24 hours.

Day Two

1. Have student groups (two to four each) brainstorm on an experimental plan, hypothesis, and prediction. Encourage the use of labeled sketches of cups to represent the experimental plan. Show them the materials that you have available for them, but stress that they can use any solutions they bring to class the next day.

2. Design share: Groups briefly share their plans with the class. You and other students should offer constructive criticisms by asking questions such as "How many variables do you have?" and "Will that experimental design allow you to answer your question?"

3. Initial data collection: Students collect data before beginning the experiments.

4. Experimental set-up: Eggs go into their various solutions. Cups should be properly labeled.

Days Three Through Five

1. Students collect data over two days
2. Lab groups work on data analysis and conclusions on the fifth day.

Assessment

The student worksheet gives instructions for a lab write-up.
Other possibilities include oral presentations using overhead transparencies, posters, or PowerPoint®.

The inquiry also lends itself to reporting by science mini poster (see "Assessing Inquiry Investigations" in the Introduction).

Implementation Strategy

- The student worksheet contains some suggested experimental questions. If your class is ready for less guidance than this, then do not use the worksheet.

- If student-designed experiments are either too complex or too simple, then guide them to improvements by posing questions for them to consider. For instance, if a group decides to simply put four eggs in syrup and see what happens, you could ask, "Is there a way to make the experiment more interesting?" or "Could you design an experiment that would give you more information than this one?"

- Don't direct the students on what type of data to collect. Challenge them to decide, but check on their plan. If a group seems to only be taking mass, then ask them how they could collect more data so that they could be even more confident of their results.

- Using four eggs per group doesn't mean there have to be four different treatments. Some groups might want to have two for each solution for verification.

- Consider having students bring in the eggs for their experiments, but have some extras on hand just in case.

- Eggs can be de-shelled in large containers filled with vinegar or students can de-shell them in the cups that they will use for the experiment.

- Eggs can be left in vinegar for 48 hours or more, but they begin to swell from osmosis as soon as the shell is gone.

- Possible outcomes:

  Eggs in syrup will shrink dramatically.

  Eggs in distilled or tap water will swell.

  Eggs in sugary sodas surprisingly gain mass, but they show a lower percentage mass gain than eggs in sugar-free sodas. Thus, diet soda is more hypotonic to an egg than regular soda.

  Eggs in salt solutions gain water, which is unexpected! Students need to attempt to explain the unexpected results. Maybe the membrane is permeable to salt?

  Eggs in soy sauce lose mass.

The Osmosis Inquiry Egg

Introduction

A chicken egg is a cell. Once you have removed the hard outer shell, water will move across the membrane of the egg based on the principles of osmosis, just as with any other cell. Since the membrane is selectively permeable, some solutes will move across and others will not. In this inquiry you will use chicken eggs to investigate osmosis.

Your Task

To experimentally answer a question of your own concerning chicken eggs and osmosis. Some possibilities are "Is a chicken egg hypo or hypertonic to _____?" or "What will happen to eggs placed in _____ and _____?" or "What is the concentration of solutes in an egg?" or "Which is more hypertonic to an egg: _____ or _____?" or . . . .

Day 1: Remove the Shells

Place all eggs (carefully) into a container filled with vinegar. Leave for 24 hours and the shell will dissolve.

Day 2: Design Day

1. Decide on an experimental question.

2. Formulate a hypothesis and prediction.

3. Design (with words and a sketch) your experiment.

4. Discuss your question and experiment with the teacher and/or other groups for constructive feedback.

5. Collect initial egg data. Make initial measurements of your own choosing. Think of how many ways you could detect and document evidence of change caused by osmosis.

6. Set up your experiment.

Day 3: Collect Data

Day 4: Collect Data

Day 5: Collect Data and End Experiment

1. Take final measurements.

2. Brainstorm on conclusions. Was your hypothesis supported?

The Osmosis Inquiry Egg *Cont'd.*

Lab Write-Up

Include at least the following in your report:

Introduction—Discuss the concepts involved. Be sure to define key terms (should be one or two paragraphs).

Hypothesis and Prediction

Procedure—List in step-by-step format. Make a visual depiction also.

Data—Tables and/or graphs would be useful to make and include.

Conclusion—Explain your results using your understanding of osmosis. Was your hypothesis supported?

What is your evidence? Discuss (one to two pages).

Mitosis Sequencing

Prior to any study of cell division, students are challenged to sequence a group of draw-ings of mitotic events based primarily on abstract reasoning.

Topic Connections

Cell Division, Mitosis, the Cell Cycle

Introduction

In this activity learners construct an understanding of the underlying logic to the sequence of events in mitosis. The lesson precedes discussions or readings on cell divi-sion so that the students are not encumbered with the memorization of new terms. After a comprehension of the flow of events has been achieved, then names for various struc-tures and stages can be more successfully introduced.

First, students independently attempt to sequence the fifteen drawings without knowing anything about them. Then learners articulate, defend, and debate their sequences with classmates in small groups. Finally, each group explains their sequence as the class reasons the way to a teacher-facilitated consensus.

Mitosis is the nuclear division that occurs during somatic cell division. Mitosis provides for equal distribution of hereditary information to the daughter cells. The drawings for this activity focus on the movements of the chromosomes.

Materials

Student worksheet of mitotic events—one per student

Time Approximation

45 minutes

Lesson Outline

1. Distribute the student worksheet to each member of the class.

2. Students work independently at sequencing the fifteen drawings. They should write a number from 1 to 15 next to each drawing.

3. Group idea development: In groups of four, students should exchange ideas on their sequences. Encourage students to explain the reasoning behind their ideas. Groups should work toward developing a consensus sequence that makes sense to all members.

4. Classwide discussion: Ask each group to offer its choice for the first drawing in the sequence. Have one or two students justify their groups' choice. If there is disagreement, then facilitate a debate and guide the class toward understanding the best choice.

5. Continue as in Step 4 for the other fourteen drawings in the sequence.

6. Concept introduction: Through classroom lessons, outside reading, or Web research, students learn the terminology to describe and explain the events observed in the worksheet drawings.

Follow-Up

While students are learning more about mitosis (via a classroom or home assignment, have them label each drawing with the IPMAT phase of the cell cycle).

Later in the unit, ask students to explain the sequence from 1 to 15 in narrative form. As an end-of-unit reflection, ask students to write a paragraph explaining how (if?) the sequencing activity helped them to understand cell division.

Implementation Strategy

- It is essential to do this activity *before* assigning readings or leading other lessons on cell division.

- Students will ask what the drawings are. It is best not to tell them. Depending on the group, some or most of the students may recognize them as cells with chromosomes.

- If they call out that these are cells, simply shrug or refrain from responding.

- Tell the students that it does not matter whether they know what the drawings actually represent. Their task is simply to apply logic to organizing the sequence based solely on what they see on the page.

- Be sure to have individuals complete the sequencing alone before encouraging exchange of ideas. It is important for each person to struggle with the puzzle of the activity so that each of them can build an understanding for himself or herself.

- Recommend to students that they write in pencil on their worksheets to accommodate later changes.

- When discussing the drawings, refer to them as first row center or second row left, and so on.

Teacher Key

#1 is a cell in interphase. The genetic material is confined within the nucleus and not visible.

#2 shows the nuclear membrane gone, releasing the still condensing chromosomes throughout the cytoplasm.

#3 shows the butterfly (or x) shaped chromosomes in prophase.

#4 shows initial spindle formation.

#5 shows spindle fiber attachment to the chromosomes.

#6 represents metaphase. The chromosomes have been moved to the cell equator so that they can be split apart with a chromatid for each side (new cell).

#7 represents anaphase with the sister chromatids pulled apart at each chromosome.

#8 through 10 continue anaphase with the chromatids (now individual chromosomes) being pulled to opposite cell poles.

#11 through 13 are telophase.

#14 shows, with nuclear division complete, the chromosomes revert to their uncondensed, chromatin form.

#15 now cytokinesis is complete and two daughter cells are formed.

Reference

Danieley, H. (1990). Exploring mitosis through the learning cycle. *The American Biology Teacher, 52*(5), 295–296.

Sequencing Teacher Key

Reprinted with the permission of the National Association of Biology Teachers. Danieley, H. (1996).

Exploring mitosis through the learning cycle. The American Biology Teacher, 52(5), 196.

WORKSHEET 3.9
Mitosis Sequencing

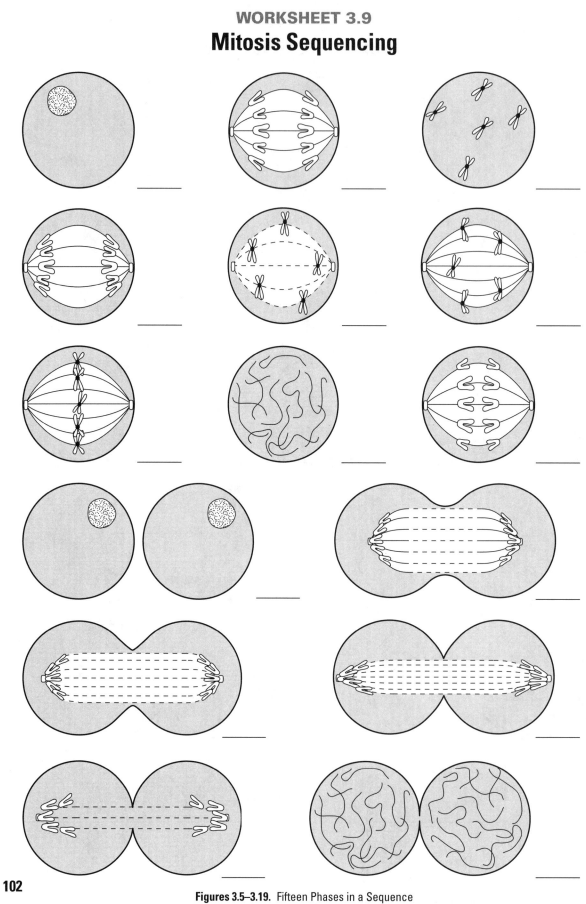

Figures 3.5–3.19. Fifteen Phases in a Sequence

Reprinted with the permission of the National Association of Biology Teachers. Danieley, H. (1996).

Exploring mitosis through the learning cycle. The American Biology Teacher, 52(5), 196.

Chapter 4

The Molecular Basis of Heredity

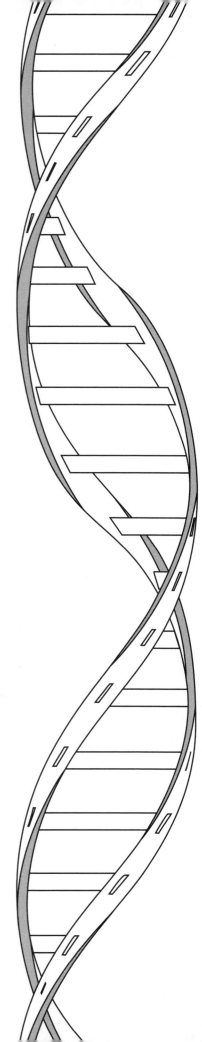

The lessons in this chapter explore principles and concepts found in the Life Science standards of "Reproduction and Heredity" and "The Molecular Basis of Heredity." Two of the inquiries guide learners through some of the thinking experienced by Mendel, Chargoff, Watson, and Crick. So, these lessons advance understanding of heredity and DNA but also address the "History and Nature of Science" standard. Other inquiries strive to move students beyond the simple Mendelian understanding of heredity to consider interactions among genes and between genes and the environment.

Mendel's Data

Students begin an introduction to heredity by analyzing Mendel's pea plant data.

Topic Connections

Heredity, Punnett Squares, Probability, History of Science

Introduction

In this partial inquiry, students begin a study of heredity by attempting to predict the results of Mendel's crosses. The actual F_1 result will be discrepant for many. Then by looking at the actual F_2 results, students propose possible explanations for the inheritance pattern. At this point students are poised to acquire background information on concepts such as dominance in order to explain Mendel's data.

The second part of this lesson is used after students have been introduced to Punnett squares. They make Punnett squares for Mendel's crosses and then attempt to reconcile the slight disparity between the predicted ratios and the actual results. This addresses the common misconception that Punnett squares show what *actually* will happen instead of what is *likely* to happen. Thus, a brief exploration of the probabilistic nature of Punnett squares ensues. An activity lesson on probability involving coins or dice would complement this exploration well.

Materials

None

Time Approximation

45 minutes

Lesson Outline

1. Lead a prior knowledge discussion on inheritance. Solicit ideas on questions such as:
   - How are traits inherited?
   - Where does a person get their eye color, hair color, and so on?
   - What if one parent has brown hair and the other one is blonde? What hair color will their children have?
2. Tell students that Gregor Mendel wondered about these sorts of questions about 150 years ago. Share Mendel's "story" with the class to set the stage for an exploration of his experiments.

3. Distribute the student worksheet.

4. Have students read the introductory paragraph. Then lead a class-wide discussion based on the "Discussion Questions." Proceed through the sequence, discussing each question before moving on to the next. A visual representation of Mendel's three generations would be helpful. For example, on an overhead transparency or on a whiteboard draw the tall and short parents and, at the appropriate time, add the tall F_1 below.

   Do not reveal the F_2 3:1 results at this point.

5. *Analysis:* In small groups or individually have students work through the questions.

6. *Background Information:* Via readings, research, and/or classroom lessons students learn about dominance, recessiveness, segregation of alleles, Punnett squares, and so on.

7. *Predicting and Probability:* Students work through the questions.

8. *Assessment/Reflection:* Lead a discussion addressing early preconceptions that the students revealed in the prior knowledge discussion. For example, ask students what they now think of the notion that certain traits "skip a generation" (a very common preconception).

Implementation Strategy

- Use this lesson *before* any readings or lessons on heredity.
- Consider preceding the lesson with a flower dissection so that students will comprehend cross-pollination and self-pollination.

Possible Responses for Selected Student Worksheet Questions

Discussion Questions

1. Many will predict medium
2. All tall plants
3. What happened to shortness? Various possible crosses might be suggested.
4. Mendel allowed the F_1 plants to self-pollinate. Predictions will vary.

Analysis Questions

1. Accept any attempts at explaining the results.
2. Responses will vary. For each, ask what new information would be revealed about any patterns. Guide the class toward seeing the value of computing ratios for each cross.

3. Tall:Short   2.84:1
    Purple:White flowers   3.15:1
    Axial:Terminal   3.14:1
    Yellow:Green seeds   3.01:1
    Round:Wrinkled seeds   2.96:1
    Inflated:Constricted pods   2.95:1
    Green:Yellow pods   2.82:1

Predicting and Probability

1. Parental cross result = 100 percent tall

2. F_1 cross result = 3:1 Tall:Short

3. They are close but the actual results are not exactly 3:1. Accept all reasonable attempts to explain the difference.

4. The more times a coin is tossed, the truer the results will be to probability-based predictions. It is quite conceivable to get three heads in a row or even ten in a row. But it is hard to imagine getting one hundred heads in a row or 10,000! The results of 10,000 coin tosses would fall very close to 50 percent heads and 50 percent tails. The results for ten tosses might be 50/50, but they could easily stray far from that.

5. Seed color and seed shape. They have the largest sample sizes so these crosses yielded results truer to the probability-based predictions.

6. Many possibilities.

Name _____ Date _____

Mendel's Data

Introduction
Gregor Mendel studied the inheritance of a number of characteristics in pea plants such as flower color, seed shape, and height. For all of these characteristics he carefully conducted breeding crosses between plants with different forms of the trait. For instance, Mendel crossed purple-flowered plants with white-flowered ones, tall plants with short, and round-seed plants with wrinkled-seed ones. In all cases he started with plants that were pure-bred. His tall plants, for example, came from parents that produced only tall offspring.

Discussion Questions
1. Mendel crossed (bred) tall pea plants with short pea plants. Predict what the offspring were like.

Tall x Short

?

Give a rationale for your prediction.

2. Your teacher will show you what Mendel actually got when tall and short plants were crossed.

3. What questions do you have now? If you were Mendel, what would you have done next?

4. Your teacher will show you what Mendel did next. It is called an F_1 (first filial) cross. Predict what the offspring of this cross were like.

_____

_____

5. The table below shows Mendel's actual F_2 results for the tall-short experiments and six others.

Table 4.1. Mendel's F_2 Generation Results

Characteristic	Trait and Number of Plants		Trait and Number of Plants	
Height	Tall	787	Short	277
Flower color	Purple	705	White	224
Flower position	Axial	651	Terminal	207
Seed color	Yellow	6022	Green	2001
Seed shape	Round	5474	Wrinkled	1850
Pod shape	Inflated	882	Constricted	299
Pod color	Green	428	Yellow	152

Mendel's Data, *Cont'd.*

Analysis Questions

1. Are the F_2 results for height what you expected? Propose a tentative explanation for these results. Consider what could have happened to the factor for shortness in the F_1 generation. How did it show up in the F_2 generation if it isn't observed in the F_1 plants?

   _____

   _____

   _____

   _____

   _____

   _____

2. What are some mathematical computations that you could do with Mendel's data to more clearly detect a pattern?

   _____

   _____

   _____

3. After thinking about and discussing the last question, your class will decide on one especially useful calculation. Do that calculation for all of Mendel's data and record your results in a table.

   _____

   _____

   _____

Background Information

You will need to acquire background information on inheritance in order to fully explain Mendel's F_1 and F_2 results. Also you will need to understand how to use a Punnett square before continuing this inquiry.

Predicting and Probability

1. Make a Punnett square for Mendel's two crosses (parental and F_1) for height.

Mendel's Data, *Cont'd.*

2. Explain in words how these Punnett squares predict what Mendel actually got for F_1 and F_2 results. How do they explain the "disappearance" of shortness in the F_1 generation?

_____

_____

_____

_____

3. Compare the F_2 ratios that you computed earlier with the predicted F_2 ratio in the above Punnett square. Propose possible explanations for why they differ slightly.

_____

_____

_____

_____

4. (Thinking question) If a coin is tossed, what is the probability that it will land heads-up? Is it possible to toss a coin three times and get heads each time? How about if you toss it ten times? One hundred times? Ten thousand times? Which of these scenarios will most reliably result in the predicted 50 percent heads and 50 percent tails?

_____

_____

_____

_____

5. Which two of Mendel's crosses came closest to a 3:1 ratio in the F_2 generation? Propose an explanation for this.

_____

_____

_____

_____

6. What further experimental questions would be interesting to explore on pea plant heredity?

_____

_____

_____

_____

Multifactorial Inheritance

By measuring and graphing a trait, students discover that the phenotype must be influenced by more than one gene.

Topic Connections

Heredity, Polygenic Traits, Nature/Nurture, Human Genetics

Introduction

When addressing heredity, most introductory biology textbooks focus primarily on single gene traits such as pea plant height, cystic fibrosis, Huntington's Disease, and so on. Studying the inheritance of such phenotypes allows for relatively simple Punnett square problem solving and predicting. They involve basic patterns that are accessible to teenagers. However, an overemphasis on 19th century Mendelian genetics is a disservice to student learning. Modern genetics has revealed the vast majority of phenotypes to result from the interactions of multiple genes. And the expression of most genes is also modified by both environmental factors and chance.

A trait determined only by combinations of two alleles at one gene locus can result in, at most, three phenotypes. There could be phenotypes produced by two dominant alleles, two recessive alleles, or, if there is incomplete or co-dominance, by heterozygotes. Most human traits show no such breakdown into two or three possible phenotypes. Skin color, height, intelligence, and most other traits reveal a wide continuous range of phenotypes. Thus, these traits must be multifactorial. They are influenced by complex interactions of multiple genes (polygenic) and environmental factors.

In this activity, students measure a trait such as index finger length. Graphing of the class data reveals a wide spread of phenotypes approximating a bell curve. Students then use this data to develop insight into the complexity of human inheritance.

Materials

- Metric rulers
- Graph paper or computer graphing program

Time Approximation

One class period

Lesson Outline

1. Either distribute the student worksheet or use it as a guide for the lesson sequence and discussion topics.

2. Solicit student ideas on the "Initial Questions." For question number 3, solicit some answers but do not discuss or resolve the issue yet.

3. Students measure their index finger or whichever trait is used. Students then exchange data. Consider having them decide how to most efficiently do this.

4. Students make bar graphs of the class data, with "length" along the X axis and "number of students" along the Y axis. Guide them to decide to do the graph this way.

5. Students answer the questions either before or within a classwide discussion.

6. Introduce the students to the concepts of polygenic inheritance, continuous variation, and multifactorial inheritance.

7. Student reflection writings give students a chance to process, organize, and make sense out of new understandings.

Implementation Strategy

- Any measurable trait could be used, such as student height, leg length, or eye span. Nonhuman traits would work as well. It might be productive to use both human and nonhuman phenotypes so that students realize that multifactorial inheritance is the norm in all species.

- Measure index fingers from the webbing between the middle finger and the index finger to the tip. Explain to the students how to measure the trait so that technique is standardized.

- *Expected data:* Graphs should reveal a wide range spreading out from a cluster in the middle. The larger the data pool, the better the chance of a bell-curve line distribution. All that is needed though is a range of phenotypes.

Possible Responses for Selected Student Worksheet Questions

Initial Questions

1. Two—Tall or short, for pea plants. For disorders, either one has it or does not, although for many disorders there are also variations in severity, onset, and so on.

2. Three—For example: red, pink, white in certain flowers.

3. No—Most occur in continuous variation.

Analysis Questions

1. Answers will vary, but should be multiple.

2. The trait must be determined by more than one gene locus with two alleles. Otherwise there could not be more than three possible phenotypes, and the graph shows many more than three.

3(a). Many possibilities.

3(b). Most human traits occur in many more than two or three phenotypes.

Students may argue that hair color or eye color exist in a small number of
phenotypes, but even these show wide ranges of variation in shades of color.

4. Multiple phenotypes resulting in continuous variation. These traits, like most,
are influenced by polygenes and also by environmental influences.

Reference

Bloom, M., & others. (2000). *Genes, environment and human behavior.* Colorado
Springs, CO: Biological Sciences Curriculum Study. (Available as a free
download at www.bscs.org)

Name _____ Date _____

Multifactorial Inheritance

Initial Questions

1. How many different phenotypes are there for a trait such as pea plant height, Huntington's Disease, or Sickle Cell Disease? Explain.

    _____

    _____

    _____

2. How many different phenotypes are there for a trait whose alleles exhibit incomplete or co-dominance? Explain.

    _____

    _____

    _____

3. Do most human traits occur in just two or three forms? Think about this question as you proceed through the next part of the lesson.

Data Collection

1. Use a metric ruler to measure a trait suggested by your teacher. Record your data here or in a lab notebook.

    _____

    _____

    _____

2. Make a graph of the data collected by the whole class for the trait.

Analysis

1. Based on your graph, how many phenotypes are present in the class for the given trait?

    _____

2. Based on this data, what can you conclude about the number of genes that determine the trait? Explain.

    _____

    _____

    _____

    _____

Multifactorial Inheritance, *Cont'd.*

3(a). List ten human traits other than genetic disorders.

_____

_____

_____

_____

3(b). How many of these ten traits occur in only two or three possible phenotypes? Which ones?

_____

_____

_____

_____

4. How many phenotypes are there for height, intelligence, or skin color in humans? What can you conclude about these traits from this?

_____

_____

_____

_____

Reflection

Write a paragraph explaining how you think differently about heredity after this activity/ lesson. What was the purpose/point/message of the lesson?

_____

_____

_____

_____

_____

_____

_____

_____

_____

Nature *and* Nurture

A discussion lesson in which students construct an understanding that both genes and environmental factors influence human behavioral traits.

Topic Connections

Genes, Human Behaviors, Multifactorial Inheritance, Human Genome Project

Introduction

Is intelligence genetic? What about athletic ability? Is musical ability genetic? Or are these things learned and developed? If asked these questions, students will have a lot to say! Through life experiences, teenagers have formed their own explanations, many of them misconceptions, about the inheritance of complex human traits. Given the opportunity, they will share all sorts of stories (and their own explanations) involving their families or those of others. These stories often end with statements like "so . . . must be genetic" or ". . . can't be genetic."

High student interest, widespread misunderstanding, and societal importance make human behavioral genetics a good classroom study topic. This lesson begins by eliciting student preconceptions with the questions above. Playing devil's advocate, you question students to help begin the process of them critiquing and modifying their previous ideas. As a result, learners are primed to acquire information on the genetics of various human behavioral traits via Web sites and other sources. Finally, reflection and a post-research discussion help students to develop a more scientifically accurate understanding of the inheritance of behavioral traits.

Heritability is a measure of the extent to which inheritance may contribute to the occurrence of a trait in humans. Research has been conducted on the heritability of many human behavioral traits, such as shyness, novelty seeking, intelligence (although defining the trait is controversial), alcoholism, optimism, and homosexuality. Easy-to-comprehend summaries of such studies are available on government-sponsored Web sites such as Online Mendelian Inheritance in Man (OMIM).

The most important outcome of this lesson for students is to comprehend the complexity of human behavioral traits. These traits are influenced by multiple genes interacting with each other and interacting with environmental factors and internal regulatory factors. Statements that begin with "*The* gene for . . . in humans" should be met with much skepticism. Unlike for Mendel's pea plants, there are very few human traits that follow simple, single-gene inheritance patterns. Behavioral traits are especially complex and very incompletely understood by science.

Materials

Web access is recommended

Time Approximation

- For the introductory discussion, about 30 minutes
- For the Web/book research, time will vary
- For the post-research discussion, about 20 minutes
- The reflection can be completed outside of class

Lesson Outline

Introductory Discussion

1. Draw out student preconceptions by leading a discussion around the three central questions listed on the student worksheet. Either have them write individual answers to the questions ahead of time or simply begin the discussion.

   Focus on one of the questions at a time. Put the question out there and then solicit some opinions. Ask students to support/justify their responses with evidence. Do not correct inaccuracies at this point. If students challenge claims by other students, then facilitate some debate, but don't step in with "the right answer" at this point.

2. After hearing from a number of students, begin to stimulate new thinking by playing devil's advocate and asking secondary questions. Refer to some earlier student claims and ask whether the opposite of their explanation wouldn't also be possible. For example, if a student claims intelligence to be genetic because a smart friend has rocket scientist parents, then ask, "Is it possible that the parents value education and they provided the friend with extra stimulating experiences that helped his or her brain to develop in a certain way?"

   The goal of these questions is to get students to doubt their previous positions and to prepare them to construct a new, more accurate or complete understanding.

Secondary Questions

1. Toward the end of each discussion, wrap up the topic by leaving students to ponder a final, guiding question about each of the following topics.

   - *Intelligence.*

     Ask: "If Albert Einstein had been raised in a stimulation- and nutrition-deprived atmosphere as a child, would he have become the genius that he was?" and "Could you make *any* child highly intelligent if you raised him or her in an ideal high stimulation environment?"

- *Athletic ability.* Ask: "If [*local sports star*] never picked up a ball could he or she one day walk on and be a star player?" and "Could [*use yourself*] have become a superstar/MVP player if I'd started playing at age three and been trained for hours every day?"

- *Musical ability.* Ask: "If a violin virtuoso never took lessons, heard music, or practiced would he or she still have an exceptional musical talent?" and "Could anyone in this room have become an exceptional violinist if he or she had practiced for hours a day beginning at a very young age?"

2. The point of these questions is to guide students into developing an intuitive understanding considering the importance of *both* genetic and environmental influences.

Web/Book Research

Students gain content knowledge on twin studies, heritability, and the results of studies on various human behavioral traits.

See "Implementation Strategy" for recommended resources.

Web Information Approach

1. Have student pairs find and summarize information on research results on the heritability of various human behavioral traits. The site Online Mendelian Inheritance in Man (OMIM) is ideal for this. See "Implementation Strategy." This could be done in school or outside of class.

2. Student pairs share their findings on a particular trait with the class as a lead-in to the step that follows.

Post-Research Discussion

1. Lead a discussion that revisits the initial three questions and asks students to apply new knowledge to them.

2. Lead the class to make general conclusions about human heredity. Help them realize that it is not nature versus nurture but nature *and* nurture. Phenotypes are not *determined* by genes. They are influenced by genes along with environmental and chance influences.

3. To drive the above point home, have students focus on a purely physical trait like height. Ask them to agree with you that height must be entirely genetic. Then ask, "But what if [*a very tall person/local basketball player*] had been raised on a diet low in calcium and protein? Would he or she have achieved the same height?"

Reflection

The reflection questions on the student worksheet could be incorporated into the above discussion or completed on the worksheet as homework.

Implementation Strategy

- Use this lesson after students have learned basic genetics. Students need to understand how twin studies are used in genetics. This could be learned before or during the lesson.

- For the intelligence question, begin with a disclaimer that "intelligence" is a controversial concept that is difficult to define and measure. But because people have a general intuitive idea of what it is and a high interest in the topic, it makes for fruitful discussion. Some students may raise the concept of multiple intelligences. Students may confuse knowledge with intelligence, but usually other students will point this out. Often students eventually equate capacity to learn with intelligence. Again, a definition of intelligence is a side issue that can be discussed briefly, but can more completely be addressed at another time.

Web Resources for Students and the Teacher

Human Genome Project Information site, maintained by the Department of Energy at www.doegenomes.org. Look under HGP Information/Ethical, Legal and Societal Issues/Behavioral Genetics.

Genes, Environment and Human Behavior is a teaching module loaded with content information as well as five inquiry-based lessons. Available as a free download from BSCS at www.bscs.org

Online Mendelian Inheritance in Man (OMIM), a database from the National Center for Biotechnology Information (NCBI). Access the site by doing a search for OMIM or through the NCBI Web site at www.ncbi.nlm.nih.gov (then find the OMIM link on the menu). It summarizes research findings on human traits. Even though it contains mostly health-related gene information, includes novelty seeking personality trait; handedness (right versus left); alcoholism; musical perfect pitch; arm folding preference; tobacco addiction; homosexuality; obesity; panic disorder; stuttering; and hand clasping pattern.

The summaries are brief and written at a level that high school students can comprehend. Younger students will need help with terms such as monozygotic, dizygotic, familial, autosomal, and so on. Usually the meaning of the summary can easily be ascertained despite a bit of jargon.

To use the Web site simply enter the trait into the search engine on the OMIM home page and then click on the link for the trait.

Magazine Resources for Students and the Teacher

Kuehn, K., Colt, G., and Hollister, A. (1998, April). Were you born that way? Genes for insomnia, optimism, and obesity may be inherited but may not be destiny. *Life,* p. 21. Although dated, the article provides a good review of the issue for the teacher.

Wheelright, J. (2004, August). Study the clones first. *Discover,* 25, 44–51.

Nature *and* Nurture

Consider these three questions. Be prepared to discuss your ideas with the class.

1. Is intelligence genetic? Or does it result from external (environmental) experiences? What is your evidence?

_____

_____

_____

2. Is athletic ability genetic? Or does it result it from environmental experiences? What is your evidence?

_____

_____

_____

3. Is musical ability genetic? Or does it result from environmental experiences? What is your evidence?

_____

_____

_____

_____

Web/Book Research
What has been learned about the inheritance of human behavioral traits? How are these things studied? You will find information on these topics as directed by your teacher.

_____

_____

_____

_____

_____

Nature *and* Nurture, *Cont'd.*

Reflection

Think about your initial responses to the three questions at the beginning of this worksheet. How would you answer them now? How has your thinking changed on the topic?

2. Pick one example given by another student during the initial discussion (for example, about a friend or family member). Now explain that example using your current understanding of genetic and environmental influences on human behavior.

_____

_____

_____

_____

_____

_____

_____

_____

_____

_____

_____

_____

_____

_____

_____

_____

_____

_____

_____

_____

_____

_____

_____

_____

_____

Chargaff's DNA Data

An introduction to DNA structure and the process of discovery that contributed to the double-helix model.

Topic Connections

DNA, Molecular Biology, History of Biology

Introduction

In the 1940s Erwin Chargaff made critical discoveries about DNA that eventually helped Watson and Crick assemble their double-helix model. Textbooks often include some of Chargaff's data to support an explanation of DNA structure. This lesson reverses the order and presents students with Chargaff's data to analyze first before they have learned about the double helix.

With a very limited knowledge of biochemistry, there is not a lot that high school students can do with molecular biology data. But Chargaff's results present simple and very significant patterns. By considering and manipulating Chargaff's data, even in a simple fashion, students begin to construct a foundation of understanding of the logic of the double-helix model. Also, they are introduced to the history of the DNA structure discovery process by experiencing some of the thinking that occurred at the time.

Materials

None

Time Approximation

45 minutes; portions could be completed outside of class

Lesson Outline

1. Ask students what they know about DNA. Encourage them to brainstorm and free associate at first. Then focus on these central questions:

   • What is DNA?

   • What does it do?

   • How does it do it?

   By the end of the discussion be sure that students understand the general concept of DNA containing the genetic code/blueprint/instructions.

2. Distribute the student worksheet. Have the class read the introductory portion individually.

3. Consider having students work in small groups to discuss and respond to these questions. At the end of this section, lead a classwide discussion to be

sure that everyone is focused on the central pattern (A occurring in direct proportion to T and G with C).

4. Consider showing a transparency or book drawing of purine and pyrimidine shapes, then have students answer the questions in small groups.

5. Show an overhead of the DNA double helix that shows A pairing with T and G with C. For advanced classes, use one that clearly shows double-ringed purines paired with single-ringed pyrimidines. Then have students respond to final questions.

6. Introduce the students to "Chargaff's Rules" at the end of the lesson or in subsequent discussions.

Implementation Strategy

- Use this lesson before any significant learning of DNA structure has occurred.

- It is important to find out what students know about DNA before beginning with the student worksheet.

- Have students work on the analysis questions in small groups to facilitate discussion, debate, and idea development. The last two sections could easily serve as the template for a classwide discussion lesson.

- Analysis question 2 will require varying degrees of guidance depending on student math abilities.

Possible Responses for Selected Student Worksheet Questions

Analysis

1. For each organism the percentage of A is very similar to the percentage of T. The same applies to G and C.

   The percentage of A + G = T + C

   Each species has different proportions of the bases.

2. Proportions of A/T and G/C. These will be very close to 1 for all species. Or ratios of A:T and G:C, which will be very close to 1:1. Students will make other calculations as well, such as averages or A + T/G + C. But none of these will yield patterns that are constant among species in the table.

3. All are different.

4. DNA does provide variation between species. Therefore it could be the hereditary molecule.

5. Many possibilities. Accept all reasonable ideas.

Background Information

    1. Purine: pyrmidine ratios are all very close to 1:1.

    2. For every purine there is a pyrimidine.

Piecing It Together

    1. Nitrogen bases point towards the inside.

       A pairs with T

       G pairs with C

       Purines pair with pyrimidines

       Double-ringed bases pair with single ringed, allowing for constant diameter.

    2. Accept all possible/reasonable ideas.

Reference

Chargaff, E., & Davidson, J. (1955). *The nucleic acids.* New York: Academic Press.

Rothwell, N. (1993). *Understanding genetics: A molecular approach.* New York: Wiley-Liss.

Name _____ Date _____

WORKSHEET 4.4
Chargaff's DNA Data

Introduction

DNA was first discovered in 1869, but not much was known about the molecule until the 1920s. Early researchers discovered that DNA was comprised of repeated units called nucleotides. Each nucleotide contains a part called a nitrogen base. There are four different nitrogen bases found in DNA:

Adenine (A)

Cytosine (C)

Guanine (G)

Thymine (T)

In the 1920s it was believed that these nitrogen bases occurred in all living things in the same repeated pattern, such as ATGC ATGC ATGC. If this were true, then DNA could not be the hereditary molecule. With the same repeated pattern in all species, DNA could not provide the variety needed for a molecule containing the genetic code.

After World War II the biochemist Erwin Chargaff made some major discoveries about the nitrogen bases in DNA. His research revealed the percentage of each base (A, C, T, and G) found in an organism's DNA. The table below includes some of Chargaff's data and some more recent additions.

Table 4.2. Nitrogen Base Make-Up of Different Organisms' DNA (in Percentages)

Organism	A	T	G	C
Mycobacterium tuberculosis	15.1	14.6	34.9	35.4
Yeast	31.3	32.9	18.7	17.1
Wheat	27.3	27.1	22.7	22.8
Sea Urchin	32.8	32.1	17.7	17.3
Marine Crab	47.3	47.3	2.7	2.7
Turtle	29.7	27.9	22.0	21.3
Rat	28.6	28.4	21.4	21.5
Human	30.9	29.4	19.9	19.8

Name _____ Date _____

Analysis

1. What observations can you make about the data in the table? What patterns do you notice?

   _____

   _____

   _____

   _____

2. What mathematical calculations could you make with the above data that would reveal more information about important patterns? Make calculations and record your results in a table.

   _____

   _____

   _____

   _____

3. What does the data show about the make-up of DNA for different species? Explain.

   _____

   _____

   _____

   _____

4. After seeing data like this in the 1940s, what do you think researchers concluded about DNA's potential to carry the genetic code? Explain.

   _____

   _____

   _____

   _____

5. Before concluding that the pattern seen in the data is universal, which other species would you want to test? Why?

   _____

   _____

   _____

   _____

Chargaff's DNA Data, *Cont'd.*

Background Information

Adenine and guanine are similarly shaped nitrogen bases called purines. Thymine and cytosine are similar in shape and they are classified as pyrimidines.

1. For at least four species in the data table, calculate the ratio of purines:pyrimidines and organize your results in a table.

   _____

   _____

   _____

   _____

2. What can you conclude about the purine:pyrimidine make-up of DNA?

   _____

   _____

   _____

   _____

Piecing It Together

Chargaff's data was a central piece of evidence used by James Watson and Francis Crick in 1953 to successfully describe the structure of DNA.

Look at a drawing of the DNA molecule that has labeled nitrogen bases. Such drawings are easily found in biology textbooks and on the Internet, or your teacher may show you one.

1. What do you notice about the arrangement of the nitrogen bases? Record as many observations as you can.

   _____

   _____

   _____

   _____

2. How do you think Chargaff's data helped Watson and Crick to predict that DNA looks like this?

   _____

   _____

   _____

   _____

Classifying Oaks with DNA

Using morphological data and DNA sequences students attempt to classify three oak leaves.

Topic Connections

DNA, Genomes, Taxonomy, Biological Species Concept

Introduction

How do biologists determine whether two populations of organisms belong to the same species or not? Taxonomy has long been a fluid, exciting, and controversial area of biology. The biological species concept defines a species as a group of organisms capable of reproducing and leaving fertile offspring. But according to this definition dogs and wolves, which readily hybridize, are the same species. However, most sources describe them as different species, *Canis lupis* and *Canis familiaris*. The value of the biological species concept is its focus on how a species came to exist—the evolution of an isolated gene pool. In reality most species are identified by the morphological species concept. In this approach a species is recognized as distinct based on unique structures (morphology).

Molecular biology has added a powerful new tool to the arsenal of taxonomists. The more closely related two organisms are, the more similar their DNA, RNA, and amino acid sequences. New molecular data have revolutionized some longstanding classifications. But like the other methods of identifying a species, the molecular approach has some limitations. For instance, how similar do DNA sequences need to be for two populations to be considered of the same species? How can we decide?

Students grapple with these questions in this lesson. First they observe and compare the two-dimensional shapes of three oak leaves (Handout 4.1). They then compare and analyze DNA sequences representing the three leaves (Handout 4.2). Combining both types of data, students are challenged to decide how many species are represented by the leaves. By morphology and DNA, one of the leaves (white oak) is very different from the other two. But pin oak and red oak are similar enough to provoke student uncertainty and debate.

An optional but recommended expansion of the lesson is provided in which students collect and analyze morphological data from a large sample of leaves collected locally.

Materials

- Copies of the handouts as well as the worksheet
- Metric ruler
- Several copies of any field guide to North American trees

Time Approximation

60 to 90 minutes

Lesson Outline

Introductory Discussions

1. Distribute Handout 4.1 with the three leaf drawings.

2. Initiate a discussion by asking, "How could you determine whether or not two organisms are of the same species?" Accept all answers and avoid correcting inaccuracies at this point. Also ask, "What is a species?" Be sure at this point that students at least understand a species to be a group of organisms generally more similar to one another than they are to another group. You might want to introduce the biological species concept as well. And "Are an oak tree and a dog the same species? A dog and a cat? How about a dog and a wolf? A Labrador retriever and a golden retriever?" Again, accept varied thoughts. Finish with a rhetorical question: "How similar do two organisms have to be to be considered the same species? How do biologists decide?"

3. Call the students' attention to the leaf drawings. In small groups have them discuss the questions in the introductory part of the student worksheet.

4. Pick a few of the groups to share their ideas on the worksheet questions. Guide the class to decide on four or five quantitative characteristics to measure and compare. To help in discussing the leaves, you will want to introduce some vocabulary at this point. Distinguish the leaf blade from the leaf petiole (stalk). The oak leaf indentations are sinuses and the extended portions are lobes.

Data Collection and Analysis

1. Students make and record measurements on the leaf drawings. For actual data for the three species, see "Implementation Strategy." Students could use this actual data for additional analysis.

2. Distribute Handout 4.2 with the DNA sequences. Tell the students that the same gene was sequenced for each leaf and that these are the results.

3. Student groups devise a way to compare the three sequences. Press them to use a quantifiable approach rather than just "eyeballing it." Guide them to focus on similarities at base locations. They could focus on the number of spots at which each leaf is different from the other two. It is easiest to compare pairs: 1 with 2; 1 with 3; 2 with 3. A percentage that is similar could then be calculated between each pair.

Wrap-Up and Reflection

1. Have one or more field guides available. Challenge students to identify the three leaves. From the drawings alone it will be easy to identify white oak

(no bristly points on its lobes) but more difficult to distinguish the other two from each other and to distinguish red oak from black oak in the field guide. Guide the students to focus in on the depth of the indentations and presence or absence of pointy lobe tips.

2. Students write responses to final questions on their worksheets.

Implementation Strategy

- A limitation to the lesson is the use of one leaf to represent each species. Eventually when the students realize (via the field guide) that they are three species, you should discuss with them that it is impossible to physically/structurally characterize a species from one leaf. There is tremendous variation in leaf size and shape on any given tree, not to mention within a whole species. The possible add-ons to the lesson discussed below remedy this limitation.

- The DNA sequences in Handout 4.2 are from identical portions of the genomes of the three species. The white oak sequence is seven bases longer than that of the other two. The sequences are for "internal transcribed spacers and a gene for 5.8s ribosomal RNA."

- The DNA sequences were retrieved from the National Center for Biotechnology Information's (NCBI) Gene Bank sequence viewer. To directly access the sequences use the following locus numbers:

  White Oak—AF098419

  Northern Red Oak—AF098418

  Pin Oak—AF098417

Table 4.3. Sample Morphological Data

	Leaf 1 (White Oak)	Leaf 2 (Red Oak)	Leaf 3 (Pin Oak)
Sample size	60	50	184
Leaf length (cm)	13.71	18.32	18.19
Leaf width (cm)	7.13	11.14	11.11
Sinus depth (cm)	3.25	4.39	4.52
Blade length (cm)	11.79	14.52	13.88
Petiole length (cm)	1.84	4.20	4.49
Petiole diameter (mm)	0.67	0.94	0.66
Number of lobes	6.02	5.14	5.09

Collected by the students of R. McMaster, Holyoke Community College. These are mean values for seven traits measured.

- If you give the data in Table 4.3 to students for analysis, be sure to exclude the species names on the top.

  For advanced students. Have them use the above data to calculate a similarity index called Euclidian distance. The formula is shown in Figure 4.1 below.

$$\sqrt{\sum (x-y)^2}$$

Figure 4.1. Euclidean Distance

- This formula is used to compare two species at a time. The symbols x and y are the means for a trait for the two species. The difference between x and y is squared. All squared differences (seven in the case of the above data) are then summed and the square root of that value is determined. For example, to compare red and pin oak, take the difference between 18.32 and 18.19 (.13) and square it (.0169). Then do the same for the other six traits in the table. Sum the seven values (.6093) and take its square root to get the Euclidian distance of .78 (rounded to 0.8). The smaller the Euclidian distance, the more similar two species are. Notice how similar red oak and pin oak are by this measure. On the other hand, white oak is dissimilar to both pin and red oaks.

Red Oak—Pin Oak	0.8
Red Oak—White Oak	7.3
White Oak—Pin Oak	7.1

- *Recommended extension:* If time and circumstances permit, have students collect data on a larger number of locally collected leaves of two or three species (oaks if available!) and follow these steps.

  1. Collect about ten leaves per species per lab group. Give each group a mixed pile of the leaves.
  2. They attempt to sort leaves into species. Groups discuss/debate how many species are present.
  3. Groups decide on traits to measure, collect data, calculate means using class totals, make graphs for selected traits, decide on number of species present, and identify species.
  4. Proceed to molecular data portion of the lesson.

Possible Responses to Worksheet Questions

Molecular Data Analysis

1. Leaf 2 (red oak) and Leaf 3 (pin oak) are 98 percent similar in their DNA sequences. About 36 percent of Leaf 1's (white oak) bases are the same as those of Leaves 2 and 3.

2. Leaf 1 is much less closely related to Leaves 2 and 3 than they are to each other. Leaves 2 and 3 might be from the same species. Students could conclude there to be two or three species.

Wrap-Up and Reflection

1. Three species: white oak (#1), red oak (#2), pin oak (#3)

2. Answers will vary. Molecular data was more concrete and less subject to student decisions on what to observe.

3. Many more samples, such as observing whole trees, trunks, branching patterns, flowers, fruits, seeds, reproductive timing, potential for hybridization.

4. An open and controversial topic.

Reference

McMaster, R. (2004). Exploring the taxonomy of oaks and related species. *The American Biology Teacher, 66*(2), 137–143.

HANDOUT 4.1
Leaves

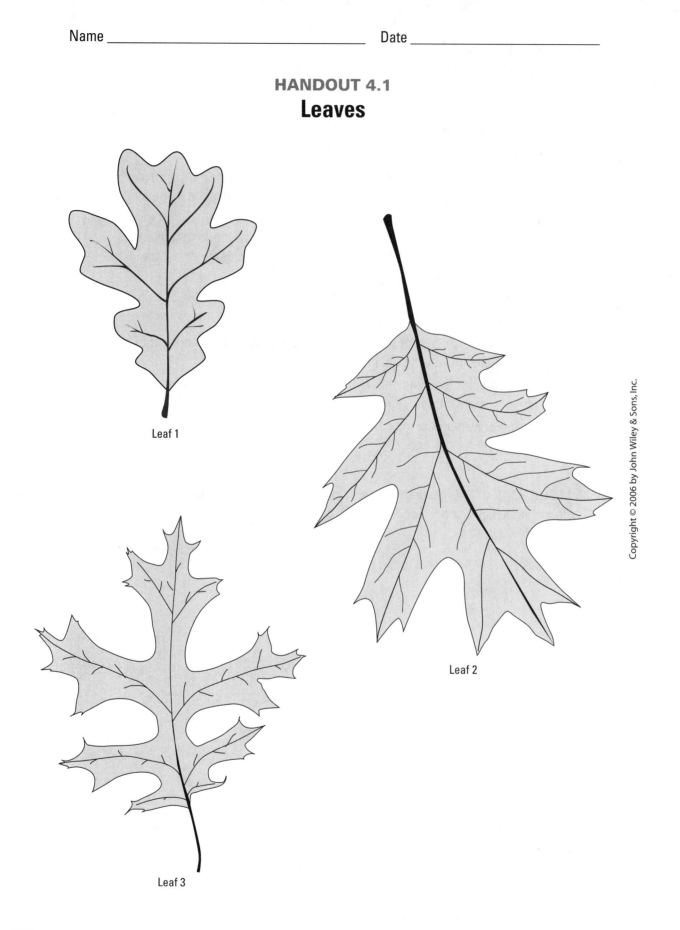

Leaf 1

Leaf 2

Leaf 3

Name _____ Date _____

DNA Sequences for the Three Leaves

Leaf 1

1	tcgaaacctg	cccagcagaa	cgacccgcga	attggttaca	accgacgggg	ggcggggggc
61	gttcgtcgcc	ccctcgcccc	ctcctgcggg	gggggcctcg	cgtctcctgc	ccgcagaccg
121	aaccccggcg	cggaacgcgc	caaggaaatc	taaccaagag	agccatgtcg	gaggccccgg
181	acacggtgtg	cccccggcgt	cggcgtctta	tgaattattc	aaaacgactc	tcggcaacgg
241	atatctaggc	tctcgcatcg	atgaagaacg	tagcgaaatg	cgatacttgg	tgtgaattgc
301	agaatcccgc	gaatcatcga	gtttttgaac	gcaagttgcg	cccgaagcca	ttcggccgag
361	ggcacgtctg	cctgggtgtc	acgcatcgtt	gccccccca	aactccggtt	cgggcggggc
421	ggaagttggc	ctcccgtgcg	tgcctgcacg	cgcggttagc	ccaaaagcga	gtcctcggcg
481	acgagcgcca	cgacaatcgg	tggttttttt	accctcgttc	ctcgtcgtgc	gtgccccgtc
541	gcccgaacgc	gctcctgcga	ccctcacgcg	tcgcctcggt	ggcgctccca	acgc

Leaf 2

1	tcgaaacctg	cacagcagaa	cgacccgcga	attggttaca	accgacgggg	ggcggggggc
61	gctcgtcgcc	ccctcgcccc	ccctgcgggc	ggggagacct	gcctgcaaac	cgaaccccag
121	cgcggaacgc	gccaaggaaa	tctaaccaag	agagccacgc	tggaggcccc	ggacacggtg
181	tgcccccgac	gtcggcgctt	tacgaattat	tcaaaacgac	tctcggcaac	ggatatctag
241	gctctcgcat	cgatgaagaa	cgtagcgaaa	tgcgatactt	gatgtgaatt	gcagaatccc
301	gcgaatcatc	gagtttttga	acgcaagttg	cgcctgaagc	cattcggccg	agggcacgtc
361	tgcctgggtg	tcacgcatcg	ttgcccccccc	aaaactccggt	tcgggcgggg	cggaagttgg
421	cctcccgtgc	gtgcctgcgc	gcgcggttag	cccaaaagcg	agtcctcggc	gacgagcgcc
481	acgacaatcg	gtggtttct	tgccctcgtt	cctcgtcgtg	cgcgccccgt	cgcccgaacg
541	cgctcctcga	ccctcacgcg	tcgtcgcctc	ggcggcgctc	ccaacgc	

Leaf 3

1	tcgaaacctg	cacagcagaa	cgacccgcga	attggttaca	accgacgggg	ggcggggggc
61	gttcgtcgcc	ccctcgcccc	ccctgcgggt	ggggagacct	gcctgcaaac	tgaaccccag
121	cgcggaacgc	gccaaggaaa	tctaaccaag	agagccacgc	tggaggcccc	ggacacggtg
181	tgcccccgac	gtcggcgctt	tacgaattat	tcaaaacgac	tctcggcaac	ggatatctag
241	gctctcgcat	cgatgaagaa	cgtagcgaaa	tgcgatactt	gatgtgaatt	gcagaatccc
301	gcgaatcatc	gagttttga	acgcaagttg	cgcccgaagc	cattcggccg	agggcacgtc
361	tgcctgggtg	tcacgcatcg	ttgcccccccc	aaaactccggt	tcgggcgggg	cggaagttgg
421	cctcccgtgc	gtgctcgcat	gcgcggttag	cccaaaagcg	agtcctcggc	gacgagcgcc
481	acgacaatcg	gtggtttct	tgccttcgtt	cctcgtcgtg	cgcgccccgt	cgctcgaacg
541	cgctcctcga	ccctcacgcg	tcgtcgcatc	gacggcgctc	ccaacgc	

Source: National Center for Biotechnology Information online database

133

Classifying Oaks with DNA

Introductory Discussions

1. In small groups carefully observe the three leaf drawings. Discuss the following questions. Be prepared to share your ideas with the class.

   - How many species are represented—one, two, or three?

   _____

   - On what are you basing your answer?

   _____

   - What distinctive features do the leaves have?

   _____

   - How do these features vary in the different leaves?

   _____

   - What traits could you *measure* to document differences/similarities among the leaves?

   _____

Data Collection

The class will decide what sort of data to collect. Make measurements and record your results below or in a lab notebook.

Molecular Data Analysis

Molecular biology provides powerful approaches to studying similarities and differences between organisms. The sequences on Handout 4.2 are for the same gene in the three different leaves.

1. How can they be compared for degree of similarity? Devise a strategy with your group members and then make your calculations. Record your results below or in a lab notebook.

   _____

   _____

   _____

   _____

Name _____   Date _____

Classifying Oaks with DNA, *Cont'd.*

2. Based on your calculations and those of other groups, what can you conclude about the three leaves? How closely related are the three? How many species do they represent?

_____

_____

_____

_____

Wrap-Up and Reflection

1. Use a field guide or other sources to identify the three leaves. How many species are represented? What are they?

_____

_____

_____

_____

2. Compare your analysis based on observing and measuring the leaves (morphological) to your analysis of DNA sequences. How did the two complement each other? In what ways was one more effective than the other?

_____

_____

_____

_____

3. What other information about the three leaves would have helped in deciding whether they were different species?

_____

_____

_____

_____

4. How similar do DNA sequences need to be for two organisms to be considered the same species? How is this decided?

_____

_____

_____

_____

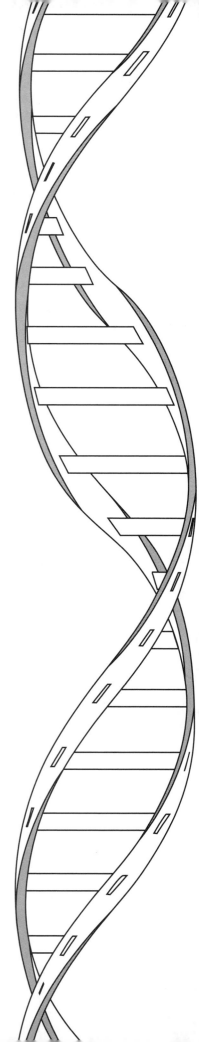

Chapter 5

Biological Evolution

Evolution is the central, unifying principle of biology. Entries in this chapter develop an understanding of some of the mechanisms and consequences of natural selection. Misconceptions about evolution are widespread and deeply entrenched. But, as pointed out in the *Standards*, the misconceptions can be changed if they are directly addressed. Two of the lessons in this chapter begin by eliciting student misconceptions that are then focused on by students. The final entry intends to integrate the concepts of adaptation and evolution into a common lab, the frog dissection.

Teacher Pages

Explaining Evolution

Students attempt to explain the evolution of an animal structure. After learning Darwin's theory, they revisit and critique their initial explanations.

Topic Connections

Natural Selection, Macroevolution, Darwin's Theory

Introduction

It is essential that students be given opportunities (and time) to develop deep understanding of the "big ideas" of biology such as evolution. This constructivist lesson goes beyond vocabulary memorization by involving students in written and verbalized explanations of how certain structures might have evolved. Two common misunderstandings addressed are Lamarckian explanations and the tendency of students to believe that structures develop in organisms because they "need" them.

Students are presented with a familiar animal structure such as a bird wing, canine tooth, hoof, or something like that. To assess preconceptions on evolution, the students then write an explanation of how the structure might have evolved over time from a pre-existing structure such as a foreleg (in the case of the bird wing). Later, after learning about natural selection and other aspects of evolution, they critique their original explanations with a red pen. Students exchange papers and then discuss how each other's thinking has changed on the topic.

Finally, students are challenged again to explain the evolution of at least one additional structure as an assessment in the latter part of the unit. Careful selection of the structures to be explained can serve the parallel purpose of teaching additional concepts. For example, if a photo of a poison dart frog is used, then a discussion of the adaptive value of warning coloration is integrated into the lesson.

Materials

Animal structures or photos of animals (see "Preparation")

Time Approximation

- Initial Explanations: 20 minutes
- Content Acquisition: time will vary
- Post-Content Acquisition and Advanced Explanations: 30 to 40 minutes
- Reflection: 20 minutes

Preparation

Any familiar animal structures will work.
Some suggestions include:

- Bird wing, if a preserved wing is available. Otherwise just use a feather or a photo of a bird flying.
- Mammal jaw with canines
- Turtle shell
- Animal claw
- Horse hoof
- Amphibian with legs, live, preserved, or photo
- Hair/fur, such as a rabbit foot or photo of snowshoe hare paw
- Photos of animals with warning coloration, cryptic coloration, or defensive structures

Lesson Outline

Initial Explanations

1. Determine student preconceptions. Show them an animal structure. In a journal or on the student worksheet have learners write an explanation of how the structure evolved from an ancestral structure. Be sure to identify the ancestral structure so students know where to begin their explanations. For a bird wing the ancestral structure would be a foreleg. For a turtle shell it would be a scaly back.

2. Students share explanations. In a classwide grouping, ask some students to share their explanations. Do not criticize or correct their thinking at this point. But after hearing from a number of students you might finish this segment by leaving them with a couple of pointed questions to think about. For example, to respond to Lamarckian thinking, ask something like, "How are new traits passed on to offspring?" or "If someone builds up their muscles at the gym, do they have muscle-bound children as a result?"

Content Acquisition

1. Via other readings, discussions, labs, and activities, students learn about evolution by natural selection and related concepts.

2. Be sure that they keep their initial writings to be used later.

Post-Content Acquisition

1. After students have developed an understanding of evolution by natural selection, have them look at their initial explanation from the beginning of this lesson. Have them critique these explanations using a red pen. They should also add new explanations when appropriate.

2. Have students exchange papers with other students. Each reads the other's initial explanations and self-critiquing. Then the students discuss each other's changes. They should also exchange ideas on the best explanation for how the structure evolved.

Advanced Explanations

1. Show the students another animal structure. In a journal or on Part 2 of the student worksheet they explain how the structure evolved.

2. Have some students share their explanations. Encourage listeners to critique any misconceptions in the explanations. Alternatively, this could be used as a summative assessment.

Reflection

1. In a journal or on Part 3 of the worksheet students write about how their understanding of evolution has changed since their first writing on the subject.

2. Class discussion follows.

Implementation Strategy

- Use the first part of this lesson at the beginning of a unit on evolution *before* any study of Darwin's theory has occurred.

- Of course any structure of any organism could be used, but relatively familiar structures keep the focus on the concepts of evolution.

- Be sure to identify the pre-existing ancestral structure for the class. If using a bird wing, then ask them how it evolved from a front leg. If a feather, then how did it evolve from a reptile scale?

- Steer away from antlers, horns, and display feathers unless your intention is to introduce a parallel discussion of sexual selection.

- Many students will begin with Lamarckian explanations for evolution. Help them to realize for themselves why Lamarckian ideas are flawed.

- Even after content acquisition students may still explain that animals developed a trait because they "needed" it for protection or something. With pointed questions help them to realize that organisms don't "need" to adapt—they either do or don't. The ones that don't become extinct. It is critical to continually focus the students on connecting adaptations to genes, mutations, and genetic variations. Without an understanding of the physical basis of characteristics it is very difficult to comprehend the origination and inheritance of new traits. Even with such an understanding, students require continual help connecting genetics, DNA, and evolution.

Name _____   Date _____

Explaining Evolution

Part 1: Initial Explanations

Carefully study the animal structure shown to you by your teacher. Think about how it evolved over time from a different pre-existing structure. For example, how did a bird wing evolve from the foreleg of its reptile ancestor? How did amphibian legs evolve in fish ancestors that had no legs? In the space below, give a detailed, step-by-step explanation of how the structure you are looking at evolved. Do not worry about being "right" or "wrong" at this point. Simply give your best explanation of how it could have happened.

_____

_____

_____

_____

_____

_____

_____

_____

_____

_____

_____

_____

_____

_____

Part 2: Advanced Explanations

Now that you have learned about Darwin's theory, you will attempt to explain the evolution of one or two other animal structures. Look at the structure presented by your teacher. Incorporating what you have learned, give a detailed, step-by-step explanation of how the structure evolved from a pre-existing structure.

_____

_____

_____

_____

_____

_____

_____

Explaining Evolution, *Cont'd.*

Part 3: Reflection

At the beginning of this unit you were asked to explain the evolution of an animal structure. After that you studied Darwin's theory and related concepts. Then you were asked to again explain the evolution of an animal structure. Compare your more recent writing ("Advanced Explanations") with that of your first ("Initial Explanations"). Discuss specifically how your more recent explanation is different from the first.

_____

_____

_____

_____

_____

_____

_____

_____

_____

_____

_____

_____

_____

Is your more recent writing (thinking) improved compared to the first? Explain.

_____

_____

_____

_____

_____

_____

_____

_____

_____

_____

The Lost World

Acting as paleontologists, students deduce an unknown animal's body structure and natural history based on its skull.

Topic Connections

Evolution, Adaptation, Paleontology, Ecology, Structure/Function

Introduction

Virtually every aspect of an organism's form, physiology, and behavior can be explained by natural selection. Selection theory explains why some frogs are a well-camouflaged green while others catch the eye with a bright orange skin. It explains why trees grow tall. It explains why many bees sacrifice their own reproduction to help to raise the young of the colony. In every case there must have been a selective advantage to the trait that helped it to persist and be passed onto the next generation.

Paleontologists rely on selection theory to explain their reconstructions of the bodies and the habits of fossil discoveries. In this activity students will engage in the analytical processes employed by fossil researchers. Given a skull of a species unknown to them, the students will use evidence to deduce such basic characteristics as size, posture, and diet. These deductions will result from careful observations of such features as skull shape, eye socket positions, teeth shape/variety, and the position of the foramen magnum. The foramen magnum is especially informative. It is the opening at the base of the skull through which the spinal cord enters to articulate with the brain. If this opening projects off the posterior of the skull (see Figure 5.1), then the animal had a horizontal (or at least linear) body plan in the way a salamander does. If the foramen magnum opens at a 90-degree angle to the skull anterior, then the animal had a vertically oriented neck like a human. An angled opening is typical of many four-legged animals. And of course, teeth reveal a tremendous amount about an animal's niche.

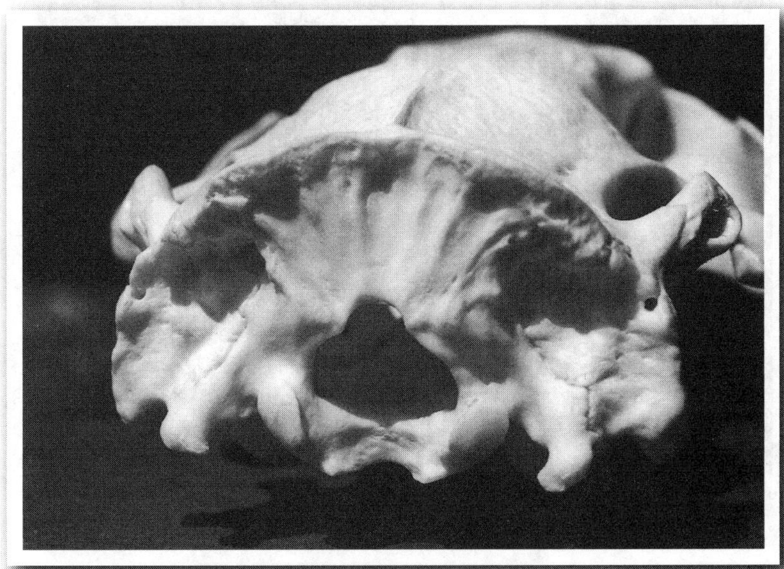

After this first round of evidence-based conclusions, the students move on to increasingly more speculative, secondary inferences and hypotheses that are based on their original framework of observations. The student paleontologists re-create a hypothesized body and a proposed habitat. They

Figure 5.1. Foramen Magnum of a Skull

then explain how the organism moved, fed, defended itself, and so on. Finally, students provide a Darwinian explanation for how their species evolved from a known ancestor.

Materials

- Skulls, one per group of two to four students (See "Preparation" section for suggestions.)
- Graph paper, 8–1/2 inches by 11 inches, one piece per group
- Construction paper, large, one piece per group
- Ruler, one per group

Time Approximation

Two to four 45-minute periods. Some of the project could be assigned for outside of class.

Preparation

Skulls can be obtained from biological supply companies. One company, Skulls Unlimited, exclusively sells skulls. They vary considerably in price. Those from common animals or animals that are routinely harvested by people are quite inexpensive. Less expensive second- or third-quality skulls are offered by some companies, and these are perfectly useful for this activity.

If necessary you could gradually build a skull collection by purchasing one or two a year. If skulls are limited, you could have the different groups all use the same one(s). Just position it centrally in the class for easy observation access. Alternatively, skull photographs from text or Web sources could be used.

Ideally, each group works with a different species. The less familiar the skull, the better. Some favorites are armadillo, mudpuppy (*Necturus*; its bony gill arches make it especially challenging), and mink.

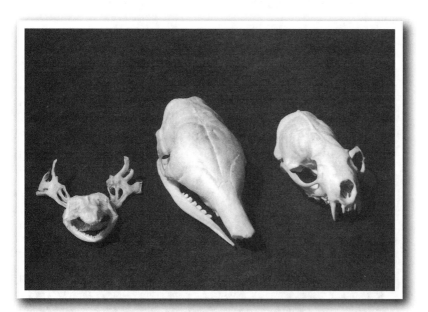

Figure 5.2. Mudpuppy, Armadillo, and Mink Skulls

Lesson Outline

1. Hold up a skull or a picture of a fossil of some other animal part. Ask the students what could be known about the animal just from the part shown. Ask them how these things could be known. Solicit ideas from the class on what is known about dinosaurs based on their fossils. Ask them how these things are known *and* with how much certainty they are known.

2. Distribute copies of the worksheet. Have them read the introduction and procedure.

3. Divide the class into groups of two to four and give each group a skull and other materials. Keep the skulls in large glass observation bowls or other containers to facilitate safe transport.

   At the end of each period collect the skulls for storage.

4. When the groups are finished, schedule the oral presentations, which are discussed below and on the worksheet.

Assessment

Have the students give oral presentations to the class summarizing their ideas. The presentations provide rich opportunities for learning. Do not be shy about interjecting with questions for the groups about their assumptions and prodding them to explain and justify their reasoning. Also, other students should be encouraged to ask questions and comment on alternative possible explanations for the skulls. If these critiques and additions are made in a con-

Figure 5.3. Sample Student Poster

structive and nonthreatening fashion, they will enhance the educational value of the activity for the whole class.

Implementation Strategy

- Stress to the students that the goal *is not* to figure out what species the skull actually is. Let them know that they will learn more from this activity and they will be more successful in the final evaluation if they analyze their skull as if it were a fossil of a species that is new to science.

- To best advance learning with this activity, don't let the students get away with completely unjustified guesswork. Sure, there is much room for varied interpretations and some creativity, but ideas should build on evidence and a sound application of adaptation and selection theory. Circulate among the groups while they are working and challenge them to defend their deductions and hypotheses.

Source

Joyce Gleason, Norwood Senior High School, Norwood, Massachusetts.

Name _____ Date _____

WORKSHEET 5.2
The Lost World

Introduction

Why do leopard frogs have green backs? The ultimate explanation for the frog's coloring (and for every trait in every organism) lies in natural selection theory. The species evolved to be green because this color was well adapted to the frog's environment, and individuals with green backs survived better and left more green-backed offspring to the next generation.

If you were given an unknown organism, could you, by observing it, explain what its natural habitat is probably like? What it normally eats? How and where it normally spends its time? With an understanding of adaptation and natural selection theory you could. Organisms' colors, structures, and habits (all of their characteristics) are shaped by an environment that includes their physical surroundings and their interactions with other organisms. So an animal's features, such as body covering, teeth type and limb shape, provide clues about how and where that animal lives.

What if you only had part of an unknown animal that was no longer present on earth. Could you figure out what the rest of the animal looked like and how it lived? This is what paleontologists do. Often using just fragments of evidence from partial fossil skeletons, they try to deduce what the whole animal looked like. They then make educated guesses about how the animal interacted with other organisms and with its physical surroundings. In this activity you will be challenged to think like a paleontologist. From a skull of an unknown, "extinct" animal you will attempt to recreate its body structure, habitat, and niche.

The Task

1. Begin to observe the skull with your group members and brainstorm possibilities for what the animal looked like and how it lived. *Note:* The skull is not really from an extinct animal, but act as if it is! You will learn more from this activity and you will do better on the final evaluation if you do not try to make your animal a copy of an existing animal that you think it is.

2. Make a side-view drawing of the skull on the graph paper. Make the drawing large enough to fill much of the paper. Use the squares on the graph paper to keep the skull's proportions right. For example, if the skull is 3 cm long and 2 cm high, you might make it fifteen boxes long and ten boxes high.

3. Affix the graph paper with the skull drawing to your construction paper. Now draw your idea for the animal's body on the construction paper coming out from the base of the skull drawing. Unlike your skull drawing, though, make the body drawing complete with your idea for the outer covering (skin, hair, feathers, scales, and so on).

4. Around the body draw in features of its habitat. You might include predators or prey if applicable.

The Lost World, *Cont'd.*

5. Give a scientific name to your animal. A scientific name consists of two words, the genus and the species. The words are Latin and they are always either underlined or in italics. Also, the genus is capitalized and the species begins with a lower-case letter. For example, *Homo sapiens* is the scientific name of humans.

6. Organize the ideas and explanations that are to be included in your final report (see below). The report will be oral and/or written.

Evaluation

Each group's report should include:

1. Drawing—skull, body, habitat

2. Scientific name

3. Summary table of inferences (see next page)

4. Explanations of the animal's:

   • Body design as seen in the drawing

   • Mobility—How did it move around?

   • Habitat

   • Niche—What did it eat? How did it find food? What else did it spend its time doing? Was it solitary or did it live in groups?

   • Defense—How did it escape or protect itself from predators?

   For each, be sure to also explain the evidence and reasoning that your ideas are based on.

5. Darwinian explanation of the animal's evolution—Use Darwin's theory of evolution by natural selection to explain how your animal evolved from a known ancestor. For example, if you think your animal is related to salamanders, then explain how the unique features of your animal evolved from a salamander-like ancestor.

The Lost World—Inferences Summary Table

To infer is to arrive at a conclusion based on evidence and reasoning. Inferences may even be based on only slight evidence. Most of your ideas about your animal's appearance and habits will be reasoned deductions or inferences.

Fill in the summary table below for all of your group's inferences about your animal.

Inference	Evidence to Support the Inference

Teacher Pages

Are Humans Still Evolving?

A constructivist writing and discussion lesson to deepen understanding of natural selection.

Topic Connections

Natural Selection, Micro/Macroevolution, Adaptation, Biotechnology

Introduction

Year after year my students tell me that humans will soon evolve to lose the pinky toe and the appendix. They inform me that we are evolving to be taller and also, because of computers, that we will evolve to be more intelligent. It is especially revealing that these misconceptions come from even the best students and even *after* exposure to Darwin's theory. In short, a vast gulf separates the ability to recite the elements of natural selection theory and the ability to actually use the theory to explain real-life situations. Memorization of facts and vocabulary words does not imply deep understanding. And even if students can apply selection theory to the evolution of paper chips or wooly worms in a lab exercise, they may still need opportunities to transfer their new knowledge to other organisms such as humans.

Pinky toe misconceptions are deeply entrenched. Replacing these misunderstandings requires specifically addressing them and then giving learners the chance to modify them on their own. This lesson solicits the misconceptions by starting with an individual journal writing activity on the topic, "Are Humans Still Evolving?" Then students exchange ideas via a period-long circle discussion. At first, ideas are expressed and left uncritiqued. Eventually facilitate student-student debate and ask pointed questions during which learners begin to self-adjust their misunderstandings. A number of interesting side topics, such as the impact of genetic engineering on evolution, arise along the way. Students become quite animated in the discussion.

Of course, there is no doubt that human populations undergo microevolutionary changes in allele frequencies due to natural selection and other factors. Some advanced students will realize this immediately. But humans behave differently enough from other species to make the question interesting to discuss anyway. And even in the most advanced classes, many students will initially focus on the popular misconceptions that they have encountered repeatedly in the past. Also, the purpose of this lesson is not to quickly arrive at a definitive answer to the question. The lesson's value lies in student application, debate, and discussion of the nuances of natural selection theory.

Materials

None

Time Approximation

- Essay/journal writing can be assigned for homework
- Group discussion takes one 45-minute period
- Post-discussion reflection can be assigned for homework

Lesson Outline

1. *Student essay or journal writing:* Have students write one or two pages on the topic: "Are humans still evolving?" The essay could be completed in a journal, on a word processor, or on the student worksheet. This could be assigned as homework.

2. *The class discussion:* Arrange students in a circle for discussion. Choose a student to begin and ask them to offer his or her opinion on the question. Refrain from critiquing any misconceptions at this point. Continue by asking another ten or so students to offer their opinions.

3. Open the discussion to volunteers. Ask whether anyone wants to respond to any of the claims that they have heard. Facilitate debate between students. Try to keep the group focused on one human trait or issue at a time. Periodically pose a question for debate. Pick a misconception that was aired, repeat it to the students, and ask for opinions on its validity.

   Occasionally you might need to ask a student to temporarily defer an idea until a current topic has been successfully discussed and accurately resolved.

4. If students don't raise societal issues on their own, then you should. Ask: "*Which* people are we talking about? (North American? Third-World? Wealthy? Impoverished?) Does it matter?"

   Also ask for opinions on the effects of biotechnology on the evolution of humans.

5. After the discussion have students write the "follow-up reflection" on the worksheet.

Implementation Strategy

- Use this lesson at the end of a unit on evolution when students will have as much topic knowledge as possible to apply to the question.

- *Adapting for different levels:* In lower grade levels or lower-ability level classes, a distinction might not have to be made between microevolution and macroevolution. With these groups the focus centers simply on whether or not certain traits (for instance, the pinky toe) are favored by natural selection and passed on more than others.

   In more advanced classes, students should apply their knowledge of population genetics to the question. In this case students will tend to subdivide the question into: (1) Are humans still subject to microevolution and (2) Are they still undergoing macroevolution?

- *The essay/journal write:* This step is important. It allows for individual idea development. Stress to students that they will not be graded according to the side of the issue they choose to argue. You don't want to restrict students by making them afraid of presenting the "wrong" answer.

- *The discussion:* Arranging students in a circle improves student-to-student interaction. It removes you from being the physical focal point.

  Begin by calling on a number of students going around the circle. Don't accept volunteers at first. You don't want to go immediately into debate. It is best to initially elicit a variety of ideas (some valid, some not) that can later be debated by students. Do not critique student statements during this initial phase, as you want other students to do that later. Also, you don't want to inhibit students at this point. You want the misconceptions to be aired.

  As much as possible your role should be as moderator to student-student discussion, but when the group can't come to an accurate explanation of a debated point, you need to weigh in to assure an accurate resolution. The key is to subjugate the "teacher as information source" role to allow as much as possible for student-constructed knowledge.

- *Typical student responses:* The following table shows some topics frequently raised by students in the lesson. The right side provides accurate application of selection theory to the topic.

Table 5.1. Typical Topics Raised by Students

Student-Generated Topic	Appropriate Explanations
Pinky/pinky toe getting smaller or disappearing "Wisdom teeth" will disappear	Variant forms do not provide survival advantage or disadvantage so allele frequencies should not change (large and small pinky toes will be passed on with equal frequency). Thus these traits are not still evolving.
Appendix getting smaller or disappearing	Possible that allele(s) for smaller/less-likely-to-become-infected appendixes could be favored in areas without access to quality health care. But this is probably not an issue where infected appendixes are easily treated.
Aren't humans taller than in the 1700s?	If true, then based on differences in nutrition/health care, not natural selection.

Student-Generated Topic	Appropriate Explanations
Lethal diseases	Alleles for lethal disorders or predispositions for diseases are selected against, especially if they kill the individual before reproductive age.
	Alleles that confer resistance are selected for. For example, individuals with two mutated CCR5 alleles do not acquire AIDS even if infected with HIV. These alleles should increase in frequency where AIDS mortality is high (Africa). Thus, this is evidence that we are still evolving.
People evolving to be smarter in response to new technologies	Ability to use technology is not gene based or normally related to survival/reproduction and thus should not be subjected to natural selection. Also, "intelligence" is difficult to define.
Modern medicine	People with potentially lethal alleles may have life prolonged by modern medical care, thus maintaining those alleles in populations. For example, the PKU allele probably exists in higher frequency in countries where the disorder is diagnosed and treated. Natural selection no longer acts on this allele in wealthy Western societies.
Biotechnology, such as "genius sperm banks," embryo screening, and gene therapy/"designer babies"	These are forms of artificial selection, further removing humans from the influence of natural selection.
	If genetically engineered offspring were available only to the wealthy, could it lead to an evolutionary gene pool divergence between rich and poor people?
Skin color, race	Skin color probably has little if any effect on survival today due to clothing, housing, behavior, nutrition, and sunscreen. Recent research suggests a benefit to light skin for vitamin D production in northern latitudes.
	Existence of distinct human races is not supported by human genome analysis.
Speciation/macroevolution	Not occurring. If anything, there is less gene pool isolation today due to advances in global travel.

- Students continually need to be reminded of the connection between evolution and genes. Beneficial traits will not emerge or increase in frequency unless the same happens to genes that code for those traits.

- Students will claim that people "need to be more. . ." Point out that "need" has nothing to do with evolution. Populations either adapt to change or they don't (and they are extirpated!). Those that adapt are successful because some individuals possess beneficial traits born of random genetic variations that gave them a survival advantage.

- After a trait such as the pinky toe or intelligence has been debated, to resolve the issue ask: "Does the trait affect an individual's ability to survive into and through the reproductive years (relative to individual's lacking the trait), *and* does it affect an individual's ability to produce fertile offspring? For many of the traits students will be thinking of, the answer is a resounding "No."

- Point out that humans are a very unusual species. We do not strive to maximize our reproductive potential. Many of the "most fit" humans with the "best" genes choose not to reproduce at all. In what other species do many of the most adapted individuals withhold their genes from the gene pool because they don't want their lifestyle to be hindered by having children? This, along with modern medicine and other technologies, dramatically reduces the impact of natural selection on our species.

- The notion of *which* people we are talking about will arise. It is likely that populations with access to high-quality health care are less influenced by natural selection than others.

Reference

Shields, M. (2004). Are humans still evolving? A natural selection discussion lesson. *The American Biology Teacher, 66*(1), 21–25.

Name _____ Date _____

Are Humans Still Evolving?

Respond to the title question using what you know about evolution and natural selection. Cite as many specific examples as you can to back up your argument. Do not worry about being on the "right" or "wrong" side of the issue. It is legitimately open to debate. What matters is a thoughtful application of natural selection theory to the question.

_____

_____

_____

_____

_____

_____

_____

_____

_____

_____

_____

_____

_____

_____

_____

_____

_____

_____

_____

_____

_____

_____

_____

_____

_____

_____

_____

Are Humans Still Evolving?, *Cont'd.*

Follow-Up Reflection

After participating in a classwide discussion on whether humans are still evolving, how has your thinking changed? Reread your initial writing on the topic and discuss any misunderstandings that you may have had.

Dissecting Frog Evolution

An inquiry supplement to a frog dissection that focuses students on the adaptive value of structures.

Topic Connections

Adaptation, Natural Selection, Frog Dissection, Vertebrate Anatomy

Introduction

Why do frogs have lungs? Why are some green above and lightly colored on their ventral surface? Why are their eyes on top of their heads? Why is their small intestine so long? Every one of these questions can, of course, be explained with natural selection. A frog dissection is an ideal opportunity for learners to further develop an understanding of evolution while studying vertebrate anatomy. Many dissection protocols almost exclusively emphasize identification and memorization of structure names. This lesson challenges learners to see frog structures in light of their adaptive value. Learners develop an ability to explain why structures exist the way they do. The lesson can be used in conjunction with a traditional dissection.

So why do frogs have lungs? Duh, as our students would "articulate," to breathe. Except that "to breathe" does not answer the question! Frogs can breathe *because* they have lungs. They don't have lungs *because* they can breathe. The "to breathe" answer reverses cause and effect and is, at best, a circular argument. Answering "why" questions in biology requires application of natural selection theory (see Shellberg, 2001, for an expanded discussion).

Frogs have lungs because in early amphibians there was a survival and reproductive advantage to having structures that collected oxygen from air, so the genes for such a structure were passed on. Such a selection theory response to a why question is an example of "ultimate cause." Survival advantage/disadvantage is the ultimate reason for the existence or form of most traits in all organisms.

While working through a frog dissection, students will attempt to infer the adaptive value of observed structural features. Subsequently, they will combine their observations and inferences with information from outside sources to develop explanations for why the frog is structured as it is.

Materials

- Frog—*R. pipiens* or similar
- Dissection tools
- Dissection manual

Time Approximation

Time will vary. The lesson is intended for integration with a frog dissection, which can be done in varying numbers of class periods. The second part of the worksheet, "Explanations," could be completed outside of class.

Lesson Outline

1. Write the following on the board: "Why do snowshoe hares turn white in winter?" Then solicit some opinions. Some students will probably respond "for camouflage." Politely inform them that they are wrong. Snowshoe hares are camouflaged because they are white. They are not white because they are camouflaged. The camouflage does not create the white fur. Rather, the white fur creates the camouflage.

2. Now send them back to again attempt to answer the question in small groups. After a few minutes again solicit ideas and lead a discussion on the topic. Steer the discussion toward natural selection. If students haven't arrived at the explanation, then guide them toward it. Snowshoe hares turn white in winter because individuals with genes for turning white in winter survive better and leave more offspring, thus passing on the genes for doing so.

3. Distribute the External Anatomy Worksheet. When students have a frog in a dissection pan they record observations on the handout. Then they make inferences as to the adaptive value of what they have observed.

4. Students proceed with dissection manual instructions you provide.

5. Students conduct book/Web research if necessary to refine their ideas about the value of various frog anatomy features.

6. Students write the "Explanations" portion of the worksheet. (This could be assigned for homework.)

7. Repeat the above steps for the thoracic and abdominal cavities.

Implementation Strategy

*   Have students work on the observations and adaptive value inferences *before* extensive use of dissection manuals or other references. You want them to make inferences from their observations—to apply natural selection thinking to what they see. You want to avoid students simply finding information to copy into the tables.

*   Some students will complain that they "have no idea" for the adaptive value of some of the frog features. Press them to continue thinking about it and to discuss the issue with classmates. Let them know that they will not be penalized for inaccurate ideas if they come from an honest effort.

*   Sometimes (such as with lungs) the adaptive value refers to the value of having the structure. Usually though, the adaptive value refers to the form of the structure. For example, why is it a survival advantage for a frog to have a *long* small intestine.

*   See the "teacher key tables" for possible responses.

Teacher Key Tables

Table 5.2. External Anatomy

Structure/Feature	Observations	Adaptive Value
Dorsal color	Green/brown/spotted (depends on species)	Camouflage with algae or swamp water
Ventral color	Beige color	Camouflage to blend with sunlight to an aquatic predator looking up at it
Location of eyes	Top of head	Frog can be vigilant for predators with only head above water
Location of ears	Top of head	Same as for eyes
Location of nostrils	Top of head	Frog can breathe with only top of head above water
Shape of head	Tapered, wedge shape	Streamlined to reduce friction when swimming
Shape of tympanic membrane (ear)	Flat against head	Same as above—streamlining
Vomerine teeth	Pointy, angle back into mouth	Help keep captured prey in mouth
Hind legs—form, length	Long!	Jumping to escape predators
Feet—form	Back feet are like flippers	Surface area for swimming

Table 5.3. Thoracic Cavity

Structure/Feature	Observations	Adaptive Value
Ribs	They do not have ribs	Frog lighter—can jump farther, swim faster; if present might be prone to breakage when landing
Lungs	Yes, sack-like	Allow for life outside of water
Pericardial membrane	Transparent membrane, very thin	Allows for friction-free environment for heart to expand, contract
Number of heart chambers	Three chambers	More efficient than two chambers; some separation of oxygen and deoxygenated blood. Double-loop circulatory system brings blood from lungs to heart for re-pumping.

Table 5.4. Abdominal Cavity

Structure/Feature	Observations	Adaptive Value
Shape, texture of stomach	Hard, tapered at ends	Break down insects, tapered ends keep large undigested food in
Size of liver	Very large, multi-lobed	Aquatic life—exposed to more fluids to detoxify
Length of small intestine	Very long, coiled	More surface area for nutrient absorption
Body cavity	Yes, spacious	Room for organs, eggs
Villi	Under microscope visible folds lining inside of small intestine wall	Increased surface area for nutrient absorption
Number of blood vessels in mesentery	Many! Going to and from small intestine	More efficient to carry away nutrients from intestine
Number of eggs (in pregnant female)	Many!	To increase chance that at least some will survive

Reference

Shellberg, T. (2001). Teaching how to answer "why" questions about biology. *The American Biology Teacher, 63*(1), 16–19.

WORKSHEET 5.4
Dissecting Frog Evolution

External Anatomy

Why are trees tall? Why do zebras have stripes? Why do cheetahs have long, narrow legs? These questions can all be answered using Darwin's theory of evolution by natural selection. In fact, virtually every trait of an organism can be explained using natural selection theory. While learning the anatomy of a frog you will use Darwin's theory to explain why the animal and its structures take the form that they do.

For the features in the table below, make and record descriptive observations. Then infer the adaptive value of the feature. Attempt to describe how the feature makes the frog better adapted for its environment.

Structure/Feature	Observations	Adaptive Value
Dorsal color		
Ventral color		
Location of eyes		
Location of ears		
Location of nostrils		
Shape of head		
Shape of tympanic membrane (ear)		
Vomerine teeth		

Dissecting Frog Evolution, *Cont'd.*

Structure/Feature	Observations	Adaptive Value
Hind legs—form, length		
Feet—form		
Other		

Explanations

In a paragraph, explain *why* a frog looks the way it does. Why is it colored the way it is? Why is it shaped the way it is? Why are structures located where they are? Refer to specific structures and use the language of natural selection theory.

_____

_____

_____

_____

_____

_____

_____

_____

_____

_____

_____

_____

_____

_____

_____

_____

_____

_____

Name _____ Date _____

WORKSHEET 5.5
Dissecting Frog Evolution

Thoracic Cavity

Fill in the table below after you have opened the frog's thoracic (chest) cavity.

Structure/Feature	Observations	Adaptive Value
Ribs		
Lungs		
Pericardial membrane		
Number of heart chambers		
Other		

Dissecting Frog Evolution, *Cont'd.*

Explanations

Explain *why* amphibians have a three-chambered heart, whereas fish only have two chambers. You may need to use book or Web resources to acquire some information on the topic. Use natural selection theory to develop your explanation.

_____

_____

_____

_____

_____

_____

_____

_____

_____

_____

_____

_____

_____

_____

_____

_____

_____

_____

_____

_____

_____

_____

_____

_____

_____

_____

Dissecting Frog Evolution

Abdominal Cavity

Fill in the table below after you have opened the frog's abdominal cavity.

Structure/Feature	Observations	Adaptive Value
Shape, texture of stomach		
Size of liver		
Length of small intestine		
Body cavity		
Villi		

Dissecting Frog Evolution, *Cont'd.*

Structure/Feature	Observations	Adaptive Value
Number of blood vessels in mesentery		
Number of eggs (in pregnant female)		
Other		

Explanations

Choose three features from the abdominal cavity and explain *why* they are the way they are in a frog. Use natural selection theory to develop your explanations.

_____

_____

_____

_____

_____

_____

_____

_____

_____

_____

_____

_____

_____

_____

_____

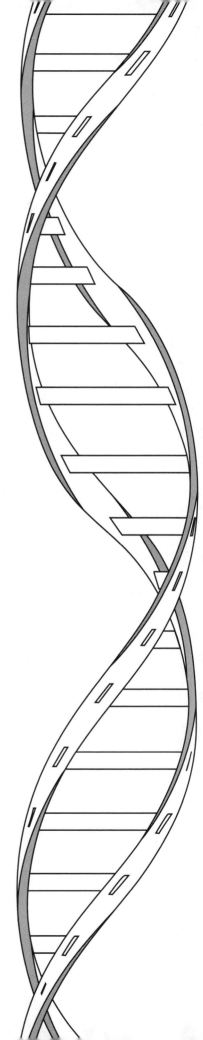

Chapter 6

The Interdependence of Organisms

Energy flow, food webs, the cycling of matter, interrelationships, changes within ecosystems . . . these are some of the concepts explored in the lessons of this chapter. The first two, "History of a Carbon Atom," parts 1 and 2, attempt to move learners beyond simple memorization of nutrient cycles. They try to get students connecting their own bodies to the processes that rearrange atoms in ecosystems. In the final inquiry of the chapter, students research and explain changes in a biological community.

History of a Carbon Atom

Part 1

A constructivist discussion introduction to nutrient cycling

Topic Connections

Biogeochemical Cycles, Carbon Cycle, Biochemistry, Food Chains

Introduction

Most people do not know what they are made of! Even after studying nutrient cycles and organic molecules, many students remain unable to explain what their hands are comprised of or how the materials that make them up got to be where they are. This introduction to nutrient cycles has two main objectives. One is to assess the prior knowledge of students on this fundamentally important topic. The second objective is to focus the study of nutrient cycles on something concrete to teenagers—their own bodies. By connecting biogeochemical cycling to the student, the whole process becomes less abstract and, one hopes, real understanding supplants memorization of terms.

Materials

None

Time Approximation

20 minutes

Lesson Outline

1. Ask the students to look at the palm of one of their hands.
2. Ask them: "What do you see?"

   Responses include: skin, lines, fingerprints
3. Ask: "What is that skin made of?"

   Responses include: blood, lines, stuff, cells (hopefully)
4. Say: "Good, now I want you to take a closer look at one of those cells. Focus in on one . . . you're going to have to concentrate . . ."

   Students will protest that cells are microscopic. Ham it up here and have some fun. Tell them to "increase the magnification" of their eyes to look inside one of the cells.

5. Ask the students what they see inside the cell.

   Responses will vary. Usually a student who gets the gag will call out that they see a mitochondria or some such structure.

6. Compliment the students for their keen eyesight and now ask the class to focus in on a mitochondrian (or any other structure) in that one cell in their hands. Ask them to look closer to see what the mitochondrian is made of. Continue like this until you have gone through the four types of organic molecule to the elements that are most abundant in those molecules: C, H, O, N, P, and S.

7. Now ask the students to focus in on one carbon atom in a molecule in a structure in that one cell in the palm of the hand. Ask them: "How did that carbon atom get there? Where did it come from?"

8. Either:

   (a) have students discuss the question in Step 7 in small groups and then report to the class for continued discussion;

   (b) have the students respond directly and continue the teacher-facilitated discussion; or

   (c) leave the question dangling. Move on to Step 9 without the question being resolved yet. Return to the question after the students have learned more about nutrient cycling.

   The answer, of course, is from food eaten by the student (you are what you eat!). Students may suggest that the atom came from their parents. Ask them to think about the quantity of matter that they actually received from each parent . . . only one microscopic fertilized egg. We receive the blueprint (DNA) for constructing ourselves from our parents, but the atoms to build our growing bodies must be consumed as food.

9. Via other lessons/assignments students learn about the carbon cycle and other nutrient cycles.

Follow-Up

As an eventual assessment/reflection on nutrient cycling, have students do the "History of a Carbon Atom" creative writing assignment, Part 2 of this activity, on the next page.

Implementation Strategy

- Use this lesson *before* the students have learned anything about nutrient cycling.

- Students should be familiar with the four types of organic molecule and the major elements that comprise organisms (C, H, O, N, P, S) before this lesson. If not, this information can be introduced during the discussion.

History of a Carbon Atom

Part 2

This is an assessment/reflection creative writing assignment on the carbon cycle. Students speculate on the history of atoms currently found in their hands.

Topic Connections

Biogeochemical Cycles, Carbon Cycle, Biochemistry, Food Chains

Introduction

Organisms are comprised of atoms that have been in existence for at least millions of years. And these atoms will eventually be returned to the ecosystem to exist in varied states for millions more years. Organisms use energy to swim upstream against the current of entropy to maintain themselves as an organized assemblage of atoms. But this achievement is only temporary. Entropy always wins in the end.

A fairly profound message of nutrient cycling is that organisms only borrow the matter that comprises them. Many of a person's atoms were in the past parts of other organisms. In the future many of these atoms will be claimed by other organisms to construct themselves. It is exciting for students to realize that their atoms have long and possibly storied histories. It is possible that one of a person's carbon atoms, for example, was in the past part of a *T. rex,* a redwood tree, a cockroach, a bacterium, or Elvis.

In this assignment students create a speculative creative story on the history of one of their atoms. Writing and eventually hearing these stories advances student understanding of cycling. And the assignment helps you to assess the extent to which the carbon cycle is comprehended.

Materials

None

Time Approximation

The writing assignment can be completed at home, but
20 minutes are needed for the reading and critiquing of some stories in class the next day.

Lesson Outline

1. *Day One:* Distribute the worksheet that explains the assignment. Have the students write their stories as a home assignment.

2. *Day Two:* Student volunteers read their stories. Choose volunteers to read their stories aloud to the class. After each story compliment the reader, and then ask the class to critique any misapplications of the carbon cycle.

Have students make notes on misconceptions on their worksheets.

Implementation Strategy

- Use this assignment after the students have learned about nutrient cycling.

- It is critical to have some of the stories read aloud to the class for two reasons. First, it provides for modeling of "what could have been" for the listeners. Second, it allows for critiquing of misconceptions. Even after studying nutrient cycles, there will still be misunderstandings. The reading critiquing reveals persistent misconceptions and launches discussion to address them.

- Do not be shy about critiquing (or better, encouraging students to) student work. If it is done in a nonthreatening, nonpunitive way, it will benefit the class tremendously by advancing understanding. Remind the class that if one student (who should be commended for taking the risk and reading aloud) has a certain misunderstanding it is likely that others do as well.

Some Common Misconceptions

Carbon atoms become part of a heterotroph by respiration/breathing.

> Although CO_2 is breathed into vertebrate lungs in air it is then expelled. Carbon is only assimilated into structures by heterotrophs via food. Plants, of course, assimilate carbon into organic molecules via CO_2 from the air.

Carbon becomes part of a human hand by floating onto it from the air.

> No, not possible.

The carbon stays as CO_2 inside organisms.

> Carbon atoms become part of carbohydrates in plants during the Calvin Cycle. In heterotrophs they are part of any type of organic molecule but can be released as CO_2 resulting from cellular respiration.

History of a Carbon Atom

Introduction

Consider a carbon atom in the palm of your hand. It has existed for millions of years. It will continue to exist for millions of years more. In essence, you are simply borrowing this atom for your relatively short stay on earth.

Think about where your carbon atom has been in the past. It might have a very interesting history! Has it been in oceans, lakes, soil, fossil fuel, air? Has it been part of a bacterium, alga, frog, dinosaur, poison ivy plant, or a famous movie actor? Chances are it has been in many places and part of many different organisms.

Biogeochemical cycles (nutrient cycles) explain how matter moves from one organism to another, between organisms and the environment and from one part of the environment to another. In this assignment you will use your understanding of the carbon cycle to write a fictional but scientifically plausible story.

The Assignment: Day One

Here's what you'll do:

Write a fictional, creative story entitled, "The History of a Carbon Atom." The story will detail the history of an atom that currently resides in the palm of your hand.

Write the story in a journal or notebook.

The story should:

- Have your atom spend time in multiple inorganic and organic parts of ecosystems.

- Explain how the atom gets into and out of each organism or part of the ecosystem. For example, is it taken in by ingestion (feeding) or by diffusion for photosynthesis? Does it go in through a mouth, through stomata?

- Mention the molecule type that the carbon atom is part of at each step. Is it taken in/released as CO_2 or as a protein, a carbohydrate?

- Be fun and creative, *but* also depict an accurate representation of the carbon cycle.

- Begin millions of years ago or more recently—your choice.

Day Two

Some volunteers will read their stories to the class. Fill in the answers to Question 1 below while listening.

1. Make note of any misapplications of the carbon cycle that you detect in a classmate's story.

   _____

   _____

History of a Carbon Atom, *Cont'd.*

2. After hearing and critiquing the stories of other students, what inaccuracies are included in your own story? Explain how they could be improved.

_____

_____

_____

_____

_____

_____

_____

_____

_____

_____

_____

_____

_____

_____

_____

_____

_____

_____

_____

_____

_____

_____

_____

_____

_____

Life or Death Food Chain Decision

Students debate responses to a challenging question. It is a brief discussion assessment that also develops deeper understanding of energy flow in ecosystems.

Topic Connections

Energy, Food chains, Cellular Respiration, Trophic Levels

Introduction

Energy transfer is a central theme in biology. Often the topic is studied in different learning units spread across a course. Learning on photosynthesis and cellular respiration often occurs in isolation from a study of energy flow in ecosystems. Students may learn that available energy decreases in successive food chain trophic levels, but do they truly understand why? A deep comprehension of energy pyramids requires an application of cellular respiration concepts. Much energy is lost from a trophic level when organic molecules produce heat as a byproduct. This discussion lesson promotes integration of these topics through discussion and debate of a challenging question (see the student worksheet for the question).

There are two approaches to using the lesson. First, it could be used to assess prior knowledge and pique curiosity as an introduction to food chains. The question would then be revisited for accurate resolution after content learning on food chains has occurred. Or, second, the lesson could serve as a culminating assessment after students have studied food chains (and cellular respiration). Either way, the lesson is formative assessment in that it reveals student comprehension level and also facilitates construction of new, better understanding.

Materials

None

Time Approximation

30 minutes

Lesson Outline

1. Either distribute the worksheet or pose the central question in another format.
2. Students individually consider the question.
3. *Small-group idea exchange and debate:* Students break into groups of four or so to discuss/debate ideas on the question. They should choose the best response and attempt to rank all of the responses. They need to develop a

justification for their ranking. A group ranking and justification should be summarized in writing.

4. *Class-wide discussion:* Representatives from each group will explain their group's choices and justifications. The next step will depend on student comprehension revealed at this point. If the students produce at least close to accurate explanations, then facilitate inter-group discussion and debate. On the other hand, the responses might reveal a need for more content knowledge of cellular respiration, food chains, and energy pyramids. In this case, direct the students to appropriate readings or implement other lessons. Then revisit the discussion of the central question and follow with the reflection.

5. Reflection: Students complete Question 4 on the worksheet, reflecting on what they have learned in the discussions. This could be completed in class or as homework.

Implementation Strategy

- Use the lesson in a study of food chains and energy pyramids, but after learning on cellular respiration has occurred. Alternatively, if ecology learning happens first, then the lesson could be used during or after the study of cellular respiration.

- Students may need a hint to consider cellular respiration at some point in the discussions. But only do this late in the process. Allow them ample opportunity to struggle their way to making the connection through thinking and discussing with peers.

- De-emphasize the goal of identifying the *one* right answer in the final discussion. It is hard to precisely determine whether the best choice is A or B or some other combination of the choices. The value of the lesson lies in developing sound explanations and justifications for the issue.

The Answer Choices

There are two main points to consider. First, if the cow is alive it is burning calories, converting organic molecules into waste products, ATP, and heat. These energy conversions reduce the cow's energy value to the people.

Second, energy transfer from one trophic level to another is extremely inefficient. If the cow eats the wheat, then much of the energy in the plant will be lost as heat and cow feces and will be unavailable to the people.

So the best choices are A and B. Choice A allows for consumption of the cow's energy before much of it is wasted by cellular respiration. Choice B is similar, but it allows for harvesting the energy in the cow's milk. It may be a better choice then A if the cow is milked right away. But if the cow continues producing milk over time (Choice C) then it will probably waste energy in the process (biosynthesis requires energy, energy is lost whenever converted) *and* it will continue losing energy as heat via cellular respiration.

Choices D and E are not good because of the previously discussed inefficiency of energy transfer between trophic levels. Choice F keeps the cow alive, burning off calories.

Source

Mark Krotec, Pittsburgh Central Catholic High School, Pittsburgh, Pennsylvania.

Name _____ Date _____

WORKSHEET 6.2
Life or Death Food Chain Decision

The Question

A small group of people are stranded on a barren desert island. They have 500 bushels of wheat and one cow. What should they do to survive for the greatest length of time?

A. Eat the cow and then eat the wheat.

B. Drink the cow's milk, eat the cow, and then eat the wheat.

C. Don't feed the cow, drink the cow's milk, eat the cow when milk production ceases, and then eat the wheat.

D. Feed the wheat to the cow and drink the milk.

E. Feed the wheat to the cow, drink the milk, and then eat the cow.

F. Eat the wheat and then eat the cow.

1. First, think about the question by yourself. Which answers do you think are the best ones? Which one makes the most sense? Why?

   _____

   _____

   _____

2. When your teacher indicates, get into a discussion group and exchange/debate ideas on the question. Try to rank the responses from best to worst. Your group will be called on to *explain* and *justify* your choices. Summarize your group's thinking below.

   _____

   _____

   _____

   _____

   _____

3. Next, there will be a classwide discussion wherein each group will share its ideas on the question to the class.

4. After the classwide discussion, write a reflection on the following: How has your thinking on the question changed after the group and class discussions? What new connections and understandings have you now developed? Explain.

   _____

   _____

   _____

Investigating Forest Succession

In this inquiry students evaluate the successional status of a local wood lot based on data that they collect.

Topic Connections

Ecological Succession, Tree Identification, Scientific Inquiry

Introduction

This investigation requires access to a wood lot of at least half the size of a football field. If accessing a forest is impossible, sample data are provided that could be used for graphing and data analysis.

Ecological succession is the process of communities of organisms replacing previously existing ones. Forest succession is often stimulated by the disruption of a community by fire, wind, avalanche, or logging. When a forest (or even as little as one tree) is cleared, the newly available sunlight on the ground promotes the growth of opportunistic grasses and weeds. Often these herbaceous plants are then supplanted by shrubs. Eventually certain species of trees may replace the shrubs. Often these first trees are later replaced by other species that are better adapted to growing in forest conditions created by the first trees.

With some knowledge of trees and succession, an observer can read the history of a forest by studying its current species composition. Also, with data on the age structure of the various species, one can predict how a forest will change in upcoming decades. In this lab students will collect and analyze species age distribution data for transects of a wood lot. Pooled data will then be entered into spreadsheets and graphed for analysis.

Materials

- Field guides to local trees or copies of pages showing the area's most common ten or twenty species
- Meter sticks, one per student
- Clipboards for recording data in the woods

Time Approximation

- Data collection: 45–60 minutes
- Data analysis: data pooling, spreadsheet forming, and graphing can be one to three 45-minute periods depending on how computer savvy the students are and how many graphs you require.

- Species learning: one 45-minute period (optional, but recommended if there is local access to the species to be studied in the lab)

Safety Precautions

Scout the location ahead of time to be aware of any hazards including poison ivy and other noxious weeds.

Lesson Outline

1. *Leaf learn (optional but recommended):* Students learn to identify the trees they will encounter in the lab. If possible, walk the students to an example of each species and challenge them (with copied pages from a field guide) to identify each one. Point out central characteristics for them to focus on, such as smooth versus jagged margins, lobes, pattern of venation, and so on. Bring a sample of leaves from each species back to the classroom for further study. Consider quizzing the students on identifying the different leaves.

   Or bring into the classroom samples of the leaves and proceed as above.

2. *Data collection:* Distribute the worksheet and clipboards and be sure that they are clear on the methodology. Students then walk their study transects and collect data. They should have field guides or photocopied pages for identifying trees. Circulate among lab groups to help them with identification and other issues.

3. *Data analysis:* Student groups pool their data. The larger sample reveals a truer picture of the forest trend. Smaller sample sizes are more subject to the vagaries of random chance. Challenge the class to devise a method for efficiently pooling data.

4. Students enter data in spreadsheets, make graphs, and do calculations. Some or all of this portion could be completed in class (or in a computer lab). Or some could be completed outside of class.

5. Assign and explain the lab write-up expectations.

Implementation Strategy

- Obviously the lab works best for a school within walking distance of a wood lot. Otherwise the field portion of the lab could easily be completed in a half-day field trip or combined with another field experience.

- If time permits you could have the student groups actually measure and mark off their 15- by 200-foot study plots. They could use plastic surveying tape to mark the boundaries. This would require another 30 minutes or so of field time, but it is not necessary.

- The actual size of the study plots does not matter, but it is important to keep the size fairly uniform among different lab groups.

- The most interesting wood lots for this lab are those in a state of transition. In these ecosystems there are certain species found mainly as large, old trees. These may have been the pioneers after a disturbance. At any rate they were the dominant species in the past. Other species are found mainly as small, young trees. These will grow to replace the current large trees, and they will become the dominant breeding trees of the forest.

- The sample data in Table 6.1 was collected by a class of students in a northern New Jersey wood lot. The data reveals that tulip tree, sweet gum, chestnut oak, white ash, and black oak dominated the forest in the past. With very few young of these species, there is evidence that they are being replaced by a community of sugar maple, black birch, red maple, and flowering dogwood. These latter species seem to grow better in the current environmental conditions of the forest floor—perhaps shadier, cooler, more humid than when the previous community got started.

The data were collected by four lab groups walking 15- by 200-foot transects. Thus, the total area sampled was 12,000 square feet.

It should be noted that flowering dogwood is an under-story tree. It never reaches the height or girth of the other species in the table.

Table 6.1. Forest Succession Data

Species	Saplings	Young	Adult	Mature	Old	Over-Mature
Black Birch	23	17	0	1	0	0
Dogwood	9	11	4	0	0	0
Tulip Tree	5	0	0	0	4	19
American Beech	8	17	5	7	16	3
Sugar Maple	578	57	3	0	0	0
Black Cherry	2	3	5	4	0	0
Black Oak	0	0	0	0	5	4
White Ash	0	3	0	0	3	5
Chestnut Oak	1	0	0	3	11	8
Red Maple	22	21	4	9	3	0
Sweet Gum	0	0	0	6	12	27

Investigating Forest Succession

Introduction

In nature, communities of organisms experience frequent change. Sometimes, existing plants create environmental conditions in an ecosystem that promote the growth of a new and different community of producers. The replacement of a community by another is called "ecological succession." Many different factors initiate succession in forest ecosystems. And many different environmental variables influence the types of trees that grow to replace an existing forest. Nevertheless, by studying a forest one can infer much about the history of that ecosystem. And by analyzing the age structure of different species, one can also predict how the forest will change over time. In this investigation you will learn to "read" the dynamics of a forest community.

Data Collection

1. Working in groups of three or four you will study an area in the forest that is approximately 15 feet wide by 200 feet long. To approximate the 15-foot width, have three group members stand next to each other with their arms outstretched to the side and fingertips of adjacent group members touching. This width approximates 15 feet.

2. Within the 15- by 200-foot plot, you will identify the species of *every* tree. It is critical not to skip trees. If you are having trouble identifying a species because it is so tall or otherwise challenging, seek help from other students or the teacher.

3. Also every identified tree must be categorized by an estimate of its age. Tree ages will be estimated using their diameter at breast height (DBH). These are the categories:

   Sapling: < than 1 inch DBH (anything shorter than breast-height is also a sapling)

   Young: 1 to 3 inches DBH

   Adult: 3 to 5 inches DBH

   Mature: 5 to 9 inches DBH

   Old: 9 to 15 inches DBH

   Over-Mature: >15 inches DBH

4. Designate one person as data recorder. Move through your study plot with group members identifying and aging trees. They should call their findings out to the data recorder, who keeps a tally on the data page.

Data Analysis

1. Lab groups will pool data to come up with class totals. (Why is this a good idea?)

   Devise a system with other students to do this efficiently.

2. Enter the class total data into a computer spreadsheet.

Investigating Forest Succession, *Cont'd.*

3. Calculations to make (using class totals):

   Total tree density (total of all trees/square feet)

   Density for each species (total of each species/square foot)

   For each species, percentage at each age

4. Graphs (using class totals):

   Choose five of the species that yielded the most data. For each, graph the distribution by age.

   Graph the distribution of all species by density.

The Lab Write-Up
Your lab write up should include at least the following:

I. An introduction: Explain, discuss the concepts of the lab (such as ecological succession)

II. Procedure followed

III. Data: Spreadsheet, calculation results, graphs

IV. Analysis and conclusions:

    A. Discuss and *explain* your results

    B. Refer to data in your explanations

    C. Address the following in your conclusion:

        (1). What was this forest like (in terms of species composition, species densities) 50 to 100 years ago?

        (2). Predict what the forest will be like in the future.

        (3). Why is the forest changing?

        (4). How confident are you about the data?

Name _____ Date _____

Forest Succession Data Table

Group Members:

_____

_____

_____

_____

_____

_____

_____

Species	Saplings	Young	Adult	Mature	Old	Over-Mature

Forest Succession Data Table, *Cont'd.*

Species	Saplings	Young	Adult	Mature	Old	Over-Mature

Chapter 7

Matter, Energy, and Organization in Living Systems

Obviously overlapping with the concepts explored in Chapter 6, this section of the book is based on the broadest section of the Life Science content standards. Concepts investigated in the inquiries of this chapter include autotrophy, heterotrophy, photosynthesis, cellular respiration, energy conversion (with a focus on body heat), photosynthetic pigments and color, the properties of water as relevant to life, and the evolution of varied molecular energy storage strategies.

Teacher Pages

Water Discrepancies

Students construct understanding of some properties of water after observing and attempting to explain a series of surprising demonstrations.

Topic Connections

Water, Cohesion, Surface Tension, Adhesion

Introduction

Discrepant event demonstrations offer an exciting way to launch inquiry. This lesson begins with a series of demonstrations revealing some surprising behavior of water. The demonstrations are performed in a "magic show" atmosphere. The unexpected observations pique curiosity, elicit prior knowledge, and create a "desire to know" in the minds of learners. After observing the demonstrations, students discuss and attempt to explain them. Then they access scientific explanations of water's properties. Finally, they use the newly acquired facts and concepts to develop accurate explanations for the initially unexpected behavior of water. The interaction between visual experiences, preconceptions, temporary (hopefully!) confusion, and new science content leads to student construction of lasting understanding.

It has been said that "the chemistry of life is water chemistry." Because of its chemical properties, water is the medium in which most of life's chemical reactions occur. Life first evolved in water, it resided there exclusively for three billion years, most life is now concentrated in water-rich areas, and the cells of organisms are about 70 to 90 percent water. Also, water is the source of electrons and hydrogen ions needed for the reactions of photosynthesis.

Because of its polarity, water molecules attract to each other forming hydrogen bonds. This attraction of like molecules is called *cohesion*. Because water is cohesive, it remains liquid at normal temperatures over much of the earth. Cohesion allows water to move up a plant following transpiration. And it results in the tension that allows some organisms to live on the surface of water. Water's polarity results in many important characteristics, such as its adhesion, high specific heat, high heat of vaporization, and versatility as a solvent.

For "Materials" and "Preparation," see each individual demonstration in the "Lesson Outline."

Time Approximation

- The Demos and Initial Explanations: 30 minutes together
- Properties of Water Research: Outside of class
- Refined Explanations: 15 to 20 minutes

Lesson Outline:
The Demonstrations

Begin class by conducting the following demonstrations. Have the class gather around you for close observation. Do not use any terms such as polarity or cohesion or offer any explanations at this time. Perform the demos in a magic show sort of atmosphere. The goal is to "wow" the students, to engage their minds, and leave them wondering.

When students ask questions do not answer them, but encourage them to write them down. Also encourage them to record observations on the worksheet or in a lab notebook.

Demonstration 1: Thy Cup Does Not Runneth Over

In this demo water cohesion prevents the liquid from overflowing an over-filled container.

Materials

- Plastic cup, filled to brim with water
- Fifty paper clips
- Paper towels

Instructions

Place the cup on top of a paper towel. The towel will make it easier to notice whether any water overflows. Have students note that the plastic cup is completely filled with water. Ask them how many paper clips you could put into the cup before the water spills over. Invite a number of students to hypothesize on this. Now gently add paper clips, one at a time. Check for water spillage after each paper clip is added. Students will be amazed by how many paper clips you will be able to carefully add before the water spills over the top of the cup. Depending on size you may be able to add fifty or more.

Demonstration 2: Break the Tension

This demo shows how cohesion results in surface tension allowing polar materials to float on water. Then a nonpolar substance (soap) is introduced to break the surface tension.

Materials

- 2-L battery jar or beaker or other large glass container
- Ground black pepper
- Bar of soap

Instructions

Fill a clean, 2-L battery jar or beaker with tap water. Sprinkle pepper on the surface of the water. The pepper will float. Point this out to the students. Carefully dip the corner of the bar of soap into the surface of the water in the middle. The pepper will immediately shoot out toward the edges, away from the soap, and it will start to fall to the bottom of the container. Have students observe the falling pepper.

Demonstration 3: Rising Above

A capillary tube reveals how adhesion and cohesion can help water counteract the downward pull of gravity.

Materials

- Beaker, 250 ml or so
- Capillary tube
- Water with five to ten drops blue food coloring to make it easier to see the water

Instructions

Hold the capillary tube so that part of it is in the blue water. Colored water will rise in the tube above the level in the beaker. Pass the beaker and tube around for students to try it themselves.

    Ask: "How can this be happening? How can water defy gravity like this?" Do not answer or even solicit answers. Leave the question hanging out there and move on to the next demonstration.

Demonstration 4: Stringing Along

Adhesion allows water to move along a string from one cup to another without dripping off.

Materials

- Tap water
- Cotton string, 2 m in length
- Two beakers, 250 ml
- Food coloring, blue

Preparation

Soak the string in water for at least 30 minutes before doing the demo.

Instructions

Fill one beaker about three-fourths full with water that has been made blue with food coloring. Have an assistant hold one end of the string over the empty beaker. Stretch the string taut at approximately a 30-degree angle and carefully pour the water from the beaker down the string. Continue until the beaker is completely empty. The water moves along the string and then drops into the second beaker.

Initial Explanations

1. Organize students into small discussion groups.

2. Ask them to discuss and attempt to explain each demonstration. Also have them discuss any questions that they had during the demonstrations.

3. Have students address the questions on the worksheet individually. These can then be discussed by the class and listed on the board, if desired.

Research on the Properties of Water

Via text or Web assignments students read about polarity, hydrogen bonding, and the effects of these on water. This could be assigned for outside of class.

Refined Explanations

In either small-group or whole-class discussions, students use their new knowledge of polarity and hydrogen bonding to explain each of the demonstrations.

Reflection and Assessment

1. Students respond to the questions on the worksheet.

2. Challenge students to create a new demonstration that exhibits a property of water. They should try it outside of class. If time permits have them show it to the class and explain it.

   Prevent them from simply finding other demos (such as water drops on a penny) that are posted on educational Web sites. Let them know that you are familiar with ones posted on the Web and that you are asking them to use their understanding of water to create a *new* demo.

Implementation Strategy

- Use this lesson *before* any recent learning on the properties of water. The core value of the lesson is the creation of temporary confusion, surprise, and curiosity. Student engagement in the learning process will not be the same if they are merely watching a verification of something that has already been explained.

- The demonstrations could all be done by the students themselves in small groups, but there are advantages to doing them as teacher-led demos. As written, the lesson creates the aura of a magic show. It also allows you to maintain a class-wide intensity and a focus on questioning.

Possible Responses to Student Worksheet Questions

Initial Explanations

Water sticks together, attracts to itself, stays together;

water rises;

water sticks to string, glass;

soap breaks water apart or causes it to move

Demo 1

The paper clips displace volume but cohesion prevents the water from spilling over until a large enough quantity is above the rim of the cup. The water above the cup "sticks together," preventing it from flowing over.

Demo 2

The pepper floats on top of the water because of surface tension. The polar water molecules attract by H bonding, forming a cohesive surface through which light polar substances don't penetrate.

The nonpolar soap molecules broke the surface tension by interfering with inter-molecular attractions of the water molecules.

Demo 3

Water moves up a capillary tube because the polar water molecules are attracted to the polar glass molecules above them (adhesion) and they are pulled slightly up. Upward-moving water molecules pull (cohesion) others below them.

Demo 4

Water moves along the string without falling because of adhesion. The polar water is attracted to the polar organic molecules in the string.

- Upward water movement in plants (cohesion)
- Keeps water from dropping in Xylem (adhesion)
- Surface tension
- Ecosystem stability (high specific heat, high heat of vaporization)
- Ice floats
- Sweating to cool (high heat of vaporization)
- Good solvent

Reference

Bilash, B., & Shields, M. (2001). *A demo a day: A year of biological demonstrations* (pp. 24-25). Batavia, IL: Flinn Scientific.

WORKSHEET 7.1
Water Discrepancies

Observations and Questions

Record below the observations and questions that occur to you while you watch the demonstrations.

Observations	Questions

Initial Explanations

Discuss and attempt to explain the demonstrations in small groups. Then respond to the following questions on your own:

1. What general statements can you make about water based on your observations?

   _____

   _____

   _____

   _____

2. What questions do you still have about what you observed?

   _____

   _____

   _____

   _____

Water Discrepancies, *Cont'd.*

Properties of Water Research
Using book, Web, or teacher resources, you will learn more about the properties of water.

Refined Explanations
For each demonstration observed, explain why water acted the way it did.

_____

_____

_____

_____

Reflection and Assessment

1. What were the commonalities among all of the demos in the way water acted?

_____

_____

_____

_____

_____

_____

2. In what ways are the properties of water important to organisms?

_____

_____

_____

_____

_____

_____

3. Create a new demonstration that would exhibit a property of water and would be surprising to observers who had not studied water.

_____

_____

_____

_____

Why Are Plants Green?

Students graph and interpret absorption spectra data for chlorophylls to begin developing an understanding of light, color, and pigments in photosynthesis.

Topic Connections

Photosynthesis, Pigments, Visible Light Spectrum, Energy

Introduction

In this partial inquiry, students begin a study of photosynthetic pigments by making and analyzing absorption spectra graphs for chlorophyll a and chlorophyll b. First introduce (or review) the visible light spectrum to the class. By analyzing their absorption graphs, students then attempt to explain why leaves are green. In doing so they may construct an understanding of reflected light resulting in perceived color. If not, they gain this understanding in subsequent background research.

When light hits pigment, it is either absorbed, reflected, or transmitted. Wavelengths of light that are absorbed disappear to the viewer. Nonabsorbed wavelengths are transmitted and reflected. When white light such as sunlight hits chlorophylls, the wavelengths at the blue and red ends of the spectrum are absorbed. Green wavelengths are not well absorbed, so they reflect back to our eye making a leaf appear green to us. Chlorophyll a and b maximally absorb slightly different wavelengths. As a result chlorophyll a is blue-green in color while chlorophyll b is yellow green. Their different absorption peaks provide the adaptive advantage of wider energy collection.

The lesson could be used in conjunction with an investigation testing plant growth or O_2 production variations with different colored lights.

Materials

- Graph paper
- Colored pencils

Time Approximation

45 minutes (portions could be completed outside of class)

Lesson Outline

1. Lead a prior knowledge discussion to determine what the students know about light/color and the electromagnetic spectrum. Hold up a colored object and ask why it has the color it does. Ask: "What causes color?" Write answers on the board but do not respond to them at this point. Next ask

why leaves are green. Again, solicit a wide sampling of student ideas, but do not affirm or correct them yet. Use a prism or an overhead transparency to introduce (or review) the concept of the visible light spectrum.

2. Distribute the worksheet, colored pencils, and graph paper.

3. After student graphs are made, provide the color associations for the different wavelengths (see "Implementation Strategy"). Alternatively, if you have a color transparency of the visible light spectrum, have them extract this information from it. Students color-code their graphs by shading or labeling the different colors of the spectrum.

4. After graphing and analysis, students will need information on color creation by light absorption/reflection. Either lead a discussion on the topic or have them find the information via research.

5. After the "Follow-Up" section of the worksheet, lead a discussion on student responses. This might be a good time to introduce the class to T. W. Englemann's experiment using oxygen-seeking bacteria and *Spirogyra*.

Implementation Strategy

- Use this lesson *before* any assignments or discussions on pigments.

- Students need to be familiar with the visible light spectrum before analyzing their graphs, but do not discuss light absorption/reflection with them until after they have struggled to develop an understanding themselves.

- Graphing instructions on the worksheet are purposely vague so that students will think about how best to set them up. Graphs should have the independent variable (wavelength) along the X-axis and the dependent variable (absorption) on the Y-axis.

- Student graphs will not exactly mimic the absorption spectra found in textbooks because they are only plotting thirteen wavelength points. Via a transparency or Web page, you might show them more complete absorption spectra after they have made their own.

- Here is an approximation of the colors that correspond with the different wavelengths. Of course the light spectrum is a continuum so this is only a rough guide.

400	violet
425	violet
450	blue
475	blue
500	blue/green

525	green
550	green
575	green/yellow
600	yellow
625	orange
650	orange/red
675	red
700	red

Possible Responses for Student Worksheet Questions

Analysis Questions

1. Both have two peaks. For both the peak is higher on the blue end. Both have a valley in green. Chlorophyll b peaks more in blue, whereas a has its peak to the left in violet.

2. Students may struggle on this question depending on their background in the physics of light and color. Accept any attempts to provide an explanation connected to the data.

3. Accept any attempts to explain.

Follow-Up Questions

1. White light hits the chlorophylls in the leaf. Blue and red wavelengths are absorbed and disappear. Green wavelengths are reflected, so they travel to the eye and the leaf is seen as green.

2. Blue and red. Especially blue. Grow light bulbs usually concentrate in blue light for this reason.

3. Answers will vary.

Why Are Plants Green?

Introduction

A pigment is a molecule that absorbs light in the visible portion of the electromagnetic spectrum. The leaves of most plants are rich in pigments. These pigments absorb light and convert it into chemical energy to fuel the production of sugars. The primary photosynthetic pigment is chlorophyll a. Other pigments such as chlorophyll b and carotenoids are referred to as accessory pigments. These absorb light and funnel the energy to chlorophyll a.

Different pigments absorb different types (wavelengths) of light. Some pigments might absorb blue light better than other wavelengths of light, for example. Others may absorb all of the colors well, or none.

A spectrophotometer is a machine used by scientists to measure the absorbance of light by substances. The better a pigment absorbs a color (wavelength) of light, the higher its percent of absorbance reading. The data in the Table 7.1 give possible spectrophotometer absorbance readings for the two plant chlorophylls.

Graphing

Graph the data for chlorophyll a and chlorophyll b on the same graph. The line for each is an approximation of the absorption spectrum for that molecule.

Table 7.1. Data

Wavelength	Chlorophyll a % Absorption	Chlorophyll b % Absorption
400 nanometers	32	8
425 nanometers	60	29
450 nanometers	10	62
475 nanometers	3	51
500 nanometers	0	8
525 nanometers	0	0
550 nanometers	4	3
575 nanometers	2	4
600 nanometers	4	2
625 nanometers	3	20
650 nanometers	21	29
675 nanometers	44	4
700 nanometers	12	0

Why Are Plants Green?, *Cont'd.*

Analysis

Using information provided by your teacher or other available resources, find the colors of light that correspond to each wavelength in the data table. Some wavelengths may fall in the transition range between two colors. Color code your graph in a way that clearly shows the color range between 400 and 700 nanometers.

1. Based on the data and your graphs, what can you conclude about the two chlorophylls and their absorption spectra? In what ways are the two similar? Different?

   _____

   _____

   _____

   _____

   _____

2. Chlorophylls are the predominant pigments in leaves. Based on the data and your graph, give a possible explanation for why plants are green.

   _____

   _____

   _____

   _____

   _____

   _____

   _____

3. If some wavelengths (colors) of light are absorbed by chlorophylls, what happens to the other wavelengths that are not absorbed? Give any possibilities you can think of.

   _____

   _____

   _____

   _____

   _____

   _____

   _____

Why Are Plants Green?, *Cont'd.*

Background Information
Find out more about how color is created by light and pigments. Use the Internet or resources provided by your teacher.

Follow-Up

1. Explain why leaves are green. Begin your explanation with white light coming from the sun and ending in your eye.

_____

_____

_____

_____

_____

_____

_____

2. Based on the above data and your graph, which type of light is most important to plants for photosynthesis? Explain.

_____

_____

_____

_____

_____

_____

_____

3. Design an experiment to collect evidence that supports your answer for Question 2 above.

_____

_____

_____

_____

_____

_____

_____

Why Are Plants Not Always Green?

By comparing graphs, students discover that chlorophyll a and b cannot alone account for plant photosynthetic light absorption. Then the absorption spectrum of carotenoid pigments is graphed and interpreted.

Topic Connections

Photosynthesis, Accessory Pigments, Energy, Chromatography

Introduction

The yellow-orange carotenoids in leaves absorb wavelengths of light that chlorophyll a and chlorophyll b cannot. While partly overlapping the absorption spectra of the chlorophylls, carotenoids absorb blue-green and green light that is only reflected by green pigments. The energy collected by carotenoids through light absorption is channeled to chlorophyll a in photosynthesis.

In this lesson students compare a photosynthesis activity graph (an action spectrum) with the absorption spectra of chlorophyll a and b. In this way it is observed that photosynthesis occurs under exposure to some light wavelengths that are not absorbed by chlorophyll. Subsequently, students graph the absorption spectrum of carotenoids to discover the yellow-orange pigment's role in assisting in photosynthesis. The role of carotenoids in autumn leaf coloration is also explored.

This lesson could be used in conjunction with a chromatography investigation of leaf pigments.

Materials

Graph paper

Time Approximation

20 to 45 minutes. Portions can be completed outside of class.

Lesson Outline

1. Distribute the student worksheet and graph paper. Students compare the photosynthesis action spectrum to the absorption graphs (from the previous lesson, *Why Are Plants Green?*) for the chlorophylls.

2. Lead a discussion centered on the "Discussion Questions" from the worksheet.

3. Students graph the absorption spectrum of carotenoids.

4. Analysis questions.

5. Web/library research.

Implementation Strategy

- The lesson is best used after "Why Are Plants Green?" If used alone you will need to provide absorption spectra for chlorophyll a and chlorophyll b to be compared to the action spectrum and to carotenoids.

- The discussion questions lead students through a logical progression. Discuss each question before having students consider the next.

- If possible have students add their carotenoid graph to the one done in "Why Are Plants Green?" to facilitate visual comparisons.

Possible Responses for Student Worksheet Questions

Discussion Questions

1. Both show two peaks and a valley in the middle. But the photosynthesis action spectrum valley is not as deep and its left peak is wider than the left peak for the chlorophyll's. The photosynthesis spectrum shows activity in the blue-green and green range, where chlorophylls do not.

2. Photosynthesis occurs even in light that the chlorophylls cannot absorb.

3. There must be something else (other pigments) absorbing light and contributing to photosynthesis.

4. Many possibilities. One is to isolate different molecules from leaves and determine their absorption spectra.

Analysis

1. Because carotenoids absorb light well at 500 to 525 nm, whereas the chlorophylls do not.

2. Yellow or orange. They reflect light from 550 nm to 700 nm, which includes yellow, orange, and red.

3. They collect energy for the plant that the chlorophylls cannot.

Web/Library Research

1. Trees stop synthesizing chlorophyll. Existing chlorophyll breaks down, revealing yellow-orange carotenoids that were present before but masked by the more abundant chlorophylls.

2. Much information will be found on this.

Reference

Campbell, N., Reece, J., & Mitchell, L. (1999). *Biology* (6th ed.). Menlo Park, CA: Benjamin Cummings.

Why Are Plants Not Always Green?

Introduction

Suppose a researcher tested the effect of light wavelength on photosynthetic activity. In the experiment photosynthesis rate was measured by O_2 production. A graph of the results, called an action spectrum, would look something like Figure 7.1.

The graph resembles the absorption spectra for chlorophyll a and chlorophyll b, but there are some subtle but important differences. Compare the graph to the absorption spectra for the chlorophylls.

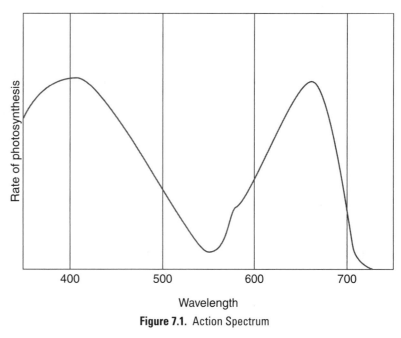

Figure 7.1. Action Spectrum

Discussion Questions

1. What observations can you make about similarities and differences?

   _____

   _____

   _____

   _____

2. Now focus on the left half of the graphs. Notice that the photosynthesis graph has a wider left peak than the chlorophyll absorption graphs. It doesn't bottom out until 550 to 600 nm. What does this mean?

   _____

   _____

   _____

   _____

Why Are Plants Not Always Green?, *Cont'd.*

3. The action spectrum shows that photosynthesis occurs even in light that is not absorbed by chlorophyll a or b. Propose an explanation for this.

_____

_____

_____

4. How could you collect evidence to support your hypothesis?

_____

_____

_____

_____

Graphing

Use the data from Table 7.2 to make an absorption spectrum graph for carotenoids, as you have done previously for chlorophyll a and b. Your teacher might have you put it on the same graphs as those.

Table 7.2. Data

Wavelength	Carotenoids % Absorption
400 nanometers	22
425 nanometers	23
450 nanometers	49
475 nanometers	43
500 nanometers	55
525 nanometers	34
550 nanometers	0
575 nanometers	0
600 nanometers	0
625 nanometers	0
650 nanometers	0
675 nanometers	0
700 nanometers	0

Why Are Plants Not Always Green?, *Cont'd.*

Analysis

1. By looking at your graph, explain why the action spectrum for photosynthesis shows wider activity than the absorption spectra for the chlorophylls.

   _____

   _____

   _____

   _____

2. What color are carotenoids? Explain.

   _____

   _____

   _____

   _____

3. What is the adaptive value of accessory pigments like carotenoids? That is, what advantage do they provide plants?

   _____

   _____

   _____

   _____

Web/Library Research
Find information to explain the following:

1. Leaves of trees in many parts of North America change color in the fall or before a dry season. Explain why and relate your explanation to carotenoids.

   _____

   _____

   _____

   _____

2. What is beta carotene? Where is it found? What does it do for plants? Why is it beneficial in a human diet?

   _____

   _____

   _____

   _____

Autotroph Inquiries: Comings and Goings

A unit-initiating inquiry in which learners discover for themselves that plants consume carbon dioxide and release oxygen when photosynthesizing.

Topic Connections

Photosynthesis, Energy Transfer, Plant Metabolism, Interdependence

Introduction

Fundamental to understanding the role of producers in ecosystems is knowing that photosynthesis consumes carbon dioxide and produces oxygen gas. The carbon is fixed into organic molecules that begin food chains. The oxygen allows for aerobic respiration, which helped spawn the evolution of complex multi-cellular life. The inverse and interdependent relationship between photosynthesis and cellular respiration are central concepts in biology courses. However, for many learners the similar but reverse aspects of the two processes promote confusion. Learning these important concepts accurately requires special attention. Students need opportunities that provide time and thinking challenges to facilitate learner-constructed understanding.

In this inquiry students design and conduct simple experiments to determine whether plants consume or release carbon dioxide when photosynthesizing. The value of the inquiry lies in its use as an introduction to the topic. If students collect, interpret, and explain evidence on photosynthesis, they are more likely to construct lasting understanding for themselves than if they are merely told what happens. The experiments are done with *Elodea* in a bromthymol blue indicator solution or with a carbon dioxide sensor and any terrestrial leaves. Then, if either dissolved oxygen or oxygen gas sensors are available, students explore whether plants consume or release oxygen. The lesson begins with an assessment of student preconceptions and concludes with reflection on new understandings.

Materials for BTB Method

- *Elodea*—Two to four sprigs per lab group
- Flasks—125 ml, two to four per lab group
- Rubber stoppers (#5) or parafilm, two to four per lab
- Bromthymol blue (BTB) 0.1 percent solution, diluted by adding seven drops per 30 ml of water used
- Water, enough to fill all flasks
- Light source
- Drinking straws—one per lab group

Materials for Carbon Dioxide and Oxygen Sensors Method

- Computer-interfaced carbon dioxide sensor—two per lab group
- Computer-interfaced oxygen sensor—two per lab group
- Leaves, recently picked—one per sensor
- Light source

Time Approximation

- Assess prior knowledge: 15 minutes
- Demonstrating the tools: 10 minutes
- The investigation: 15 minutes to plan and discuss and
- 15 minutes to set up;
  BTB experiments are left overnight
- Experiments with sensors: 15 minutes to collect data
- Data analysis reflection: 15 minutes

Preparation

Elodea is a common aquarium plant also know as *Anacharis.* It can be purchased very inexpensively from pet stores or biological supply companies.

Dilute 0.1 percent BTB by adding (or have the students do this) seven drops of BTB to every 30 ml of water used.

Plant grow lights work well for both methods described here. They offer bright but cool light. Flood lamps will work, but keep them far enough from the plants so that their heat doesn't shut down photosynthetic activity.

If using CO_2 sensors, you will need fresh leaves. They can be picked from shrubs, trees, or houseplants. Fresh spinach leaves from the grocery store work as well.

Safety Precaution

Students should wear splash-proof goggles at all times when working with BTB. Caution students to blow very gently into the BTB when they are using the straw to add CO_2.

Lesson Outline

Assess Prior Knowledge

1. Either distribute the worksheet or have students use their notebooks/journals for the tasks and questions on the worksheet.

2. Inform the class that they will be learning about photosynthesis. Tell them that you first want to find out what they know about the topic. Ask: "What do plants need to live? What do they need to photosynthesize?" Accept all responses and don't correct any inaccuracies at this point.

3. Focus on what plants consume and what they release. Have students fill in the table on the worksheet or they could make a concept map for this.

4. Now call on various students to offer some of the ideas they put into their tables. Again, refrain from making corrections at this point.

5. Tell the students that they will focus in on carbon dioxide (and oxygen if you have O_2 sensors) and that they will investigate whether plants consume or release these things.

Demonstrating the Tools

Show the class how they will be collecting evidence of CO_2 consumption. If using sensors, provide instruction in their use. If using BTB do the following:

1. Fill a beaker half-full with the diluted BTB.

2. With goggles on, insert a straw into the liquid and gently blow until the color changes from blue to green to yellow.

3. Inform them that BTB is an indirect indicator for the presence of CO_2. The acid formed from CO_2 and water (carbonic acid) causes BTB to change to green, and with increasing amounts, to yellow. Conversely, when CO_2 is taken out of a BTB solution, the color change reverses back toward blue.

4. To see whether CO_2 is consumed over time, one needs to start with yellow BTB. If it changes back to green or blue, the CO_2 was taken out of the solution.

The Investigation

Inform the students that they will investigate the question, "Do plants consume CO_2 or release it when they are in the light, photosynthesizing?"

BTB Method

1. Provide access to two to four sprigs of *Elodea* and two to four 125-ml flasks (or other glass containers), stoppers or parafilm to seal the flasks once they've been filled, water, and straws.

2. Student groups need to devise and set up an experiment that will effectively investigate the question.

3. You might critique experimental designs as they are being set up. Or you could wait until the next day and then challenge the validity of their results and provide an opportunity for a re-do.

4. Experiments are placed under a light bank or near flood lights and left until the next day. The lights should be on for all twenty-four hours.

5. The next day students collect data and draw conclusions. Lead a discussion on student results and their meaning.

6. Have students research via book or Web sources the role of CO_2 in photosynthesis.

Computer-Interfaced Sensors Method

1. Follow the above, but use leaves and CO_2 sensors. These experiments do not need to be left overnight. They can yield conclusive data in 15 minutes or so. After 15 minutes of observing carbon dioxide consumption, students

could wrap the chambers in aluminum foil, at which point consumption will stop and carbon dioxide production (caused by respiration) may even be detectable.

2. Have the students repeat the above procedure for oxygen using an oxygen gas sensor and leaves.

Reflection

Have students respond to the questions/topics on the Post-Investigation/Reflection part of the worksheet.

Implementation Strategy

- Use this inquiry *before* you have introduced photosynthesis with book or classroom learning. The experience will be much more meaningful for students if they are using it to construct new understanding, rather than merely verifying what they have recently learned.

- Students may need help learning that their experiments have uncontrolled variables. Commonly groups will put one flask in the light source and one in the dark. The one in the light changes from yellow back to blue or green and the one in the dark does not. Ask them whether anything else could have possibly caused the color change. Could the light itself have caused the change? They can't say because they didn't control for that possibility. A better set-up would have a flask with only yellow BTB but no plant next to one with yellow BTB and a plant, but lead them to figure this out. These kinds of mistakes provide fertile opportunities for learning scientific thinking. The critiquing can be done while the experiments are being designed/set up or the next day.

Some Possible Student Experiments

To eliminate light some may put a flask in a cabinet or cover it with paper or aluminum foil.

Some may have some plants in yellow BTB and others in blue BTB (not helpful).

The best will involve a plant in yellow BTB in the light, a flask with only yellow BTB in the light, and a plant with yellow BTB in the dark.

The Post-Investigation Reflection

For Question 2, press the students to come up with a reasonable equation for photosynthesis. Younger students might use only words like carbon dioxide + water → sugar + oxygen. Students with a chemistry background should use symbols. This may be a struggle for students, whether they have learned about photosynthesis in the past or not. Tell them to focus in on what plants use (need) and they should be able to come up with light, water, and, after doing this inquiry, carbon dioxide for the left side of the equation.

For advanced students you can have them apply an understanding of mass conservation in an attempt to balance the equation.

For Question 5, the answer is to make organic molecules (sugars). It is crucial to steer students away from thinking that photosynthesis evolved to produce O_2. Oxygen gas is a waste product of the process that organisms then adapted to using.

Autotroph Inquiries: Comings and Goings?

Consider these questions. What do plants need to live? What do they need to photosynthesize?

Then fill in the following table with as many ideas as you can. Don't worry about being right or wrong. The purpose at this point is to find out what you know *before* studying photosynthesis.

Table 7.3. What Plants Need

What Do Plants Need/Use/Consume?	**What Do Plants Give Off?**

Based on what you wrote above, try writing a summary equation for photosynthesis. On the left of an arrow put the things that go into photosynthesis and to the right put the things that come out of the process. Again, don't worry about being right or wrong at this point.

The Tools
Your teacher will demonstrate the tools you will use to investigate photosynthesis.

The Investigation
Think about the following question:

Do plants consume CO_2 or release it when they are in the light, photosynthesizing?

With your group members, develop a plan to answer this question. How will you go about collecting convincing evidence?

Autotroph Inquiries: Comings and Goings?, *Cont'd.*

Post-Investigation Reflection

1. Do plants consume CO_2 or release it when they are in the light, photosynthesizing? What is your evidence for this?

   _____

   _____

   _____

   _____

2. Now again try to write the general summary equation for photosynthesis. Your teacher might ask you to attempt to balance the equation if you have learned about mass conservation.

   _____

   _____

   _____

   _____

3. Do plants consume or release O_2 in photosynthesis?

   _____

   _____

   _____

   _____

4. How do you now think differently about photosynthesis than you did at the beginning of this inquiry?

   _____

   _____

   _____

   _____

5. What is the purpose of photosynthesis?

   _____

   _____

   _____

   _____

Autotroph Inquiries: Do Plants Respire?

Students design and conduct brief experiments to investigate an area of common misconception.

Topic Connections

Plant Metabolism, Cellular Respiration, Photosynthesis, Autotrophs

Introduction

Learners of all ages may harbor the misconception that "plants do photosynthesis" and "animals do respiration." While true, the thinking omits the important understanding that plants "do both." Like all living things, plants use cellular respiration to harvest the energy stored in the bonds of organic molecules. Many students may come to your course with this misconception-by-omission. Like all preconceptions, it needs time and specific attention devoted to it if learners are to reconstruct a more accurate understanding.

When plants photosynthesize, the CO_2 that they also produce by cellular respiration is not detectable because there is a net consumption by the Calvin Cycle. Thus, in the previous inquiry, *Autotroph Inquiries: Comings and Goings,* plants in the light consume CO_2 from their surroundings. But a plant in the dark will *yield* detectable quantities of CO_2 produced by respiration. In this inquiry students use either *Elodea* and bromthymol blue or leaves and CO_2 sensors to investigate the topic.

The inquiry can be combined with similar investigations of photosynthesis and respiration. Or it can be isolated in a series of learning experiences. Either way it is important to specifically devote time and thinking challenges to the central misconception.

Materials for BTB Method

- *Elodea*—four sprigs per lab group
- Flasks—125 ml, two per lab group
- Rubber stoppers (#5) or parafilm, two per lab group
- Bromthymol blue (BTB), 0.1 percent then diluted by adding seven drops per 30 ml of water used
- Water, enough to fill all flasks
- Light source
- Drinking straws—one per lab group

Materials for Carbon Dioxide Sensor Method

- Computer-interfaced carbon dioxide sensor—two per lab group
- Leaves, recently picked—one per sensor
- Light source

Time Approximation

- Opening discussion: 10 minutes
- The tools: 10 minutes (unnecessary if done for previous inquiry)
- The investigation: 15 minutes to plan and discuss
- 10 minutes to set up
- BTB experiments: Left for 24 or 48 hours
- Experiments with CO_2 sensors: 15 minutes to collect data
- Data analysis discussion: 15 minutes

Safety Precaution

Students should wear splash-proof goggles at all times when working with BTB.

Lesson Outline

Opening Discussion

1. Ask the class whether plants photosynthesize or respire. Don't offer the ". . .or both?" option at first. You want to really find out what they are thinking. A student answering "both" to the question as phrased will be showing you a fairly confident understanding. Other students may be less clear on the subject.

2. Inform the class that they will be investigating whether plants do carry out respiration.

The Tools

1. Show the class how they will be collecting evidence of CO_2 consumption.

2. If using sensors provide instruction in their use.

3. If using BTB do the following:

   - Fill a beaker halfway with the diluted BTB.

   - With goggles on, insert a straw into the liquid and gently blow until the color changes from blue to green to yellow.

   - Inform them that BTB is an indirect indicator for the presence of CO_2. The acid formed from CO_2 and water (carbonic acid) causes BTB to change to green, and with increasing amounts, to yellow. Conversely, when CO_2 is taken out of a BTB solution the color change reverses back toward blue.

The Investigation

1. Student groups brainstorm on an experimental design to answer the question.

2. Critique the designs. Lead a class discussion where some of the groups share their plans. Encourage students to offer constructive criticisms of each other's designs. Alternatively you could critique the experiments by circulating and

discussing them with each group. Improvements should not be directly offered, rather students should be guided via questions to realize for themselves how they could change their experiments.

3. Experiments are set up and run. BTB-based experiments should be left for 24 to 48 hours.

Data Analysis Discussion

1. After students have collected evidence, lead a discussion on the meaning of the results.

2. See the student worksheet for discussion topics.

Implementation Strategy

- The inquiry could be used before any learning on photosynthesis and cellular respiration has occurred or it could be used after learning on both has occurred. It is best, however, to use it *before* any readings or discussions specifically addressing cellular respiration in autotrophs.

- If the previous inquiry, *Autotroph Inquiries: Comings and Goings,* was used, then lab design and set-up time will be reduced for this inquiry.

- Students could build on their learning from these two "Autotroph Inquiries" by investigating the interrelationships between producers and consumers. Using the same tools (BTB or CO_2/O_2 sensors), they could test predictions on CO_2 production/consumption using combinations of organisms such as *Elodea* and snails, *Elodea* and small fish, or leaves and crickets. The experiments could be run in different light conditions.

- *Elodea* produces much less CO_2 overnight in the dark than it consumes overnight in the light. Thus, the color change will not be as dramatic as when investigating photosynthesis. But there is a discernible change to greenish from blue in twenty-four hours. The color change is best assessed if the experimental flask is held next to a BTB-only control flask for comparison.

- Successful student experiments will involve *Elodea* in blue BTB in the dark and a control flask of only blue BTB in the dark. Some groups may also want to keep an additional flask in the light to compare.

- None of the experiments should involve turning the BTB yellow at first. If students want to do this, ask pointed questions such as, "What do you expect to happen in that flask?"

- The title of the student worksheet is intended to be a bit of a trick question. The goal is to emphasize the misconception and then challenge them to think deeply about it, developing a more advanced comprehension of cellular respiration.

- Dark conditions can be attained via cabinets, boxes, closets, or by wrapping containers in aluminum foil.

Discussion Question Responses

1. Plants do *both* photosynthesis and respiration.

3. The "purpose" of photosynthesis is to transfer light energy into the bonds of organic molecules.

4. The "purpose" of respiration is to release energy trapped in the bonds of organic molecules into small more useable forms such as ATP.

5. The plant would make sugars, but it would not be able to break them down to make useable (ATP) energy for cellular functions.

Autotroph Inquiries: Do Plants Respire or Photosynthesize?

Post-Investigation Analysis

1. What can you conclude from your experiment? What is the answer to the question in the worksheet title? What is your evidence?

_____

_____

_____

_____

2. How confident are you of your experimental results? How could you improve your experiment if you were going to redo it?

_____

_____

_____

_____

3. Explain the "purpose" of photosynthesis.

_____

_____

_____

_____

4. Explain the "purpose" of cellular respiration.

_____

_____

_____

_____

5. What would happen to a plant if it could photosynthesize but it lost its ability to carry out cellular respiration? Explain.

_____

_____

_____

_____

Teacher Pages

Autotroph Inquiries: Building Organic Molecules

Grappling with a challenging question leads student groups to develop an understanding of a central but commonly misunderstood concept. A brief discussion lesson follows.

Topic Connections

Photosynthesis, the Calvin Cycle, Cellular Respiration, Organic Molecules, Plant Structure

Introduction

Even after studying energy reactions in autotrophs, students may not fully understand the importance of photosynthesis in providing building blocks for plant biosynthesis. Often students learn early in the year about organic molecules and that cellulose is an important plant carbohydrate. Later in the year they learn about energy transfer and the O_2/CO_2 interdependencies of photosynthesis and cellular respiration. Students know how photosynthesis makes sugars and cellular respiration consumes sugars. But they may not appreciate or comprehend the role of photosynthesis in making organic molecules, which are then modified and combined to make polymers of carbohydrates, lipids, proteins, and nucleic acids. In short, plants photosynthesize to make more of themselves—to build roots, stems, leaves, flowers and seeds—as well as to store energy.

This constructivist discussion lesson encourages thinking connections between knowledge of organic molecules, photosynthesis/respiration, plant structure, and food chains. It works best at the end of a unit on photosynthesis and cellular respiration.

The lesson focuses on the question:

"What do plants do more of over the course of a year . . . photosynthesis, cellular respiration, or are they carried out in equal amounts? Explain."

In addition to developing understanding of biosynthesis in plants, the discussions help you and the students to assess understanding of energy reactions in general. The question generates discussion of oxygen production and use, atmospheric levels of oxygen and carbon dioxide, sugars, and food chains.

Materials

None

Time Approximation

30 minutes

Lesson Outline

1. Either distribute the student worksheet or pose the central question in another format.

2. Students individually brainstorm on possible responses to the question.

3. Small group idea exchange. Students break into groups of four or so to discuss/debate ideas on the question. A group response should be developed and summarized in writing.

4. Class-wide discussion is held with representatives from each group explaining their groups' ideas and reasoning on the question.

5. After at least some groups have presented their ideas, facilitate intergroup discussion/debate on their ideas. Be sure to challenge groups to identify evidence and reasoning to back up their statements.

6. If the students don't get there, lead them to thinking about plant structure. Hold up a plant and ask what it is made of. Ask where the materials (molecules) that make up the plant come from and, if the plant is to grow and develop, where will the new molecules come from?

7. Reflection: Students complete Question 4 reflecting on what they have learned in the discussions. This can be completed in class or as homework.

Implementation Strategy

- Use this lesson in the culminating stages of a learning sequence on photosynthesis and cellular respiration.

- To heighten engagement you might make the group response a competition. Offer candy or something for the best idea(s).

- Younger learners may need more guidance in the lesson in the form of pointed questions. They should still be able to develop an understanding of the biosynthetic purpose of photosynthesis, even if they have not specifically studied organic polymers.

Discussion Points

Evidence that more photosynthesis occurs then cellular respiration:

- O_2 accumulates in atmosphere but what about CO_2?—Carbon dioxide levels are increasing, but probably due to human oxidation of fossil fuels, in essence, artificial respiration.

- More photosynthesis than respiration has occurred in the past. Otherwise there wouldn't be a pool of O_2 for heterotrophs to use.

- There is a surplus of carbohydrates and other organic molecules. Otherwise there would be no new sources of food to start food chains.

Why they must at least occur in equal amounts:

- Plants need O_2 produced by photosynthesis to do aerobic respiration.
- Cellular respiration needs the sugars made by photosynthesis. If photosynthesis didn't keep up with cellular respiration, then respiration would shut down (after stored sugars were depleted).

Why there must be more photosynthesis than respiration:

- Plants don't only use their synthesized organic molecules to fuel cellular respiration. They also use them to build the large molecules (such as cellulose and proteins) that make new leaves, stems, roots, flowers, seeds, and cellular structures. Heterotrophs get their building blocks from food. Autotrophs synthesize theirs.

Autotroph Inquiries: Building Organic Molecules

The Question

What does a plant do "more" of over the course of a year?. . . Photosynthesis? Cellular respiration? Or are they carried out in equal amounts? Explain.

1. First answer the question as well as you can by yourself. You will have time to share ideas with classmates later.

   _____

   _____

   _____

   _____

   _____

   _____

2. When your teacher indicates, get into a discussion group and exchange ideas on the question. Summarize your group's thinking below.

   _____

   _____

   _____

   _____

   _____

   _____

3. Next, there will be a classwide discussion where each group will present their arguments on the topic to the class.

4. After the classwide discussion, write a reflection on the following: How has your thinking on the topic changed after the group and class discussions? What did you not consider before when attempting to answer the question that you understand now?

   _____

   _____

   _____

   _____

   _____

   _____

Cold-Blooded Thermometers

In this brief, partial inquiry, students use thermometers and socks to explore the source of body heat.

Topic Connections

Cellular Respiration, Energy, Endothermy/Ectothermy, Body Insulation

Introduction

There are widespread misconceptions among students about the concepts of body heat, endothermy (homeothermy), and ectothermy (poikilothermy). If asked why his or her body is warm, the typical student would probably claim that it was because we are "warm-blooded." Biology students learn many details about cellular respiration, but many don't realize that its exergonic reactions generate heat in every cell of the body. Of course this cellular heat production occurs in reptiles and other ectotherms as well. But endotherms are capable of regulating their body temperature by influencing heat generation (especially in muscle cells) and by influencing the conservation or release of body heat by a variety of structural, physiological, and behavioral means.

In this activity the students' incomplete understanding of the nature of heat sources will be exposed to them. They will be challenged with the following question: What would happen if you took three identical thermometers, all reading the same temperature, and wrapped them in three different socks—one wool, one silk, and one cotton—and then left them in the same place until the next day? What temperature would each thermometer read? (from E. Carlyon in J. Layman, *Inquiry and Learning*).

Most students will expect the thermometer within the wool sock to read a higher temperature. They will be surprised the next day to discover the three thermometers reading the same temperature as each other. At this point the students will be ready to construct for themselves a more accurate understanding of body heat via discussions.

Materials

- Socks, three per lab group (one each wool, silk, cotton)
- Thermometers, three per group

Time Approximation

20 minutes the first day and discussion time the next day

Preparation

Consider assigning the lab groups to bring in the three socks. Do this a few days before the activity to provide time to ensure that enough socks come in. Or establish a collection of old socks to keep and use every year.

Safety Precautions

Thermometers are quite fragile. Remind students to handle them with caution.

Lesson Outline

1. Present the class with the experimental question that is given in the introduction. The question could be written on the board or on an overhead transparency.

2. Ask the students to brainstorm on the question in their lab groups. They should make a hypothesis, a prediction, and a brief justification for their hypothesis.

3. Have the students set up their experiments. They should set them aside in a place where they will not be disturbed until the next day.

4. The next day have the students check the readings on their three thermometers.

5. In their lab groups have the students attempt to explain their results.

6. Have each group report their data to the class.

7. Initiate a classwide discussion based on questions such as those on the student worksheet. Or have the students work on the worksheet before then initiating a class discussion of the topics.

Implementation Strategy

- If silk socks are difficult to obtain, substitute another type (rayon? blend?) or simply do the inquiry with only wool and cotton socks.

- Do not provide the students with any initial information on the goals, purposes, or context of the activity. All of these connections will be made in the post-inquiry discussions.

- Some students may wonder how the experiment would be affected by different external temperatures (such as in a refrigerator or on a warm windowsill). Encourage them to explore these areas of interest. The results, of course, will be the same; if the three thermometers are exposed to the same ambient temperature, they will register the same reading regardless of where they are.

- It is possible that one (or more) of the groups will obtain results showing one of the thermometers at a different temperature than the others in their experiment. For instance, if a student holds a thermometer by the bulb when removing it from the sock, its reading would be errantly effected. However, most of the groups will find all of their thermometers at the same temperature, so any anomalous ones can serve as a launching pad for discussions of experimental error, importance of large sample size, and verification.

Possible Responses for Student Worksheet Questions

2. Yes. Wool is an excellent insulator.

4. Yes. Because it traps body heat more efficiently than cotton.

5. Body heat is produced as a byproduct of metabolic cellular reactions. Aerobic respiration produces significant heat. According to the 2nd Law of Thermodynamics, heat is produced whenever energy is converted from one form to another.

6. Yes, reptile cells generate heat. However, they have a slower metabolism than birds and mammals and they lack adaptations for maintaining constant body temperatures the way that endotherms can.

Reference

Layman, J. (1996). *Inquiry and learning.* New York: The College Board.

Name _____ Date _____

Cold-Blooded Thermometers

1. Explain your results.

   _____

   _____

   _____

   _____

2. Is wool a good insulator? Why?

   _____

   _____

   _____

   _____

3. Does a thermometer generate heat? Do socks generate heat?

   _____

   _____

   _____

   _____

4. Does a wool sweater keep you warmer than a cotton sweater? Why?

   _____

   _____

   _____

   _____

5. You are warm to the touch. Where does that heat come from? What is the source of body heat? Be as specific as you can.

   _____

   _____

   _____

   _____

6. Do the cells of reptiles generate heat? Why can't reptiles remain warm when the surrounding temperature falls?

   _____

   _____

   _____

Energy Storage Molecules and Natural Selection

Students attempt to apply knowledge of lipids and carbohydrates to explain why animals and plants differ in their energy storage molecules. This is a brief discussion lesson based on a challenging question.

Topic Connections

Energy Storage, Organic Molecules, Adaptation, Animal/Plant Metabolism

Introduction

Animals store surplus energy as fat, while plants tend to do so in carbohydrates. Why? This question offers a great opportunity for learners to think deeply about differences between types of organic molecules, how energy is stored in molecules, and the influence of natural selection on the molecular structure of organisms. The topics considered in this lesson are fairly complex. The lesson is most appropriate for advanced high school classes.

Lipids store more energy per unit mass than carbohydrates do. The harvestable energy in organic molecules resides in the carbon-hydrogen bonds. A carbohydrate such as $C_{12}H_{24}O_{12}$ and a lipid such as $C_{12}H_{24}O_3$ store comparable amounts of useable energy. But because it contains many fewer oxygen atoms, the lipid is considerably lighter than the sugar.

For plants, minimization of size and mass are not factors that would be selected for by the environment. On the contrary, bulk that allows for height, wide trunks, and sprawling root systems may be a survival advantage to many plants. Storing relatively heavy starches in underground roots does not weaken a plant's ability to function, escape predation, and so on. For animals, however, fats provide an adaptive advantage over polysaccharides like starch. Packing more energy into less mass and space, fats allow for energy storage that doesn't slow the animal as much, doesn't expand its size as much, and doesn't cost as much energetically to ferry around. Thus, animals that developed lipid storage mechanisms survived better and passed this trait to their offspring.

Unlike stems and roots, space considerations are important for energy storage in seeds. And as one might predict, much energy storage in seeds occurs as oils rather than as starch.

Materials

None

Time Approximation

30 minutes

Lesson Outline

1. Either distribute the worksheet or pose the central question in another format.
2. Students individually brainstorm on possible responses to the question.

3. *Small group idea exchange:* Students break into groups of four or so to discuss/debate ideas on the question. A group response should be developed and summarized in writing.

4. *Classwide discussion:* Representatives from each group will explain their groups' ideas and reasoning on the topic. The next step in the lesson will depend on student comprehension revealed at this point. If the students are close to an accurate understanding, then facilitate inter-group discussion and debate on the topic. If, on the other hand, students need significant help, then there are two options. First, you might direct learners to text or Web readings where they could gather more basic understanding of energy in molecules, then return to the discussion later. Or you could provide some of the guiding information given in "Implementation Strategy" and continue the discussion.

5. *Reflection:* Students complete Question 4 on the worksheet reflecting on what they have learned in the discussions. This could be completed in class or as homework.

Implementation Strategy

- A good time to use the lesson is when studying energy reactions in organisms and after learning on organic molecules has occurred.

- The question is challenging even for many advanced students. But even if no groups arrive at an accurate explanation at first, the lesson is still valuable. Eventually, when they are guided to understanding the explanation, it will have more lasting meaning because of their struggles/discussions/debates than if they merely read or heard the information.

- To arrive at a sound explanation for the question learners need to consider:

    Carbon-hydrogen bonds store energy that is harvested in cellular respiration to make ATP.

    Carbohydrates maintain a 1:2:1 ration of carbon:hydrogen:oxygen, whereas lipids have a much higher hydrogen:oxygen ratio. Plants don't move, while most animals do.

- If students need some clues to move them along write these two formulae on the board:

$$C_{12}H_{24}O_{12}$$
$$C_{12}H_{24}O_{3}$$

    Or show them transparency or Web diagrams of lipid versus carbohydrate structure.

- For animal/plant differences, ask them to act like a plant for a few moments (still). Then have them consider what animals often do that plants never do (be moving around the room as you say this to them).

Energy Storage Molecules and Natural Selection

The Question

Why do animals store their surplus energy in fat molecules while plants mainly use carbohydrates like starch? Explain.

1. First answer the question as well as you can by yourself. You will have time to share ideas with classmates later.

   _____

   _____

   _____

   _____

   _____

   _____

2. When your teacher indicates, get into a discussion group and exchange ideas on the question. Summarize your group's thinking below.

   _____

   _____

   _____

   _____

   _____

   _____

3. Next there will be a classwide discussion where each group will present its ideas on the question to the class.

4. After the classwide discussion, write a reflection on the following: How has your thinking on the topic changed after the group and class discussions? What new connections and understandings have you now developed?

   _____

   _____

   _____

   _____

   _____

The Behavior of Organisms

This chapter's entries address concepts found in the Life Science content standards "Regulation and Behavior" and "The Behavior of Organisms." The concepts include behavioral responses and, in multicellular animals, a nervous system with sense organs that orchestrate the behaviors. In the first inquiry students investigate a mysterious animal response to a stimulus. *Homo sapiens* is the research subject for the next two entries. In the final lesson students critically evaluate unsubstantiated claims about human memory.

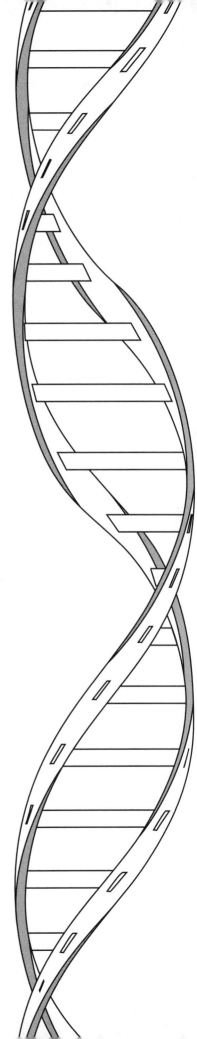

Termite Trails Mystery

Students self-initiate the inquiry process as they investigate why termites follow an ink trail.

Topic Connections

Scientific Inquiry, Animal Behavior, Insects, Animal Communication

Introduction

This lab develops scientific inquiry skills and introduces students to animal communication.

Learners initially observe a termite following a red ink trail. This strange behavior generates quite a bit of student interest and it piques their curiosity. Spontaneously at first, and later with some encouragement, students engage themselves in science by questioning, hypothesizing, predicting, experimenting, concluding, debating, and evaluating. They investigate many variables that could be attracting the termites, including color, texture, brightness, odor, pen style, pen brand, and so on. Along the way groups periodically claim to have solved the mystery. At this point they are challenged by peers and by you to back up their proposed explanations. Usually they then realize that they are still hypothesizing. They then focus their experiments on ruling out alternative explanations and supporting their ideas with defendable evidence.

Many animals communicate with other members of their species through chemical messages called pheromones. Honey bees release alarm pheromones that stimulate hive mates to attack an intruder. The human egg releases a chemical that communicates with and attracts sperm cells. And everyone has observed a line of ants following a pheromone trail from their nest to a food source.

Subterranean termites are especially reliant on chemical cues because of the dark world in which they live. These insects leave a pheromone trail as they move from one place to another. The trail can lead other members of the colony to food or help the original trail maker to find its way back to the nest. Strangely, ink in Paper Mate® (and possibly some other) pens contains a glycoprotein that is similar to a termite pheromone. A subterranean termite will quickly detect and then follow lines made with one of these pens. Red pens are used to bait students into initially looking for a termite attraction to color. Eventually through background research students learn that termites are blind. They integrate this knowledge with their experimental observations to develop more advanced explanations for the termite behavior.

Materials

- Worker termites, three or four per lab group (see "Preparation" for information on obtaining termites)
- White paper, blank sheets, two or three per lab group
- Paper Mate® pen, red, one per lab group

- Paint brush, small, soft-bristled, one per lab group
- Other pens, a wide variety of brands, colors, and styles

Time Approximation

A 45- to 90-minute period and part of a following period for discussion

Preparation

The termites must be subterranean (family *Rhinotermitidae*). Collect them by splitting open rotting wood boards, downed trees, or tree stumps or order them from a biological supply company. One of the major supply houses sells termites that are not subterranean and will not work with this activity. The termites sold by Carolina Biological work fine. It might also be possible to ask a local exterminator to collect some for you.

The best way to maintain termites is by keeping them in a chunk of wood in which they have been living. The wood offers the cover and high humidity that they require. Keep the wood in a sealed container. A very light spray of water into the container once every few weeks will help, but too much water leads to lethal fungal growth. If keeping the termites for only a week or so, I would not add any water. Of course, it is safest to use the termites soon after obtaining them.

Lesson Outline

1. Give each small group of students a blank piece of unlined paper and a red Paper Mate® pen. Have the students make a simple drawing on the paper using continuous lines from the red pen (such as a large figure 8 or a spiral).

2. Carefully drop one or two termites onto each of the group's papers. Termites are fragile so touch them as little as possible. The ideal way to move them is to tap the container or piece of wood they are in/on so that they fall onto the paper. Once they are on the paper, students can move them by folding and tapping the paper rather than by touching them or by gently moving them with the paint brush.

3. The termite will follow the ink trail of the Paper Mate® pen indefinitely.

4. Students will ask why the termite is doing this; some will call out possible explanations. During these initial 5 to 10 minutes, say nothing. Leave the students to their own impulses to question and explore.

5. Next, circulate from lab group to lab group reiterating their questions. The central question to focus on is: "Why do the termites follow the red ink trail?" The students offer possible answers (such as "the termite likes red"). Respond only with something like: "Interesting idea. How could you test that?"

6. Students propose ways to test their ideas. Encourage them to try them. Typically they will try different colors, different textures of pen, different brands of pen, pencils, indentations made without a pen, and so on to determine what it is about the ink trail that attracts the termite. Have these available

in the room in case students ask for them, but don't call their attention to these things unless they ask for them.

7. Each time a group claims to have solved the mystery, ask them to present evidence that they have ruled out all other possibilities. Play devil's advocate by offering alternative possible explanations when students claim to have "proven" a hypothesis. Even if a group comes up with the "right" answer at this point, never tell them that. Instead, prod them to collect as much evidence as possible to support their idea. The answer, of course, is not the point of this activity as much as the process. Also enlist nearby lab groups to help critique other groups' claims of having found the answer. Usually by the end of a one-hour period some groups will have ruled out vision by running simple but effective experiments with a termite following a red line but not following one that is covered by something transparent like scotch tape or an overhead transparency sheet.

8. Students should keep a log of their experiments and the results/observations during the lesson.

9. About 20 to 30 minutes into the inquiry, stop the class and initiate a short discussion. Have each group report on their observations to that point. Have them discuss what is known and what still needs to be discovered. Issue a challenge to them. Tell them that they have explored some good ideas but that they have not yet solved the mystery.

10. In another 20 minutes or so, again stop the students and lead a session in which each group reports on their findings.

11. Near the end of the period, have a classwide discussion summarizing what each group has discovered and attempting to make sense out of their findings. At this point the students usually realize that they need more basic information on termites before they can completely solve this riddle, and their homework becomes library research on termites.

12. At the end of the lab give the student worksheet to the students. The worksheet includes an assignment to find general background information on termites.

13. The next day ask students to share their new information on termites (termites are blind, leave pheromone trails, and so on). Lead a discussion challenging students to incorporate this new information into their ideas and observations from the day before. Ask them to refine their explanations for the termite ink-following behavior.

Implementation Strategy

- Use the lab in an animal behavior unit or it could be used early in a course as an introduction to scientific investigation. If doing so, then use it *before* teaching the general terms and concepts of scientific inquiry. After doing this inquiry, students can be introduced to the terminology and ideas of science process. Concepts such as hypothesis or variable will have more meaning for the students if they can connect them to their previous experiences of trying to solve the termite mystery.

- Be aware that most but not all termites will follow the ink trail. Also, some will do it more consistently and for longer than others. Discuss with the students that this is natural variation found in all species.

- Do not reveal "the answer" to the students at any time. The point is not to find "the answer" but to go through the process of using evidence and logic to attempt to explain an observed behavior.

- Early on some students are likely to guess that the termites are smelling the ink. Again, do not tell them that they are correct. After all, they are just hypothesizing. Challenge them to test their idea and to collect evidence that would be persuasive.

- The chemical that attracts termites is found in all Paper Mate® ballpoint pens (and possibly some other brands), but red is initially used to throw the students off the track a bit.

- Distribute the worksheet *after* the activity.

Possible Responses for Selected Student Worksheet Questions

2. The termites did not follow the lines by vision. Termites are blind. Students might reasonably hypothesize that the termites were attracted to a smell, taste, or feel of the line.

5(a). To control for individual differences in behavior.

5(b). To be more confident that results reflect generalized termite biology and not simply artifacts of chance or individual variations.

6. Questioned, hypothesized, designed experiments, controlled variables, drew conclusions, defended conclusions, communicated results, researched background information, modified explanations in light of new evidence and information.

Reference

Lana Hays-Access Excellence Web site, Activities Exchange Forum, www.access excellence.org/

Name _____ Date _____

Termite Trails Mystery

Introduction

You have observed some strange behavior. Termites follow ink trails. And termites follow some ink trails but not others. To both of these observations you have wondered, "Why?"

In your explorations of this mystery you have gone through the same kind of thinking as someone who researches acid rain, salamanders, or cancer. You were engaged in the process of *scientific inquiry.* You may be eager to know the complete "answer" to the termite mystery, but that is not the point of this activity. Scientists go weeks, years, sometimes lifetimes without answering certain questions. Of course, it is gratifying to find solutions to problems, but the excitement of science centers on the *process* of seeking answers, the quest for knowledge. Scientists are motivated by the challenge of the unknown, and they focus tremendous energy and creativity on ways to make pieces of science puzzles fit together.

In this activity you experienced this challenge. Now you will consider the thought processes and strategies that were most helpful along the way.

Background Information Search

Use Web or book sources to find general information on termite biology. How do they live? What do they do?

Analysis and Reflection

1. For each idea that you tested in the termite lab give:

   a. How you tested it

   b. What your test told you about the possible answer

   (It might be helpful to put this information in the form of a table.)

   _____

   _____

   _____

   _____

2. What is your best possible explanation for the termite's behavior now that you have more information on termite biology? If you had unlimited time and equipment, what would you do to see whether your current explanation is a good one?

   _____

   _____

   _____

   _____

Termite Trails Mystery, *Cont'd.*

3. Find the meaning of the following concepts and explain how you used them in the termite activity: scientific question, hypothesis, prediction, controlled experiment, controlled variable (constant), uncontrolled variable, conclusion, background information/literature search.

   _____

   _____

   _____

   _____

4. How could you have improved any of your experiments so that they would have provided more useful information?

   _____

   _____

   _____

   _____

5. Explain why it might have been worthwhile to have:

   a. Used many termites for each experiment

   b. Repeated each experiment multiple times

   _____

   _____

   _____

   _____

6. How did you act and think like a scientist in the termite lab?

   _____

   _____

   _____

   _____

7. What are some other ways that animals communicate?

   _____

   _____

8. What other animals communicate the way termites do?

   _____

   _____

Red Dot Special

Students investigate and attempt to explain the cause of afterimages created by staring at colored dots.

Topic Connections

The Eye, Nervous System, Visible Light Spectrum, Adaptation

Introduction

After staring at a red dot, if a person looks at white paper, he or she will see a greenish-blue dot that is not really there. This discrepant event captures student attention, piques their curiosity, and launches them on an inquiry quest for an explanation. To solve the original mystery, students must acquire an understanding of the human eye, color perception, and neuron function. Along the way they do Internet or library research, make predictions, design experiments with other colors/materials, and continually refine their explanations with new data and conceptual understandings.

The retina of the human eye consists of three types of color-sensitive neurons called cones. There are three different types of cone, and each responds best to a different part of the visible light spectrum. One type maximally absorbs light at 455 nm or blue light. Another best absorbs wavelengths at 530 nm or green light. The last type is most sensitive to red light at 625 nm. There is considerable overlap in the absorption ranges of the three (see Figure 8.1). By comparing and analyzing impulses from the three types of cones, our brain is able to distinguish thousands of different colors.

Upon staring at a red dot for a prolonged period, a person exhausts the red-sensitive cones in a dot-shaped area of the retina. Then when looking at a white surface they see the bluish-green afterimage. The white light coming from the white surface contains all of the colors of the visible spectrum, including red. However, in the area of the retina that had been responding to and forming an image of the red dot, the exhausted red cones will not transmit an impulse to the brain. But the blue-sensitive and green-sensitive cones in that area *will* send signals to the brain. Thus, the brain will be tricked into perceiving a blue-green dot where one doesn't exist.

The red-sensitive cones become only temporarily nonresponsive. Staring at a colored dot causes the cluster of cones to repeatedly fire, thus depleting their energy (ATP) supply. Energy is required by neurons to run the sodium potassium pump that "resets" the cell for a new action potential.

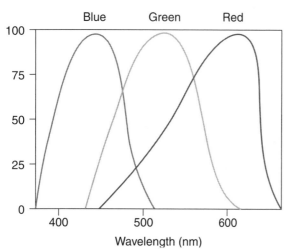

The "blue cones" have their maximum light absorption at 455 nm; the "green cones" at 530 nm, and the "red cones" at 625 nm. The brain perceives all other colors from the combined activities of these three cones' systems.

Figure 8.1. Color Vision

Source: From Raven and Johnson, Biology.

New York: McGraw-Hill. Used with permission.

Materials Per Student

- Index cards, white, unlined (if possible), 4" x 6" or larger
- Adhesive red dots, 2 inches in diameter. These can be found in stationery stores. They usually come with blue and yellow dots also.
- Other colored dots, pens, paper as requested by students
- Extra blank index cards
- Metric ruler

Time Approximation

One to three 45-minute periods;
Internet/library research can be done in school or outside of class

Preparation

Place a red dot sticker in the center of each index card.

Lesson Outline

The Red Dot Mystery

1. Begin by having students experience the discrepant event. All at once have all students raise their cards so that they can see the red dot. Then have them quickly move the card so that the dot is about 20 cm from their eyes. They should stare at the dot for one minute (keep track of the time so that they don't have to). They should continuously stare at the dot while not moving the card and trying to minimize blinking, as in Figure 8.2.

Figure 8.2. Students Observing Red Dot

2. At the end of one minute have the students flip their cards over and stare at one place on the pure white side. They should see a bluish-green dot.

3. Repeat the process one or two more times until most students have successfully seen the afterimage.

Initial Brainstorming

1. Distribute the student worksheet.

2. Have the students complete the "Initial Brainstorming" section. First have students work alone. Then they discuss and complete questions 2 and 3 in small groups.

3. Lead a class-wide discussion on student ideas for this phenomenon. Find out what their preconceptions are on the eye and color vision. Have the different groups share their hypotheses and predictions. Do not critique the hypotheses. Let students test their validity in the next segment.

Investigations

Student groups design and conduct experiments to test their predictions. Make materials available to them such as blank cards, blue and yellow dots, construction paper, and any other materials they think of.

Web/Library Research

1. Students seek background information on the biology of the eye, neurons, and color vision. This could be a home assignment or completed during class time.

2. Lead another class-wide discussion with students sharing their refined explanations for the afterimage. Challenge students to combine their direct observations with their background research when explaining the phenomenon.

3. Ask for new predictions based on the refined explanations.

Implementation Strategy

- Do not, of course, reveal to the students any of the information found in the Introduction. They need to develop understanding on their own.

- To see the afterimage it is important to hold the card still for the entire minute. It is also important to minimize blinking and to focus solely on the dot for the entire time.

- If a student sees a double image of the red dot during the one-minute stare period, have them adjust the distance from their eye to get to a single image. They should then stare for one minute from that point on.

- Usually most students see the after image, but some do not. Repeat the procedure for a second and even a third time so that at least most will get to experience it.

- Initial student explanations often revolve around previously learned concepts of primary or complementary colors. In discussions at the end of the lesson be sure that these preconceptions have been replaced by an accurate understanding of human color photoreception.

- A graph of the light absorption spectra for human cones is available on a number of Web sites. It is also commonly found in college-level introductory biology texts. If students do not find it on their own, you might make a drawing or transparency to show them.

- Student questions could lead to many possible additional lines of investigation. For instance, what variables effect the duration of the afterimage effect?

Possible Responses for Selected Student Worksheet Questions

See "Introduction" for the information they should find during research.

Follow-Up

3. Many possibilities exist. It is useful primarily for diurnal animals. Advantages could involve detecting/avoiding colored toxic food, finding fruits or flowers for food, finding prey, choosing mates based on plumage, and so on.

Reference

Thompson, R. (1996). Is seeing believing? In *Neuroscience laboratory and classroom activities* (pp. 239-258). Reston, VA: NABT.

Teacher Pages

Red Dot Special

An Investigation Into Color Vision

You have experienced a mystery. You have observed an image of a dot that hadn't been there before and probably isn't there now. Your challenge is to explain this mystery.

Initial Brainstorming

1. What do you know about the human eye? Vision? Color? Record as many things as you can think of below.

   _____

   _____

   _____

   _____

2. Propose a tentative, possible explanation for the red dot mystery. Then get together with lab group partners and exchange your ideas.

   _____

   _____

   _____

   _____

3. Develop two or three testable "if/then" predictions based on your group's ideas.

   _____

   _____

   _____

   _____

   _____

Investigate

1. Using any available materials, your group should conduct experiments to test your predictions. In the space below (or in a lab notebook) record the data from each test.

   _____

   _____

   _____

   _____

   _____

Red Dot Special, *Cont'd.*

2. Summarize the significant results from all the groups' experiments.

_____

_____

_____

_____

3. Based on these findings, propose a new, refined explanation for the red dot mystery.

_____

_____

_____

_____

Web/Library Research

1. Find information on the human eye and color vision that might help you to improve your explanation of the mystery. Summarize significant findings below.

_____

_____

_____

_____

2. Now propose yet another new, improved explanation for the red dot mystery.

_____

_____

_____

_____

Follow-Up

1. You may want to test any new predictions to support your revised explanation.

2. In what ways did your actions/behaviors/thoughts in this lab resemble those of working scientists?

_____

_____

3. What might be the adaptive value of color vision? Why do you think some animals have it and others don't?

_____

_____

The Mozart Effect

Investigating Music and Memory

Students perform experiments of their own design investigating the effects of music on short-term memory.

Topic Connections

Human Memory, the Brain, Scientific Inquiry

Introduction

In 1993 scientists at UC Irvine reported that student performance on an IQ test was improved after listening to Mozart. The results of the small study (thirty-six students) garnered tremendous attention. The media dubbed the result, "The Mozart Effect." In 1998 the governor of Georgia initiated a program to distribute free classical music CDs to the parents of every newborn child in the state. Based on a "Mozart Effect," the governor's plan aimed to improve intellectual development through exposure to classical music. Today, certain Web sites claim that classical music improves intelligence and learning. Some suggest that the music of Mozart but not others is required to produce the enhancement effect. Meanwhile, a number of controlled studies have been conducted that have found no effect whatsoever of music (Mozart or any other) on memory or spatial ability testing. Some researchers have even replicated the original study with larger sample sizes and have found no improvement in the Mozart group. Nevertheless, the Mozart Effect is treated in popular media as absolute truth and Web sites sell Mozart-based programs to increase the intelligence of children.

The underlying hypothesis of the Mozart Effect is that the complexity of his compositions stimulates changes in the brain (the hippocampus) that enhance reasoning ability. In 2004 one of the original researchers reportedly found that exposure to Mozart increased production of three neuron and synapse growth compounds in rats (reported on NewScientist.com). In response to the report, Harvard learning specialist Howard Gardner stated, "It suggests stimulation in general has measurable neurochemical effects, but whether this effect is due to music, let alone Mozart, still has to be determined." Some critics of the Mozart Effect hypothesize that enhanced mood or arousal caused by hearing pleasurable music may temporarily improve test-taking ability. Others feel that the evidence is too insubstantial and contradictory to support a Mozart Effect at all.

In this inquiry students design experiments to test the effects of music on short-term memory. Two simple tests of memory are explained. These can be shown to students as a model of a testing tool for their experiments. While designing, critiquing, performing, and analyzing experiments, students advance their understanding of valid scientific study and they learn to appreciate the complexity and challenges of studying human traits such as memory.

In the second part of the inquiry, "Are You Buying It?," students go online to access readings on the Mozart Effect. After comparing information that supports and contradicts the Mozart Effect, learners are guided to focus on evidence-based arguments. In discussion they consider the importance of repeated, verifiable studies and, hopefully, they construct a better ability to look skeptically at claims based on scant evidence.

Materials

- Personal CD or MP3 players
- Random objects, possibly needed for memory tests
- Dictionaries, possibly needed for making word lists for memory tests
- Stop watch or clock with second hand
- Separate notebooks or lab books for the research results

Time Approximation

- Introductory Discussion and the Research Tool: 20 minutes
- Experimental Design and Feedback: 30 minutes
- Collecting Data: Will vary; can occur in class or outside of class

Preparation

If necessary seek permission from school administrators for students to bring in and use personal CD or MP3 players for the investigation. Then survey students to be sure enough will be available.

Lesson Outline

Introductory Discussion

1. Ask students: "What are the conditions like when you study for a test? What works best for you?" Responses might include music, TV, or silence.

2. Then ask: "What do you know about the effects of music on memory and on learning?" Students might raise common beliefs that those who learn instruments or study music become smarter or do better in school. Some may raise the Mozart Effect. If not, ask if they've heard of it. Do not explain it at this point. If students explain the Mozart Effect as fact be sure to correct them. It is a claim made by some people and not widely accepted by scientists as fact.

The Research Tool

1. Inform students that they will be investigating the effects of music on memory.

2. You might want to show the class one or two ways to test memory. Students could either use these tools or use them as a basis for developing their own.

See "Implementation Strategy" for two examples. Also, a Web search for "short-term memory test" leads to a number of sites with simple online tests.

Experimental Design

1. Inform student groups that they will investigate the effects of music on short-term memory. Ask them to first brainstorm a list of questions that they are interested in. Then they should choose two or three variables that they are most interested in comparing. They might, for example, compare acoustic guitar music to electric guitar to silence or rap to classical music to radio news talk to silence.

2. Next, have them develop an experimental plan.

3. For the feedback session, lead a class-wide discussion in which each group presents their experimental plan. Encourage students to offer constructive critiques of other groups' plans. Also guide groups into realizing major flaws in their designs. There will be many topics to discuss. Many complex variables need to be addressed. See "Implementation Strategy" for some of these.

Collecting Data

Students conduct their experiments. Students could bring in personal CD players or MP3 players with headphones. If school rules prohibit use of these, ask administrators for a one- or two-day biology-class-only waiver. Alternatively, students could collect data outside of class using family or friends as subjects. If so, they should practice and standardize the procedure in class first.

Data Analysis

Student groups discuss their results. Encourage them to calculate means or other mathematical applications. Data should be organized in tables and represented in graphs.

Assessment

Students communicate their findings in written or oral format. See "Assessing Inquiry Investigations" in Chapter One.

The next phase of the inquiry, "Are You Buying It?," should be used before students make final conclusions on their own investigations. In the next phase students learn how even the results of practicing scientists can be overstated and difficult to support. They need to realize that their own experimental results provide *very* tentative beginnings, not definitive answers.

Proceed to the next pages for "Are You Buying It?" or initiate that portion as homework while the investigation portion of the inquiry is occurring.

Implementation Strategy

- Use this lesson in a unit on the human body or animal behavior/learning. Or the lesson works at any time to develop abilities and understandings of scientific inquiry.

- Examples of simple memory tests include:
  1. Set up a grid of sixteen random items, including things like a paper clip, pencil, bottle cap, rubber stopper, and so on. Cover the grid with a box or newspaper. Reveal the grid to the testee for twenty seconds while he or she attempts to memorize it. Cover the grid. The subject attempts to recall the grid of items by writing them on a square of sixteen empty boxes. Further trials could involve random rearrangement of the items and/or similar items. Playing cards could also be used.
  2. Use a dictionary to compile a list of random words of equal complexity and number of syllables. The researcher then either says or shows the subject a series of words to be recalled. It might include ten to fifteen words at once or it could involve a series of two, then four, then six, then eight at a time.
- Some variables that need to be considered when experimenting on human memory:

  Will different subjects be exposed to the different music types? Or will the same subject be tested under all of the experimental conditions?

  How will the tests be made consistently fair for complexity, familiarity, and so on?

  What will be the age, gender, and memory ability of the subject?

  How many trials will be done?

  How will test results be quantified?

  What will the surrounding environment be like during testing?

- The effect of factors other than music could also be investigated. Variables such as distracting sounds, stress (hand in ice water), before/after meal could be used.

Name _____ Date _____

WORKSHEET 8.3
Investigating Music and Memory

Introduction
Your group will investigate the effect of music on human short-term memory. A description of the experimental process follows. You will record your results in a lab book or separate notebook.

The Research Tool
Your teacher may show you one or more simple ways that short-term memory can be measured. You might use one of these methods, or your group might develop its own.

Experimental Design
In your lab group discuss the following:

1. Questions you have about music and its possible effects on memory. Make a list.

2. Two or three musical variables that might effect memory that you would like to investigate.

3. An experimental plan to test your variables. Be prepared to explain your plan to the class. Constructive criticism from the class may help your group improve the experiment. How will you measure the effect of music on memory? Who will you test? How many people will you test? How many times? Consider other factors to control.

Collecting Data
Your group will conduct your experiments. Develop a system for recording your data in an organized, logical way.

Data Analysis
After experimenting you will analyze your data. Use math to make more sense out of your data. Make graphs of your data. Discuss and attempt to explain your results.

Report
You will report on your experiments and results in the manner described by the teacher. Address the following questions in your conclusions:

- Can you explain your results?

- What part of the brain might be involved?

- What alternative explanations are there for your results?

- How confident are you of your results?

- What could be done to your experimental plan to increase your confidence?

- If you had unlimited time and materials, what would you do to investigate your experimental question?

The Mozart Effect
Are You Buying It?

Students research and evaluate conflicting data and claims involving the Mozart Effect.

Topic Connections
Scientific Inquiry, Skepticism, the Brain

Introduction
This is the second phase of the inquiry initiated in *The Mozart Effect: Investigating Music and Memory*. See the "Introduction" for that lesson for general information on the topic. This portion of the inquiry provides an opportunity to compare evidence that supports and contradicts the Mozart Effect. Students are challenged to weigh evidence and use it in making sound conclusions. Generalizations are raised as to how people can decide the merits of claims heard in popular media. It is hoped that students leave the inquiry with an improved appreciation for the role of skepticism in both scientific and everyday thinking.

The lesson consists of three sequential discussion sessions and a Web research phase. It could be completed as one long lesson or broken down into segments over two or three days.

Materials
World Wide Web access

Time Approximation
- The original study: 20 minutes
- Web research: Will vary; could be in class or homework.
- Discussion of findings: 20 minutes
- Further studies: 20 minutes
- Reflection: Can be done outside of class

Lesson Outline
The lesson is based on readings and discussions. Either distribute the worksheet as a guide and a place for student written responses or use the questions to facilitate the different discussions. The summary of the original study could, for example, be transcribed onto an overhead transparency and then discussed.

The Original Study
1. Students read the summary of the original study. Alternatively, the one-page *Nature* letter in which the experiment was reported could be acquired and distributed to students to read.

Teacher Pages

2. In small groups students discuss the questions about the experiment and the researchers' conclusions.

3. Lead a class-wide discussion of student ideas for these questions. Be sure to discuss that biologists never "prove" hypotheses (see "Possible Responses to Worksheet Questions").

Web Research

1. In school or at home students read Web sources on the Mozart Effect. They should find and read two or three on each side of the issue. To be sure that they find opposing views, recommend that they search for "The Mozart Effect" and also for "The Mozart Effect skeptic."

2. Students collect evidence that supports the idea and evidence that does not. Either before or after this, discuss with students the difference between "evidence" and "claims."

3. Lead a discussion in which students share information found on Web sites. Facilitate some debate on the value of some of the information based on its source, support, credibility, and so on. Solicit and discuss student opinions on the case for the Mozart Effect.

Further Studies

1. Introduce the information on the 1995 and 1999 studies as discussed in the worksheet. This could be done in class or at home. Advanced students could read the original 1999 paper. It is relatively jargon free.

2. Lead a discussion on the topics addressed in the worksheet questions for this section.

Reflection

1. Students respond to the questions on the worksheet. Be sure to either read or discuss these with students to determine whether the goals of the lesson have been achieved.

2. At some point ask students to connect what they have learned in this lesson to the conclusions they made for their own experiments in "The Mozart Effect: Investigating Music and Memory." Help them realize how very tentative their results were and guide them to understanding the need for much scrutiny and further study before confident conclusions can be made.

Implementation Strategy

- Use this lesson after or in conjunction with the preceding lesson, "The Mozart Effect: Investigating Music and Memory."

- The Web site SkepDic.com provides a good summary of the case against the Mozart Effect, or at least against the conclusions that some have made despite a lack of replicated evidence.

References

Rauscher, F., Shaw, G., & Ky, K. (1993). Music and spatial task performance. *Nature, 365,* 611.

Rauscher, F., Shaw, G., & Ky, K. (1995). Listening to Mozart enhances spatial temporal reasoning. *Neuroscience Letters, 185,* 44–47.

NewScientist.com. (2004, April). *Molecular basis for Mozart effect revealed.* A news report of a presentation given at a neuroscience symposium by F. Rauscher.

Steele, K., Bass, K., & Crook, M. (1999). The mystery of the Mozart effect: Failure to replicate. *Psychological Science, 10,* 366–369.

Possible Responses to Student Worksheet Questions

The Original Study

1. A very small sample size. Accept other possibilities. The point is to get them thinking critically about an experiment.

2. Maybe the relaxation tape and silence *impaired* testing ability instead of Mozart enhancing it.

3. No. Biologists never *prove* anything. Experiments can produce evidence to *support* hypotheses, but science is tentative. Explanations are often modified in light of further evidence. The results of one small experiment like this could be regarded as potentially interesting and cause for further study, but it should never have led to the uncritical acceptance and bold claims that it did.

Web Research

1. More studies have found no "Mozart Effect" than ones that support it. Some Web sites make claims but offer no evidence. Encourage students to be skeptical of claims that "research shows . . ." or "science has found that . . ." in the absence of cited research results. Also, the most credible sites will discuss research results from both sides of the issue. Research results are generally considered more credible if they are originally published in a peer-reviewed scientific journal, although it is difficult for students to know which sources are and which are not.

2. In general, the hypothesis is that complex music stimulates chemical releases that promote neuron growth, synaptic connection, or otherwise improved brain function. The hypothesis certainly sounds potentially plausible, but that alone does not make it true!

Further Evidence

1. One of the studies could be flawed in its design, implementation, or interpretation. Random chance might have led to unusual results not representative of true patterns.

2. In such cases it is difficult for a layperson to know what to think. Specialists may have a better understanding of the reputations of the researchers involved, the validity of the techniques used, and so on. Generally, we should conclude that much more research needs to be done before any strong conclusions can be made.

3. No. A lack of evidence *for* something does not negate its possible existence. We may not have been able to experimentally observe a phenomenon yet. Science acknowledges that future evidence may (and often does) lead us to modify explanations. But still, we can't decide that a phenomenon does exist unless there is sufficient evidence.

4. Difficult to answer. There is no magic quantity, but the more evidence, the more confidence in an idea.

Reflection

1. Responses to this question will reveal the extent to which the lesson was successful. By this point students should have constructed an understanding that the Mozart Effect commercial industry is based on ideas that, while intriguing as possibilities, are supported by thin evidence that has been unverifiable to anyone other than the original researchers.

2. A very important role for both science and everyday life, as long as it is tempered by reason.

3. Many possibilities.

WORKSHEET 8.4
Are You Buying It?

Introduction

In 1993 researchers at the University of California, Irvine, reported that college students performed better on an IQ test after listening to Mozart. The study captured tremendous attention in the news and was referred to by the media as "The Mozart Effect." Today a number of Web sites sell Mozart-based programs that they claim will improve intelligence, memory, and learning. But what evidence supports these claims? The Mozart Effect is highly controversial. You will explore information on the topic to decide whether it has any merit.

The Original Study

Read the following summary of the original study and then respond to the questions that follow. Be prepared to discuss the questions in small groups and with the class.

Method

- Thirty-six college students as subjects
- Each given an IQ pretest (a partial test called a "task") to assure they used students of "equivalent capabilities"
- Each later given three IQ tests under three different conditions
- One IQ task taken immediately after hearing ten minutes of Mozart
- One IQ task taken immediately after hearing ten minutes of "relaxation" New Age music
- One IQ task taken immediately after ten minutes of silence

Results

After Mozart, student IQ scores were 8 to 9 points higher than after relaxation music or silence. Researchers concluded that the Mozart music temporarily enhanced abstract reasoning ability.

Questions

1. Based on the information given, can you think of any possible flaws or weaknesses in the experimental design?

   _____

   _____

   _____

   _____

   _____

Are You Buying It?, *Cont'd.*

2. Can you think of any possible alternative conclusions for the results of the experiment?

_____

_____

_____

3. Does the experiment *prove* that Mozart music enhances reasoning ability? How much weight should be given to the results of a single experiment such as this?

_____

_____

_____

Web Research

Find and read a number of Web sources for information on the Mozart Effect. Try to find equal numbers of sites that support the idea and those that are critical of the idea. Fill in the evidence table below as you read the sites. Then respond to the questions that follow.

Table 8.1. Evidence Table

Evidence Supporting the Mozart Effect	Evidence Not Supporting the Mozart Effect

Are You Buying It?, *Cont'd.*

1. Which is stronger—the case for the Mozart Effect or the case against it? Explain.

   _____

   _____

   _____

   _____

   _____

2. What is the underlying biological, brain-based hypothesis for a possible Mozart Effect? Does it sound reasonable? If so, does that make it true? Explain.

   _____

   _____

   _____

   _____

   _____

Further Evidence

In 1995 the original researchers repeated their experiment but they used seventy-nine college students divided among the three experimental conditions. Again, they reported temporary enhanced reasoning ability in only the Mozart group. However, soon after, at least seven studies by other researchers failed to find any "Mozart Effect." Then in 1999 researchers used 125 college students to copy the 1995 experimental procedure as closely as possible. Their results showed no improvement in IQ tasks whatsoever after listening to Mozart.

1. How could two studies using the same methods produce such very different results?

   _____

   _____

   _____

   _____

   _____

2. When two or more research studies produce conflicting results what should we conclude?

   _____

   _____

   _____

   _____

Are You Buying It?, *Cont'd.*

3. Does conflicting evidence on "The Mozart Effect" mean that it doesn't exist? Explain.

    _____

    _____

    _____

    _____

4. How much research evidence is *enough* to make an idea accepted by scientists and acceptable to people?

    _____

    _____

    _____

    _____

Reflection

1. What is your opinion of the claim that listening to certain types of music improves reasoning ability, memory and intelligence? Explain. Should people spend money on Mozart tapes specifically to improve brain function?

    _____

    _____

    _____

    _____

    _____

2. What is the role of skepticism in science? What role should skepticism play in everyday life?

    _____

    _____

    _____

    _____

3. What are some other claims made in popular media culture or advertisements that you might be skeptical of? Explain why.

    _____

    _____

    _____

    _____

Chapter 9

Science in Personal and Social Perspectives

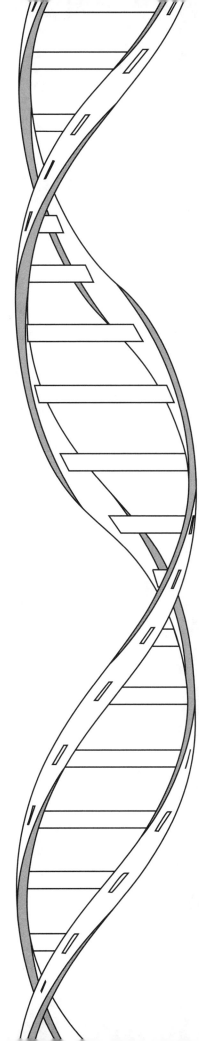

This chapter is based on a content standard that, like Inquiry, is common to all grade levels. Some of the concepts in this standard include personal and community health, natural resources, environmental quality, and science/technology in local, natural and global challenges. The entries in the chapter include an inquiry investigation of sunscreen effectiveness, a broad plan for studying a local natural resource (such as a watershed) and generic plans for writing about, discussing and formally debating bioethical/biosocial issues.

Putting SPF to the Test

In this inquiry lab, students design experiments to compare the effectiveness of various sunscreens.

Topic Connections

Scientific Inquiry, Ozone Depletion, Environmental Issues, Skin Cancer

Introduction

With publicity about thinning stratospheric ozone has come heightened public awareness of the mutagenic effects of excessive ultraviolet light exposure. Exposure to U.V. radiation has been associated with melanoma, cataracts, and premature skin aging. Consequently, sunscreen use has increased, and there has been a proliferation of "sun-blocking" products advertising various levels of U.V. ray protection.

Sodium azide, "blueprint" paper is sensitive to ultraviolet radiation. When exposed to U.V. light, the paper turns from yellow to white. The light source intensity influences the rate of the color change. Outside on a sunny day the paper may go entirely white in a few seconds. Exposed only to the ambient lighting of a classroom, the paper may take a few minutes or longer to change.

This inquiry uses blueprint paper as an indicator of relative U.V. exposure. The paper is introduced to the students as a research tool for investigating sunscreens. Students are prompted to ask their own questions and design experiments to answer them. Along the way student groups encounter a variety of experimental problems to be solved and methodologies to be refined.

Materials

- Wide variety of sunscreen products (see "Preparation")
- Light source: access to outdoors, windows, plant grow lights, or classroom lights (if none of the others are available)
- Sodium azide "blueprint" paper available at art stores; often, technical drawing or industrial arts teachers have it and will share some
- Scissors
- Lab books or notebooks for recording results
- Available in classroom for possible use but not specifically presented to students:

  Petri dishes;

  clear overhead transparency film;

  microscope slides;

  small boxes;

  stopwatches or digital watches)

Time Approximation

One 90-minute lab period

Preparation

A few days before the lab ask students to bring in a bottle of sunscreen or two from home. Mark the bottles with student initials to facilitate return after the lab. This should provide you with a wide variety of sunscreen types. If not, purchase as many sunscreens as you can of varying SPFs and brands.

To obtain blueprint paper, check with your local industrial arts or technical drawing teacher to see whether you can have a few sheets. Otherwise purchase it from a local art supply store.

Keep the blueprint paper in the dark. Keep it enclosed in black plastic. When dispensing to students, turn the room lights off and keep the paper upside down. Give each lab group one-eighth to one-fourth of a page. Warn them to be conservative with their use of the paper.

Have some possible experimental materials handy in the room, but do not point them out to students.

Safety Precautions

Caution students to wash their hands thoroughly after handling sunscreens. Warn them not to touch their eyes until they have completely washed the sunscreen off their hands.

Lesson Outline

The Introduction

1. Arrange all of the sunscreens at the front of the room. Initiate a discussion to determine what students know about ozone depletion, ultraviolet light, and skin cancer.

   Introduce a variety of sunscreens by reading their labels. Poke fun at some of the exaggerated claims made by some of them. Ask the students which they would use. Ask how one is to decide when there are so many types claiming so many features.

2. Show the class a small piece of blueprint paper. Hold it close to light so that they see it change color. Tell them that this will be a tool for them to investigate the effectiveness of various sunscreens.

3. Tell students that sunscreen cannot go directly on the paper. They must come up with a way to test them.

4. Show them how much blueprint paper they will receive for the first round of experiments.

Experimental Design

1. In lab groups students come up with a question to investigate.

2. Students then develop a hypothesis and an experimental plan.

3. In a class-wide discussion each group shares their question, hypothesis, and experimental plan with the class. Students offer critiques and suggestions for improvement to other groups. You might lead students to discovering problems in their experiment by asking pointed questions, or problems can be left to be discovered the hard way and discussed after the fact.

The Experiment

1. Hand out supplies and allow students to carry out investigations.

2. Experimental problems encountered are discussed. Revised experiments are carried out.

3. Successful experiments are repeated for verification.

Data Analysis

Students discuss and interpret their results and record them in their notebooks.

Assessment

See "Assessing Inquiry Investigation" in Chapter One. Student reports could be oral, written, or by miniposter.

Since this inquiry will involve a variety of different experiments and outcomes, it would be ideal for group presentations to the class—either orally or via miniposters.

Implementation Strategy

- One of the biggest experimental challenges faced by students is how to get the sunscreen between the blueprint paper and the light source. Tell the students NOT to put the sunscreen directly on the paper because it will interfere with the color change. But *do not* give them any suggestions as to how they should do it. They should struggle with the problem until they come up with an idea that works. Some possibilities include:

    Paper inside petri dishes with sunscreen on top of the dish cover

    Paper beneath microscope slides that have the sunscreen smeared on them

    Paper beneath blank overhead transparency film that has the sunscreens on it

- Initial student experiments will probably fail for a variety of reasons. Reinforce to students that it is OK and a normal part of scientific inquiry. Challenge them to continually improve their experimental design and try again until their methodology and results stand up to the scrutiny of you and their classmates.

- First experiments often result in all experimental papers turning completely white (especially if performed outside). Students learn from this that they must shorten the light exposure time in order to discriminate among those papers changing significantly and those not as much.

- If testing outdoors, students will need to devise a method of preventing light exposure while transporting their experiments from the classroom to the testing site.

- Some possible investigations:

  Comparing the effectiveness of different brands rated at the same SPF

  Comparing different SPFs of the same brand

  Comparing children's sunscreen to nonspecified of the same SPF

  Comparing waterproof to nonspecified

  Comparing oil to lotion

- There are many variables to be controlled in the student experiments. Encourage groups to critique each other's designs for problems with uncontrolled variables.

- Most experiments will yield qualitative results that involve comparing the extent of color change in the paper beneath the different sunscreens. You might also challenge groups to devise a way to quantify their results, perhaps by measuring the time it takes for the paper to change to white beneath a sunscreen.

Copyright © 2006 by John Wiley & Sons, Inc.

WORKSHEET 9.1
Putting SPF to the Test

Introduction

Thinning ozone has in recent years focused attention on the importance of shielding your skin from harmful U.V. rays. Shopping for sunscreen, however, can be a daunting task. There are many different brands, SPFs (sun protection factors) ranging from 0 to 45, and numerous other product claims to sort through. In this inquiry you will ask and then investigate a question pertaining to sunscreen products and their claims. You will use blueprint paper (sodium azide paper) as an indicator of U.V. light exposure. Blueprint paper quickly fades from yellow to white when exposed to sunlight.

Your Task

To experimentally answer a question of your own concerning the effectiveness of sunscreen products. Be sure to focus on only one variable and to control all other variables. You might investigate SPF claims or a comparison of brands or. . . .

Experimental Design and Data Collection

1. Your group should decide on an experimental question to pursue.

2. Formulate a hypothesis and prediction and record it in your notebook.

3. Design (with words and a sketch) an experiment to address your question.

4. During a feedback session, each group will briefly share their question and experimental plan with the class. Other groups and the teacher will offer constructive criticism and suggestions.

5. Data collection: Set up and perform your experiments. If needed, carry out second, third, and fourth trials. . . . Make modifications as necessary.

6. Analyze data and draw conclusions; discuss within your group.

Report

The teacher will assign the method of communicating/reporting your experimental findings. Incorporate your Web/book research findings into your conclusions and discussions of your investigation.

Background Research

Using Web or book resources find information on sunscreens (How do they work?); ozone depletion (causes and consequences); and ultraviolet radiation.

Other Questions to Consider in Your Report

- How confident are you of your experimental results?

- What improvements would you make to your experimental approach if you had more time and materials?

Watershed Investigations

A general approach for student investigation of local streams and rivers. Easily adaptable to other bodies of water.

Topic Connections

Ecology, Aquatic Organisms, Pollution, Scientific Inquiry

Introduction

Local ecosystems provide rich opportunities for student inquiry. As possible resources for water supply and recreation, local aquatic ecosystems are especially relevant and important to the lives of students. This entry provides a highly adaptable guide for investigating local streams and rivers. The full inquiry yields ample experiences for learners to ask and refine their own questions, to collect, analyze, and explain evidence, and to communicate research results and explanations.

Many options exist for collecting data on streams and rivers, but they can be partitioned into the categories of *physical* and *biological*. Physical data includes temperature, pH, turbidity, flow rate, and quantities of chemicals such as dissolved oxygen, phosphates, nitrogen compounds, chlorine, and so on. Biological data includes coliform bacteria counts, types of algae present, and species of macroinvertebrates such as fly larvae, crayfish, and aquatic worms. Through its Save Our Streams programs, the Isaak Walton League has developed a simple system of assessing stream water quality based on macroinvertebrate populations (see "Collecting Field Data"). Equipment for student use might include seine nets, dip nets, plankton nets, thermometers, pH paper/meters, and test kits or probes for measuring chemical quantities. Of course the data collected and equipment used will vary depending on availability, suitability, and student/teacher interests. Some interesting data can also be collected on local tap water. Some biological data can be collected with only minimal need for nets. Generally though, the best student experiences will involve at least one day of collecting data in the field.

Local streams can be assessed for water quality. Different streams can be compared, and different portions of a single stream can be compared with data analyzed by students. Data variations over time or by location are explained by students. They research, consider, and discuss possible natural and human impacts on their data. Also student data can be collected in an ongoing database that allows for monitoring of stream/river conditions over time. Students appreciate that they are doing "real science" in this inquiry by collecting meaningful data on a local resource.

This inquiry guide is broken down into three phases: "Introductory Lessons," "Collecting Data," and "Explaining and Communicating."

Introductory Lessons

In these lessons students use topographic maps to identify elements of the local watershed. They consider what they know about local waters. They grapple with questions on defining pollution and recognizing water quality. They make predictions on the water quality of the watershed. They develop and refine questions to investigate.

Materials

- For "The Swamp Water Challenge": Beakers, four (one must be new for drinking out of), cola, raisins, banana
- For "Topo Twister": USGS Topographical maps, 7.5 minute, 1:24,000 scale quadrangle series. Obtain five to fifteen of the local watershed (the more the better).

Preparation

For "The Swamp Water Challenge": Fill one beaker with tap water. Fill one with clean-looking aquarium water (if this is not available, use tap water and tell the students it is aquarium water). Fill a third beaker with greenish or brownish algae or swamp water (any water that has been colored by a natural source). In the last beaker create a concoction that looks disgusting. Try to make it look like sewage, but use things that you can consume during the demo. Diluted iced tea or diluted flat soda is a good start. Add unrecognizable solid fragments like crushed raisin pieces and small pieces of banana. The raisin fragments will settle to the bottom while the banana fragments will float. A touch of chocolate syrup might add some thickness.

For "Topo Twister": Obtain topographical maps from the USGS (www.usgs.gov) or outdoor stores. Consider laminating the maps for future use.

Time Approximation

- "The Swamp Water Challenge": 20 minutes
- "Topo Twister": 30 minutes
- For other parts, the time will vary

Lessons That Can Be Used Early in the Watershed Inquiry

1. Lead an exploratory discussion on the local stream/river/watershed. Ask students what they know about it, their impressions, if they would drink from it, if they would swim in it, if they would eat fish from it, and so on. For all responses ask the students to explain their reasoning. Ask them to back up any claims about water quality with evidence.

2. Lead a discussion on pollution. Challenge students to define the term. Have them research definitions.

The Swamp Water Challenge

1. Have the four beakers on display at the front of the room, but don't let the students get too close. Do not tell them what the liquids are. Just explain that these are four local water samples. Ask them to look at the beakers

(from their seats) and decide which one(s) they would like to drink. Hold up the tap water beaker and ask a couple of students if they would like to drink it, but, of course, do not let them. Repeat this with the aquarium water, the algae water, and finally—with much fanfare—the disgusting-looking water. Next ask the students which of the beakers they would have you drink if they could. They will choose the last beaker, and you will shock them by taking a hearty swig of "sewage" water.

2. Ask the students what the point/message of the demonstration is. Lead them to realize that you cannot assess water quality by appearance alone. Many students harbor the misconception that clear water is clean (unpolluted) and water with color is somehow degraded. In reality, many unpolluted bodies of water are brown from tannins, green from algae, or cloudy with natural sediment. On the other hand, crystal-clear water systems may contain pathogenic microorganisms or colorless toxins such as arsenic or PCBs. Some of the cleanest-looking lakes are those completely devoid of life because of acid rain.

3. Lead the discussion toward the question: How can we judge the quality of water? Solicit and discuss their ideas.

Topo Twister

1. Bring the class to an area with enough floor space to spread out the topo maps. Give them all of the topos for the watershed and challenge them to piece them all together accurately.

2. Lead a discussion on the whole watershed map. Ask students to make observations about variations in human developments, natural areas, and so on. Ask them to trace the path of water through various parts of the watershed.

3. Ask students where their tap water comes from (if they haven't already asked you!). Ask them where their waste water goes. Have some students research this information by calling local municipal agencies.

Student Questions

Throughout these early lessons, students will generate many questions. Focus their questions now on possible investigations. What aspects of the watershed are they curious about? What would they like to research? How could they obtain answers to their questions? What would be sufficient as evidence to address their questions? Guide discussion of the questions to focus on achievable projects. This will depend on the accessibility/safety of sampling field sites and availability of equipment.

Collecting Field Data

This phase of the inquiry will vary widely depending on local circumstances.

The best situation involves at least one whole-day field trip. Incorporate student input into site choices as much as possible, but the accessibility and safety of sites will of course trump other considerations.

Visit multiple sites. Sites that vary in their characteristics make for interesting analysis. Students collect data on chemical and biological parameters. Data-collecting procedures are too varied and extensive to get into here, but see the following resources for guidance.

Resources

Isaak Walton League of America (www.iwla.org), Save Our Streams Program:
Hands on Save Our Streams-The SOS Teachers Manual (215 pages)
S.O.S. for America's Streams—A Guide to Water Quality Monitoring (28-minute video)
Field Guide to Aquatic Macroinvertebrates
Global Rivers Environmental Education Network (www.green.org):
Field Guide for Water Quality Monitoring
The Network also sell nets, chemical test kits, and other materials.

Consider contacting a local nature center or environmental organization. These groups may have a naturalist or researcher who could join your field trip to help with data-collecting techniques and field identification.

Materials

Will vary tremendously; see the "Watershed Field Trip Checklist" for possibilities.

Preparation

Visit potential field trip sites ahead of time to assess their suitability and safety.

Make a field trip handout that includes an itinerary, student checklist (see the example), macroinvertebrate key (Isaak Walton League "Bug Chart" for easy classification), and data tables. See the student worksheet for sample data pages.

An interesting side trip would be a visit to a local water treatment plant or sewage treatment facility.

Watershed Field Trip Checklist

Each Individual

_____ Sturdy footwear (that can get wet, muddy), hiking boots, old sneakers . . .

_____ Lunch

_____ Raincoat, hat, warm clothes (layers)

_____ Clipboard, field trip packet with data tables, pen

_____ Sunblock, insect repellent?

_____ Waders or rubber boots (if people have access to)

The Class

_____ Seine net (for fish)

_____ Kick seine net (for macro-invertebrates in streams)

_____ Dip nets (for organisms in any aquatic location)

_____ Field unit for data sensors (such as Pasco or Vernier)

_____ D.O., pH, temp sensors (or test kits, pH paper, thermometers)

_____ Chemical test kits (Hach or Lamotte) for phosphates, nitrates, chlorine, iron, hardness, turbidity

_____ Pie plates

_____ Bug viewing boxes, hand lenses

_____ Plastic pails, water collection jugs (to bring samples back to school)

_____ Garbage bags

_____ GPS receiver to determine latitude and longitude of sampling locations

Explaining and Communicating

In this phase of the inquiry, students analyze and explain their data. Working in small groups they discuss their data. In general there are two organizing elements here. First, for every piece of data, what does it mean? If, for example, a dissolved oxygen reading for a site is 8.4, then what does that tell us about the water at that site? Does it indicate clean or degraded conditions? High or low quantities of waste? Of bacteria? Is it a reflection of water surface area or temperature? Challenge the students to discuss and explain every piece of data.

Second, all variations should be explained. If one site has a higher D.O. than another, then what is the reason for that?

Throughout this phase students will need to consult with books, Web sites, or other resources. They may want to check for state water quality standards as well as E.P.A. Web postings. They may need to refer to local topo maps again to look for possible sources of water quality impacts.

At this point data often points to new questions. A question might arise about the impact of a local industry or sewage treatment plant, for example. The class or small groups can focus in on more specific investigations in this way. Such topics also lend themselves to senior projects or independent studies by students.

Time Approximation

Time will vary. Much can be completed outside of class, but some time should be provided for group discussion/analysis of data.

Assessment

Data and explanations should be communicated by students in written and/or oral form. Many students have difficulty effectively discussing data. They tend to state conclusions without actually citing their evidence. Encourage them to cite and explain their data when assessing the water quality of a site and when comparing the quality of different sites.

If student data is substantial, consider having them present their findings at a local environmental commission meeting.

References

"The Swamp Water Challenge" was written by the author and first appeared in B. Bilash & M. Shields. (2001). *A demo a day biology: A year of biological demonstrations* (p. 282). Batavia, IL: Flinn Scientific.

"Topo Twister" comes from the *New Jersey WATERS* curriculum of the New Jersey Audubon Society (www.njaudubon.org).

Name _____   Date _____

Watershed Investigations

Use the following data table to organize the information you collect.

Table 9.1. Watershed Data Table

Site Name Latitude Longitude				
Dissolved oxygen				
Iron				
Ammonium				
Nitrogen				
Phosphate				

Watershed Investigations, *Cont'd.*

Table 9.1. Watershed Data Table *(Cont'd)*

Chlorine					
pH					
Temperature					
Odor					
Color					
Turbidity					
Solids— floating, settled, suspended					
Coliform bacteria					

Team members: _____

Watershed Investigations, *Cont'd.*

Use the following data sheet to organize the information you collect.

Table 9.2. River Data Sheet: Biological Observations

Site:

_____

Plants:

Submerged:

Floating:

_____

Algae:

Attached:

Planktonic:

_____

Zooplankton:

Watershed Investigations, *Cont'd.*

Table 9.2. River Data Sheet: Biological Observations *(Cont'd)*

Macroinvertebrates (see key):

Group 1:

Group 2:

Group 3:

Others:

Vertebrates:

Fish:

Others:

Consider the Issues

Students develop, express, and discuss informed opinions on a variety of personal, ethical, and societal issues throughout a biology course.

Topic Connections

Various Biology Topics, Values Clarification, Science/Technology/Society

Introduction

Rarely does a week pass without a new biological advance making newspaper headlines. Genetically engineered fluorescing monkeys, extended life span genes, cloning, stem cells, biodiversity loss, genetic profiles, and so on. Biology is exciting. In its impact on society, biology is fresh and provocative. It is relevant to our lives and, although they don't expect it, to the lives of teenagers.

Adolescents crave opportunities to develop and express opinions. By creating and arguing a point of view, a young person travels further along the path of self-creation and identity formation. Biology becomes meaningful to students when they use its words and concepts in the creation of a system of values.

This lesson plan goes beyond the brief beginning or end-of-class discussion. The procedure explained here provides every student an opportunity for independent written expression in a journal or short essay and then public expression via an entire class-period discussion. The issues discussed in these lessons deserve central positioning in the curriculum. They deserve to have significant time devoted to them. After all, what is more valuable to our students—understanding and forming an opinion on stem cells, germ line genetic therapy, and genetic profiles *or* memorizing the stages of mitosis? Most of our students will not major in biology at college. But all will be members of our participatory democracy. All will be needed for a thoughtful societal dialogue on critical issues in biotechnology and the environment.

The lesson plan is generic and can be included in every teaching unit of a biology course. In addition to values clarification, the lessons reveal content misconceptions and promote construction of deeper, more accurate biology understanding.

Materials

Journal (composition book) is optional

Time Approximation

- Issue Introduction: Time will vary; if it is a reading, then it can be completed as homework
- Journal Writing: 15 to 20 minutes, either in class or as homework
- Class Discussion: 30 to 45 minutes

Lesson Outline

Issue Introduction

There are varied ways to introduce the issue. Newspaper and popular newsmagazine articles usually do a good job of summarizing an issue and any opposing viewpoints. Videos or segments of TV newscasts/documentaries also work well. Sometimes the class previously has learned enough about an issue to simply begin at the next step.

Personal Opinion Development

In a journal or on the student worksheet learners write their response to the question/topic you will pose. Responses should reflect serious thought and consideration/incorporation of biological facts and theories. Be clear to students that they will not be graded based on their opinions. There are no right or wrong answers.

Class Discussion

1. Arrange the class in a circle. This facilitates student-student discussion, removes you as the focal point, and changes what is probably the routine for the class.

2. Call on students one at a time to express their opinions on the issue. Proceed around the circle in order to involve as many students as possible. With a large class, you probably will want to open the discussion up before getting to every student, and by about halfway through a large class most of the possible angles on the issue will have been raised and it becomes more fruitful to facilitate discussion of disagreements.

3. Now call on students who want to comment on issues raised by other students. Before initiating this phase, remind the class that personal attacks are not acceptable. Instead, students should critique facts and express disagreement as a personal point of view.

4. Often the students will steer the discussion into related or subcategory issues. Sometimes you might ask them to hold off on these until after a current topic has been thoroughly discussed. At other times it might be welcome.

5. Have some questions ready to raise related issues if the students do not. For example, for a discussion of deer overpopulation, secondary questions might be: "Do humans have a responsibility to control populations of wildlife?" or "Is it OK to be against hunting if you eat meat?"

Final Reflection

Many students' opinions will change as they develop better understanding of the issue by modifying preconceptions and considering new information. Provide a mechanism for crystallizing the new understanding and opinion via a final writing on the issue.

Assessment

It is recommended that opinion-based journal-type writings not be numerically or letter graded. Consider using a credit/no credit/partial credit system based on whether a serious effort was made for the assignment.

Implementation Strategy

- Students will often want to know the teacher's opinion on controversial issues. It is best to hold your opinion, at least until after the writings and discussions are finished. Voicing your opinion might influence students into saying what they think you want to hear. A goal of all teachers should be to develop independent thinking in their students.

- Stress repeatedly that there are no right or wrong answers for these issues. Stress the expectation that students give thoughtful consideration to the issues and that they weigh costs, benefits, risks, and alternatives.

- Before the class discussions, remind students that they are expressing personal opinions. They can respectfully express disagreement with other opinions, but do not under any circumstances tolerate personal attacks on students for their opinions.

- Some teachers avoid controversial topics in the classroom, fearing parent or administrator reprisals, but there should be no such fear as long as you with-hold your own opinion and it is clear that all opinion-based expressions will not be criticized, attacked, or graded.

- Although *opinions* should not be criticized, it is essential for students and the teacher to critique misunderstandings of biology. Student opinions should be supported by accurate knowledge. If they are not at first, then the discussions provide opportunity for improving and modifying biological understanding.

- Students need a foundation of content knowledge in order to make informed decisions. Thus these lesson are often most appropriate for use at the end of a unit of study. Also content research can be incorporated into the lesson plan at any stage.

A list of possible topics is given in Table 9.3 below.

Table 9.3. Possible Issue Topics

Question to Pose	Unit of Study
Is there a deer overpopulation problem? What should be done?	Ecology
Is there a bear overpopulation problem? Should they be hunted?	Ecology
Is there a human overpopulation problem? What, if anything, should be done?	Ecology
Should research on human cloning be allowed? Federally funded? Therapeutic cloning? Reproductive cloning?	Cell Division, Reproduction
Should research on embryonic stem cells be allowed? Should it be federally funded?	Cells, Cell Division, Embryology

Table 9.3. Possible Issue Topics *(Cont'd)*

Question to Pose	Unit of Study
Should we clone endangered animal species?	Cell Division, Conservation
Should we attempt to clone extinct species such as the wooly mammoth?	Cell Division, Conservation
Should we genetically modify food products?	DNA, Genetics, Biotechnology
Should the F.D.A. require genetically modified (G.M.) foods to be labeled as such?	DNA, Genetics, Biotechnology
Should people choose the gender of their children?	Genetics, Biotechnology
If one of your parents had Huntington's Disease, would you get tested to see if you had the gene? Also would you have children if you carried (or could possibly carry) the gene?	Genetics, Biotechnology
Should people use gene therapy to modify their offspring (embryos)? For any reasons? Would certain types of improvements be OK? If so, where should the line be drawn?	Genetics, Biotechnology
Do people have a responsibility to society to determine whether they carry harmful mutations?	Genetics
Would you want to see a genetic profile of yourself that possibly indicated alleles associated with heightened risk for future health problems?	Genetics
Should insurance companies or potential employers have access to a person's genetic profile?	Genetics
If prenatal testing indicated that you/your spouse carried a fetus with Down Syndrome would you want to continue with the pregnancy? What about for cystic fibrosis?	Genetics
Write a campaign statement on acid rain as if you were running for office in the Midwest . . . and in the Adirondacks of New York. Are the two statements different? Should they be?	Chemistry
What should be done to curb carbon dioxide emissions? What should individuals such as yourself do?	Chemistry, Cellular Respiration, Ecology
Should animal organs be harvested for transplant into humans?	Vertebrate Body Systems
If biotechnology developed a way to dramatically increase the average human lifespan (to 100? 120? 140?) would you want to extend your life?	Biotechnology, Cells, DNA

Name _____ Date _____

Consider the Personal/Societal Issues

Question/topic:_____

Your Task
Develop and write an informed response to the issue. What is your opinion? Be sure to explain your reasoning. As much as possible back up your statement with evidence or biology knowledge. Your understanding of biological concepts may be constructively criticized, but your opinions will not be criticized. There are no "right" or "wrong" answers to the questions—just opinions based on knowledge and values.

_____

_____

_____

_____

_____

_____

_____

_____

_____

_____

_____

_____

_____

_____

_____

_____

_____

_____

_____

_____

_____

_____

_____

_____

_____

Consider the Personal/Societal Issues, *Cont'd.*

Final Reflection

How has your thinking changed on the issue after the class discussion and/or further research on the topic? What aspects of the underlying biology do you better understand now?

_____

_____

_____

_____

_____

_____

_____

_____

_____

_____

_____

_____

What were the most compelling arguments/pieces of information that led you to either alter your thinking or become more confident in your opinion?

_____

_____

_____

_____

_____

_____

_____

_____

_____

_____

_____

_____

_____

_____

Debating Biological/Societal Topics

Students choose, research, and debate various controversial biosocial issues.

Topic Connections

Various Biology Topics, Science/Technology/Society, Informed Decision Making

Introduction

Some of the most important and engaging topics in biology are those that interface with society in ethical, legal, or otherwise controversial ways. Debate projects provide a way for students to deepen their understanding of such topics. While researching an issue, debaters learn significant biological content. And they learn the nuances of ethical, legal, economic, and political implications of the biology/society interaction.

In this project student teams of two or three choose a topic, along with another team against whom they will debate. The groups are given a number of weeks to thoroughly research and prepare their arguments. The debate fills an entire class period. Thus, a class of twenty-four could have either four or six debates depending on team size. Each debate covers a different topic, so the class is exposed to a variety of topical issues.

Students benefit by acquiring, processing, and organizing the content knowledge necessary to argue a point of view in a debate. Presenting and defending a position promotes deeper understanding than that experienced through passive learning. When observing other debates, students take notes to keep them focused and to help them develop their own informed opinions, which are then expressed in writing. Even without these tools, student interest in the debates is high. The debates are often lively and very entertaining.

Materials

Library/Web research tools

Time Approximation

- 45 to 50 minutes per debate
- A few periods in the school library for research (exact number will vary with motivation/ability level and teacher preference). Much research can be completed outside of class.

Lesson Outline

1. Assign the debate project. Student teams of two or three pick a topic and a side. Teams of two work very well, but if you need to reduce the number of debates to use less class time, teams of three will work. If more than one group wants a topic/side, then pull names out of a hat to decide.

2. Provide three or four weeks for the students to research their topics. Periodically provide time in a library/media center.

3. Determine the dates for the debates. Have multiple groups ready to go on a given day in case of student absences.

4. The day before the debates, to avoid taking time on the debate day, explain/discuss any last-minute questions about how the debates will proceed. Distribute the student worksheet for audience members to take notes.

5. On debate day, have seating arranged so that all class members can clearly see the two opposing teams.

6. Begin the debate. Follow the debate format on the student worksheet. Time each segment. Consider using a hand signal to warn the students when time is running short. Make notes on the Student Grading Sheets to help you later decide on points earned for each category.

7. Solicit audience questions for the debaters after the debate.

8. As part of post-debate reflections, have all audience members write a one- or two-paragraph reflection explaining their opinions on the topic. This could be completed as homework.

Implementation Strategy

- To heighten motivation and interest, let the students choose their debate topics. Suggest that a team (or student) find another team (or student) who wants to argue the opposite side of a topic.

- At least three days (one a week for three weeks) in the library are recommended. Library time encourages the use of more diverse information sources such as periodicals, newspapers, and books. Otherwise, students may almost exclusively rely on Internet sources.

- Distribute and discuss the Grading Sheet when the debate is first assigned. Students need to know in advance the importance of varied sources, having audiovisual aids, citing sources, and presenting from note cards or memory rather than reading. The debates can be deadly boring if students read their entire arguments. Stress the importance of eye contact and other oral presentation skills.

- Timing the debate segments (see debate format) is crucial. Use a stopwatch or digital watch. When time is up tell students to finish their thoughts.

- The "Possible Debate Topics" and "Debate Format" could be distributed as a handout to students, displayed as an overhead, or posted on a Web page.

- Students could also pick a topic other than those on the list. Certain topics are problematic though and should be avoided. The argument against researching embryonic stem cells, for example, derives entirely from a religious point of view.

- Collect the Grading Sheets back to use the day of the debate. Make notes on each person's grading sheet as he or she participates in the debate.
- Collect one bibliography from each team. The grade for this will be the same for each team member. The audiovisual grade will also be a team grade. The other categories are assessed individually.
- Try to allow time for audience questions after each debate. The observing students will want to challenge/question claims heard during the debate.

Possible Debate Topics

Should research on human cloning (reproductive and/or therapeutic) be supported by the federal government?

Should we genetically modify food products?

Should we research and develop technologies and medicines specifically to increase human life span?

Should nonhuman animals be used in medical research?

Should people be allowed to genetically modify their offspring (embryos)?

Should the Arctic National Wildlife Refuge be opened for oil exploration?

Do we need to take significant action to address global climate change?

Should we take measures to control global human population growth?

Should physician-assisted suicide be legal?

Should marijuana be legalized for medicinal purposes?

Should wolves be re-introduced into areas where they formerly existed?

Should _____ be hunted to control population size?

Debate Format

Affirmative Side (Pro)	Negative Side (Con)
Opening Statement (2 min.) ⟶	Opening Statement (2 min.)
1st Argument (4 min.) —— (1 min. prep) ⟶ Cross Exam (2 min.) ← (1 min. prep) ——	Cross Exam (2 min.) 1st Argument (4 min.)
Cross Exam (2 min.) ← (1 min. prep) —— 2nd Argument (4 min.) —— (1 min. prep) ⟶	2nd Argument (4 min.) Cross Exam (2 min.)
(2 min. prep for closing statements)	
Closing Statement and Final Rebuttal (3 min.) ⟶	Closing Statement and Final Rebuttal (3 min.)
Questions from the audience for debaters (as much time as available)	

Notes

- Both teams have one minute to discuss and prepare before their cross examination.

- Both teams get two minutes to organize and refine closing statements and final rebuttal.

- Affirmative side goes first for opening statement, first argument, and closing statement.

- Negative side leads for second argument.

- Team members can divide their time however they wish but everyone should participate equally.

Biology Debate Grading Sheet

Category	Teacher Notes	Possible Points	Points Earned
SOURCES (team grade) Quantity Variety of media (Internet, book, newspaper, periodical) Interview with expert?		20	
CONTENT KNOWLEDGE (individual grade) Knowledge of both sides Responses to cross exam Accuracy of biology content Minimal need for notes Information is well-explained		30	
PRESENTATION (individual grade) Eye contact *Not reading* Clear Well-paced		20	
ARGUMENT EFFECTIVENESS (individual grade) Uses quotes Cites data Cites sources, experts Explains credibility of sources Convincing/persuasive		20	
AUDIOVISUAL AIDS (team grade) Posters Handouts Video clip? Props? Taped interview segment?		10	
Total Points		100	

Name _____   Date _____

Debate Observer Notes and Reflection

Debate topic: _____

During the debate make notes in the form below.

Compelling Arguments Made

Affirmative Side	Negative Side

Debate Observer Notes and Reflection, *Cont'd.*

Evidence Supplied for Arguments

Affirmative Side	Negative Side

Debate Observer Notes and Reflection, *Cont'd.*

Post-Debate Reflection

Debate topic: _____

1. What is your informed opinion on the topic of the debate? Explain and cite evidence that persuaded you.

   _____

   _____

   _____

   _____

   _____

   _____

   _____

   _____

   _____

   _____

   _____

2. Did your opinion on the topic change as a result of what you heard in the debate? Explain.

   _____

   _____

   _____

   _____

   _____

   _____

   _____

   _____

   _____

   _____

   _____